Doubts and Decisions
for Living

VOLUME I
The Foundation of Human Thoughts

(Enhanced Edition)

List of Books by This Author
(As of June 20, 2020)*

Non-fiction

The Nature of Love and Relationships 2011, **2016**
Doubts and Decisions for Living:
  Volume I: The Foundation of Human Thoughts **2014**
  Volume II: The Sanctity of Human Spirit **2014**
  Volume III: The Structure of Human Life **2014**
Relationship Facts, Trends, and Choices **2016**
The Mysteries of Life, Love, and Happiness **2016**
Relationship Needs, Framework, and Models **2016**
Gender Qualities, Quirks, and Quarrels **2016**
Marriage and Divorce Hardships **2016**
Being Better Beings **2020**

Fiction

Persian Moons 2007, **2016**
Midnight Gate-opener 2011, **2016**
My Lousy Life Stories **2014**
Persian Suns **2021 (Planned)**

---

*12 older books are Enhanced Editions and printed in 2020. They were resubmitted to the Library and Archives Canada Cataloguing as well. If a book's 'print date' on the copyright page is older, the newest version is available at Amazon and bookstores.

Doubts and Decisions
for Living

VOLUME I
The Foundation of Human Thoughts

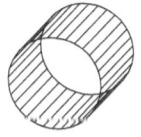

Tom Omidi, Ph.D.

Copyright © 2014 by Tom Omidi
Copyright © 2020 by Tom Omidi

All rights reserved. No part of this book may be reproduced, translated, or transmitted in any form or by any means—graphic, electronic or mechanical, including photocopying, recording, taping or information storage or retrieval systems—without the prior written permission of the publisher or author.

Omidi, Tom, 1945-, author
Doubts and decisions for living / Tom Omidi, Ph.D.

Contents: Volume I. The foundation of human thoughts
Volume II. The sanctity of human spirit
Volume III. The structure of human life.

ISBN 978-1-988351-11-7 (v. 1 : pbk.).
ISBN 978-1-988351-12-4 (v. 2 : pbk.).
ISBN 978-1-988351-13-1 (v. 3 : pbk.).

1. Conduct of life. I. Title.
II. Title: Foundation of human thoughts.
III. Title: Sanctity of human spirit.
IV. Title: Structure of human life.

Old Edition at
Library and Archives Canada Cataloguing in Publication
BJ1581.2.O45 2014   170'.44   C2014-903378-8

Cover page design by Tom Omidi

Published by Eros Books,
Vancouver, British Columbia
Canada

erosbooks2020.@gmail.com

Enhanced and Printed in 2020

For my children

"And you…!?
"Have you yet figured out
 all your reasons for living?"

Table of Contents

	Page
Author's Note	1
Introduction	5

PART I: Philosophy and Personality

Chapter One: Social Conscience and Philosophy	21
Our Habits and Life Routines	22
Our Basic Plans and Ideologies.	24
A Global Philosophy for Humanity	28
Power and Personality	30
Personality Aspects	32
Addendum: A Comparison of the Id, Ego, and Superego with Self, Ego, and Model	38
Chapter Two: Humans' Philosophical Thoughts	41
Reasons for Living	44
Means of a Happy Life	46
Making Our Lives Meaningful	48
Taking Life Easy	52
Exploring the Inner 'Self'	55
Defining the Essence of Humanness (Humanity)	57
Effecting Change and Improving Social Order	59
Choosing a Path of Wisdom	61
Gaining Our Freedom	64
Living Practically but Not Submissively	69
Nurturing Our Positive Doubts	73
Fighting but Not Fearing Depression	77
Making Major Life Decisions	81
Finding a Reliable Companion	82
Optimizing Our Physical and Mental Health	83
Appendix A: A Big Human Dilemma	88

Table of Contents (Cont.)

	Page
Chapter Three: Perceived and Real Worlds	91
Characteristic of the 'Real World'	92
Characteristic of the 'Perceived World'	92
Perceptions about Our Identity	95
Perceptions about Dependence and Independence	96
Perceptions about Love	97
Perceptions about Religions	97
A Picture of the Real World	104
Perceived and Real Realities	111
Exploring the Real World	115
<u>PART II: Facts and Myths</u>	
Precautionary Notes about Part II	122
Chapter Four: The Essence of Facts	123
Facts, Myths, and Challenges	124
Essential Facts and Myths	127
Sources of Facts and Myths	128
Awareness about Our Perceptions	130
The Complexity Level of Our Perceptions	134
Chapter Five: Main Mental Reconciliations	137
Physical Self, Spiritual 'Self', Humanness	137
Life, Freedom, Doubts	144
Nature, Love, Relationships	148
Physical Growth, Truth, Psychological Growth	152
Social Living, Happiness, Coping and Adaptation	154
Economic Constraints, Chance, Contentment	157
Personal Limitations, Enlightenment, Decisions	160
Personal Needs, Inner Strengths, Needs Alignment	164
Perceived Reality, Real Reality, Health	167
Death, Creation/Creator, Spirituality	170
The Role of Facts, Myths, and Challenges	174

Table of Contents (Cont.)

PART III: Personality and Mood
- Chapter Six: Happiness 183
  - Description of Happiness 184
  - 'Happiness' Attributes 185
  - The Happiness of 'Model' 188
  - The Happiness of 'Ego' 194
  - The Happiness of 'Self' 198
  - Personality Aspects' Role for Happiness 201
- Chapter Seven: Depression 205
  - The Depression of 'Model' 206
  - The Depression of 'Ego' 209
  - The Depression of 'Self' 211
- Chapter Eight: The Formula of Happiness 215
  - The Happiness/Depression Cycles 215
  - The Ideal Personality for Salvation 218
  - The 'Self' Aspect of the Ideal Personality 220
  - 'Model' and 'Ego' Roles for the Ideal Personality... 225
    - Addendum: The Formula 227

PART IV: Philosophy and Reality
- Chapter Nine: Thoughts and Wisdom 233
  - Three Philosophical Questions 235
  - The Ultimate Wisdom 238
  - Human Thoughts' Mishmash 243
  - Managing Our Thoughts 245
  - The Significance of No-thought Experiences 248
  - Thoughts and Sufferings 253
  - Common Sources of Suffering 258
- Chapter Ten: Life and Self 265
  - Human Life's Structure 265
  - Life's Major Decisions 268
  - 'Life' and 'Self' Decisions 274
  - The 'Self' and 'Life' Impasse 276
  - The Substance of 'Life' and 'Self' Decisions 278

Table of Contents (Cont.)

	Page
Chapter Eleven: Actions and Adjustments	281
1. Social Disorder	282
2. Destiny	283
3. Personal Negligence	286
The Morality of Our Actions	286
The Capacity to Adjust and Act	288
Changes and Adjustments	292
Awareness and Actions	297
Chapter Twelve: 'Forward Thinking' Philosophy	303
Phase Three Reference	310
Phase Two Reference	314
Phase One reference	318
Epilogue	321

List of Tables, Diagram, and Chart

Table 2.1: Humans' Philosophical Thoughts 42
Diagram 3.1: The Path of Awakening—Eros Dimension... 113
Table 4.1: Suggested List of Facts, Myths, and Challenges . 127
Chart 5.1: Nine Phases of Exploring Inner Self 179

Author's Note

The night my first child was born, thirty-three years ago, my life changed forever—for better or worse, I would never know! Many lucky (or doomed) parents probably feel the same way when suddenly a huge sense of love and responsibility hits them like a sledgehammer and keeps them anxious for the rest of their lives. At the time, I had a flourishing career in Iran with a bright prospect. However, that night, I felt I must do everything in my power to make my kids' future as solid and happy as possible. The first thing to do, then, was to find a peaceful place for them to grow up in—a free, modern society with fine opportunities. After a few months of haggling with all kinds of doubts, the need for making very serious, risky decisions became clear. I left my wife and child behind to travel to the United States in 1981 and apply for immigration to Canada, which appeared to be the best country for my children to live in. Depriving myself from the joy of witnessing my baby start to talk and walk was only one of many sacrifices I had to make in order to pursue my objective. All along, many other thoughts tortured me regarding my sanity to plan such a difficult and unpredictable future and leave behind everything I loved in my country, including my parents, family, and friends. Making all these big decisions so hastily almost fully in hopes of making my kids' future simpler was not easy.

Due to the Iran-Iraq war and border closure, only government authorities were allowed to leave Iran on official business. And the U.S. consulates had stopped issuing visitor's visas to Iranians due to the U.S.'s dislike of the Iran's new regime. Yet, I overcame all these obstacles and got our permanent residency papers from the Canadian Consulate in Los Angeles within a year, despite a ban on education-based admissions—due to the recession and high unemployment in Canada. Then, my wife and daughter had to flee Iran through Pakistan border with enormous difficulty and hardship on top of the large sum of money we paid for smuggling them on foot out of Iran. In Vancouver, I looked for a job fitting my qualifications for four years and our second child was born, too. By then we had spent our lifetime savings. We were on the verge of destitute when I finally found a relatively suitable job. Then, life became rather easier and our kids grew up away from the hassles of wars, the educational curriculum of a revolutionary Islamic regime, and the limited freedom of expression in Iran.

The above brief account of our efforts to bring our children to Canada cannot reflect the hardships my *ex-wife* and I bore on this particular project. I still believe that braving that risky adventure had entailed the toughest doubt and decision in my life, especially in terms of abandoning my newborn baby and wife in the middle of a big war for one year to start the immigration process outside my country alone. Some details about this adventure are offered in Chapter Ten of Volume II of this trilogy under the heading of *Real Experiences*. They rather reveal the gravity of my doubts and decisions at the time about my mission's expected challenges and pains, all in hopes of making our kids' future easier with an opportunity to live in a healthier and safer environment. Still, the hurdles and setbacks we bore for many years to finally make this dream come *partially* true deserves a separate book.

Overall, I often believe my decision thirty years ago has been correct. At the same time, even now my doubts about the value and results of that project and almost all my other decisions pain my brain during trying times and reflection periods. In fact, my cynicism about the value of my foresight and sacrifices during the best years of my life has increased all along in view of the sad outcome of my personal life in Canada mainly in line with my ex-wife's and children's rising apathy towards me. This feeling is unsettling, especially for those of us who believe that all major events bear divine purposes. A gloomy irony, and maybe life's funniest mystery, is our endless doubts about the wisdom of our divine faiths, while we try to grasp and honour our dreary fates!

Telling our story of immigration to Canada has been only for stressing the agony that most parents willingly bear for their kids. Yet, as my children got older, it seemed that I had an even more taxing task ahead. I felt that my main responsibility as a parent was to answer their questions and guide them during adolescence when all kids face the highest amount of doubts about themselves and life and must make very serious decisions in a short span of time. As a parent, my duty to enlighten them, if I could, appeared ten times more important and difficult than all the hardships of bringing them to Canada and providing them with a comfortable life. Preparing my kids for the hassles of living even in modern societies with inefficient economies, volatile job markets, phony lifestyles, and materialistic values, felt crucial, while hoping to teach them think rather independently, instead of getting addicted to so much vanity blindly. I felt obliged to make them understand what life was all about, but could I? Did I understand life myself? The answer to both questions seemed to be a resounding 'no.' I did not know much about life myself, and my children, like all other kids, looked unenthusiastic to listen to their old-fashioned parents' advice. Still, pursuing my mission felt rather imperative. I had to establish my opinions about the main features of human life and struggles for my own benefit at least. Maybe I could then share my plausible conclusions with others, too, especially youths who strive to build themselves and their futures in such confusing societies. Then, it dawned on me that it would be more productive to write a book gradually and systematically, instead of offering random ideas here and there. Then, maybe my kids and others would take the trouble of reading this account of a concerned parent's wisdom leisurely on their own!

I began this trilogy fifteen years ago and finished the first draft in three years. Through extensive research and contemplation, an advanced version also evolved gradually, but I failed to get my kids to read them carefully. The reasons for my failure to raise their interests are noted in the Epilogue. Apparently, we all prefer to discover our naivety about existence and societies the hard way after many years of struggling and disappointments—if at all. Maybe my kids will read this trilogy more keenly someday when their youthful egoism subsides and social artificialities become more apparent to them. Would it be too late by then to sharpen their focus and revamp their lifestyles? Would the points raised in this trilogy be convincing enough to set their life priorities more realistically before losing their stamina? Would their social and family obligations ever spare them a moment for reflection?

Not all parents have enough time and patience to explore the effects of new lifestyles objectively or delve into life's mysteries. Besides, it is hard to draw a general picture of life and its pitfalls in the 21st century. No study in this area can be easy, popular, or complete. Still, after wrestling with major doubts about the value and validity of studying this touchy topic—this dwindling social setting and humiliating humanity—I embraced this mission with a reserved optimism about its intended purpose. Let us hope my goal and the outcome would appeal to some parents interested in giving their children a somewhat more realistic perspective of life beyond social norms. In fact, it might help them personally even more if they read it patiently first and possibly agree with some conclusions in this trilogy. Maybe they feel intrigued to reflect upon some radical ideas more seriously for personal salvation and possible use in our faltering educational systems.

Happy reading
Tom Omidi, Ph.D.
Vancouver, 2014

Introduction

This trilogy strives to explore the main features of social living, which revolves around humans' innate ability to think, feel, and act. This requires an evolving Foundation of Human Thoughts (as discussed in Volume I), a divine mentality (and high spirits) for understanding and compassion (as discussed in Volume II), and an allegedly purposeful Structure of Human Life (as discussed in Volume III). Surely, our thoughts, actions, and feelings induce a large amount of excruciating doubts and decisions for us to face a lifetime. In return, our doubts and decisions reflect our deepest urges to think, feel, and act as logically as possible for grasping the meaning of life and purpose of our existence. Accordingly, the idea of learning about ourselves and choosing the right path of life depends immensely on how well we grasp the nature and consequences of our lifelong doubts and decisions.

In particular, this trilogy intends to aid the youths who face many questions and doubts regarding life, but must make timely, smart decisions for their welfare and future. Yet, the discussions are equally useful for us all, especially parents, to assess our life dilemmas. This trilogy's messages can kindle our curiosity and stir our self-awareness process, especially since our unconscious, naïve 'inner child' dominates our perceptions and relationships at all ages. They can help us explore the purposes of our struggles and grasp the means of achieving contentment and freedom more naturally. Maybe then, we could give some valuable advice to our kids and educational systems, too.

Parents' Dilemmas

Every caring, intelligent parent doubts his or her parenting skills. We keep asking ourselves many questions: Have I done right by my children? Have I been a good mentor and role model for them? Have I communicated everything I know about life that may be useful to them for developing their value systems and for making the right decisions? Most of all: Are my perceptions of life valid enough to share with others?

These and similar doubts perturb every conscientious parent, as we wish to prepare our children for escalating life challenges. Some of us are humble enough to admit that we can never be sure about the meaning of life and the kind of lifestyle that might best give our kids a peaceful future. Thus, we strive to be careful with our advice and definitely not get dogmatic with some of our lousy opinions. Still, we are concerned about their welfare and happiness in our failing societies. We hope they do not repeat our mistakes. Actually, we subconsciously wish to relive, through our children, the stages of life that have proven to be either blissful or nightmarish for us, which must be somehow corrected now at least for (or through) our children. For example, we often advise our children about their careers or relationships, because we have succeeded or failed in our own decisions.

However, advising our kids is risky and tough, nowadays, as no reliable guidelines are available for managing our lives in such overly complex, chaotic, and superficial societies. In particular, explaining the meanings of success and happiness is impossible, nowadays, as we witness the gloomy outcome of our supposedly astute search for life's virtues. How can any sensible person not doubt the validity of his or her interpretations of happiness and success? Only a few wise, selfless parents might know *something* about life's secrets. Even then, their ideas would sound absurd and radically incongruent with the alluring lifestyles that push the youths only for more pleasures and vanity.

Meanwhile, many parents overindulge their children to boost their self-image and chances of success in a materialistic setting. Accordingly, kids have become too self-absorbed and spoiled to grasp the intricacies of life or care about their parents' cautions and teachings. Some parents, especially 'mothers,' go even to the bizarre extreme of adopting their kids' whimsical lifestyles and values just to show their modernity and support. They look quite ridiculous when they behave and speak like their children. They pretend to be happy that at least their kids do not disdain them as often. **Something is definitely wrong in a society where adults imitate their children as part of parenting.**

Parents' inexperience and superficial mentalities these days hurt their kids' characters, too, whether they try to be a mentor or remain rather passive to let their kids figure out life on their own. Most of us are naïve about life and formed by social demands and the upbringing flaws of our own parents. Thus, we damage our children's psyches as well as our relationships with them by the time they reach adolescence.

Nevertheless, we finally learn that we cannot gain our kids' trust or hold enough influence over them. Both social influence and a premature urge for independence goad kids not to listen to any advice, anyway. At best, they learn to listen diplomatically without understanding. The adults' wisdom usually feels funny to them, as they quickly find their parents out of touch with the fast-changing world. They take even a small age difference as a clue for ignorance and obsolescence. Thus, even if we had something important to share with our children, the right conditions never arise, because parents lose their authority too fast, nowadays. Only a few lucky, patient, and selfless parents might succeed to build a lax, active relationship with their children and share their viewpoints without getting too pushy and dogmatic.

Youths' Conundrums

On the one hand, youths' tenacity to doubt their parents' wisdom, like a subtle rebellion, is often a blessing, because most of us have nothing useful to teach our kids, anyway, or do not know how to do it. Their resistance could *potentially* help them become freethinkers and open-minded with objective mentalities if the society and media did not confuse them so tenaciously. In fact, both parents and society cause substantial confusion and anxiety for youths with their superficial teachings, idealistic ideologies, and phony lifestyles. Peer influence during adolescence hinders youths' desire to think objectively and independently as well. As modern humans, nowadays, most parents and kids are inflicted with deep psychological flaws that prevent their abilities to teach or learn anything, anyway.

On the other hand, the absence of guidelines or a reliable role model for children, due to cultural collapse in societies, hinders youths' chance for building even a basic foundation of thoughts and developing their own life values and ways. In this passive and senseless environment, our children are helplessly at the mercy of a society that has no intention or capacity to teach them life's true meaning and issues. Instead, the effects of the rising financial insecurity and social deprivations for youths only make them more restless, desperate, and radical.

Children's tiny interest in reading is somewhat encouraging as they usually learn more from reading than listening. However, what they read, nowadays, is often misleading them, too. Sadly, very few books exist for helping the youths with their doubts and decisions for living, and for building their foundation of thoughts on a solid ground. Not enough simple and intelligent books are available to help the youths grasp the sad nature of the world they are inheriting. Books must give them enough facts and ideas to think for themselves, instead of filling their minds with trivia, fantasy, and corny conclusions. Books must offer practical tools and techniques to identify their options for living, instead of only raising their soppy sentimentalities and high expectations from life. Youths must understand the most likely consequence of their major life decisions and doubts before their hasty choices lead to lifelong depression and a stressful subsistence. These books must merely reflect humans' sincere lessons from life without pushing popular mottos to justify our own lifestyles or brainwash youths' brains in line with our demented socioeconomic values. We need books that address life issues in a plain language to discourage consumerism and crude, self-gratifying values. Good parenting, new realistic school curriculum, and books are our last chances to mitigate humans' mental collapse and distress from the influence of TV, video games, social media, and misguiding books.

Despite some positive attributes children might inherit from their parents, many irreversible psychological defects ruin their mentalities. They also imagine we hurt them deliberately. Even when they do not show hostility and anxiety, they often suppress an enormous level of traumas and cynicism about their parents—sometimes rightfully and sometimes due to their misperceptions. Sadly, even as adults, they (like the rest of us) seldom find the opportunity to recognize their idiosyncrasies and the means of overcoming them, especially the ones etched in their unconscious minds during childhood. The outcome is that every generation, in the last century at least, has become less cultured in pursuit of phonier lifestyles, instead of becoming more apprehensive and doubtful about modern societies' direction.

Social and Personal Dilemmas

Humans (especially youths) become too conditioned to think and learn anything useful outside their narrow personal perceptions and beliefs, unless some magical incentives goad them follow a long process of self-awareness. Fortunately, we all question the purpose of our struggles, while we face many complex dilemmas regularly, too. We try, mostly subconsciously, especially during adolescence and early adulthood, to find someone whose wisdom we could trust to share our thoughts with, but nobody appears clever enough. Thus, many of us live in depression most of our lives, since we cannot resolve our subconscious doubts about the validity of our thoughts and lifestyles and we cannot make the right decisions for attaining a peaceful existence.

We have an intricate nature and a delicate soul, but have fully dedicated ourselves to social rules and values that serve neither our natures nor our souls. We are born into complex, tough, and mental-conditioning societies with no capable leaders grasping or directing them for the long-term welfare of humanity. Overall, the perplexities of human nature and world have created havoc and stress for us all, while we have become disheartened with ourselves, our relationships, and socioeconomic settings. We are becoming more confused about our identities and the way we can, or should, relate to social norms and other individuals. Our relationships are mostly incomplete and stir deep sufferings and disappointments. Some of us might even feel our psychological dysfunctions and insecurities, but cannot help ourselves or trust anybody to help us. And, of course, our natural growth itself is threatened by the mere necessity of living under such meagre conditions within contaminated environments.

Social and personal shortfalls are not new revelations, but the downfall acceleration is now making us dizzy. In addition, we are expected to adapt ourselves to this hectic condition more eagerly in order to survive. We feel obliged to set our life objectives and act based on some frivolous criteria of success and individualism. We must stay positive and pretend to love and enjoy the life structure formulated around the interests of conglomerates and capitalism. Therefore, we are burdened with an immense amount of unsettling problems and dilemmas, while our inner conflicts and doubts about our life choices keep piling up.

Even for finding a remedy for our problems and anxieties, we mostly look outwardly and seek refuge in the same type of values and relationships that have created our problems in the first place. Consequently, the whole society feels more baffled and helpless every day about its options and identity. The bitterness of our life experiences, especially those related to our family relationships and careers devastates many of us, especially after counting on them all along to bring us happiness and peace. They just prove contrary to what we had expected them to be and do for us.

Nowadays, everybody, especially youths, feels defeated and doubtful about his/her purpose of living or even a simple, truthful definition of life. Without reliable criteria and guidelines, making the right choices is difficult. However, we should decide about a large variety of critical and urgent matters every day. Thus, we just make our half-hearted decisions, hope for the best, wrestle with our doubts, and life goes on. Meanwhile, we mostly scorn ourselves for our inabilities to adapt perfectly to social conditions and rules that we have taken as the reality of life. Unfortunately, all these sad clues and sufferings, evident in all aspects of our lives, do not teach us anything, either. We do not stop to think and ask, **'Is life's reality supposed to be so glum?'**

We are concerned and curious inherently, thus question the validity of our ideas, struggles, and values mostly subconsciously. Ultimately, we face two conflicting realities: The reality of social living and the reality of our 'being.' These two realities reflect the conflicting forces of external demands versus the intrinsic needs of humans. As we are mainly preoccupied by, and attracted to, external values and incentives, we have lost touch with our inner needs and dimensions. We have sacrificed our identities in hopes of developing an artificial personality through social compliance and adaptation. Thus, we suffer, because we cannot harmonize our two conflicting realities, i.e., our external (social) and internal (personal) realities. The big question is whether they can ever be reconciled. Most likely, no, since social 'living' has become too demanding and erratic to allow any kind of compromise with our sense of 'being.' This conflict highlights our dilemmas regarding our sense of living within a crooked structure of life we have laid out mostly in recent decades merely out of our sheer foolishness. We live a lifetime with this painful, tough socio-personal conflict.

Humans have many intellectual and instinctual dimensions that work together to build their characters and direct their efforts and visions. We seek psychological knowledge, philosophical notions, interpersonal skills, spiritual guidance, and inner 'self' energy to feel the essence of our being and seek solutions for our unresolved questions and problems. We guess (and also doubt) that there must be a more fundamental reality of the universe and a higher dimension of being (perhaps our soul) that is part of our existence in spite of our lack of wisdom to comprehend it readily. We read many books to find some reasonable answers, but most of these books have become too specialized and narrow in scope. They usually tackle social dimensions of humans and a related thought process or discipline to fortify our phony lifestyles. Thus, even when we attempt to grasp our identity, we do not use all our knowledge and energy. We ponder some basic ideas sporadically without learning the full potential and limitations of humans.

There is an old saying that every individual should have two lives: One to experience and one to live. Many of us believe we would do many aspects of our lives differently if we were given a second chance to start over. After reaching certain age without having had the benefit of a thoughtful and informed decision process, it is often too late for many of us to change ourselves or our lifestyles. Ironically, even if we were given a second chance by a miracle to live, we would most likely make the same or similar mistakes if we do not how to build a proper foundation of thoughts and while we are usually bound to live in such terribly designed social structures.

Nevertheless, we can reassess our values and adjust our *ways of thinking,* if our experiences have taught us anything useful. Then, we could possibly help our children, too, in their thinking processes, perhaps through passive leadership as an honest role model. Instead of being dogmatic parents and pushing our vague and distorted images of life upon our children, we could try to draw a truer picture of life for ourselves by reflecting upon our experiences and analysing their significance truthfully. The goal is to rebuild our fundamental thoughts according to, i) our honest view of the symbols that make one's life sensible or futile, ii) our interpretations of major life challenges and our relationships, iii) our awareness about our debilitating prejudices and hang-ups, and iv) our fresh set of beliefs and faiths, and their reliability for resolving our dilemmas and making decisions. We want to test, and set, our convictions before communicating them to our kids. We like to assess and accept the depressing truth about life in the 21st century. Only then, our reflections might become a worthy and truthful mirror for our children to look into as well. Maybe we could even get involved in developing a truthful and forceful set of guidelines for new generations about life's authentic values and essentialities. Alas, the existing socioeconomic forces limit the chances of pursuing this sacred mission—to think freely and open-mindedly, at least during our private contemplations.

Plausible Solutions

This trilogy suggests that we cannot resolve our dilemmas about our lives and identities by studying only a particular dimension of our being, e.g., our psyche, and by using only one discipline, e.g., psychology, to explain it. Rather, we need all our intellectual and instinctual abilities to explore and reconcile our life purposes within the context of social (dis)orders and endless pressures. It is not even enough to learn about our idiosyncrasies and become more self-aware. Instead, we should also learn how to resist the social and economic conditions that suppress our real needs and reinforce many of our psychological defects, including the ones that our parents have initially inflicted upon us, mostly due to their ignorance and confusion regarding the matter of existence versus the pressures of subsistence in our dysfunctional societies.

Our main goal is to explore our humanistic dimensions away from social norms and values, but also explain them within the context of socioeconomic facts and expectations. Our challenge is to realize and internalize our being and decide what we need—

mostly mentally and spiritually as moral humans—to survive rather peacefully within the harsh realities of our dying world. In addition, we wish to justify both our existence and our efforts for social adaptation based on our own rules of true humanness. We struggle to live practically, but also like to feel our being and the aesthetic values of life. Can we ever reach this delicate balance to get a better sense of our being—our deprived 'Self'? How?

Regardless of our age and level of social success, many of us continue, intuitively, to seek our inner being, the 'self,' in hopes of redeeming our dying spirits. Identifying and relating to our true self during youth is hard. We are merely influenced and distracted by social norms and demands that we believe address our needs the best automatically. Thus, we simply adopt and nurture a load of debilitating ideas and values. Sometimes we rebel against the rules we find offensive or annoying, but usually we do not have proper values or convictions to replace our social norms and teachings. When we grow older, we get too involved with our daily dilemmas to concern ourselves with the seemingly deprived 'self' suffering the pains of existence and mourning our demise. We just keep following the prevalent lifestyles and try to blend in, because society would not allow non-conformers to succeed. Some of us have become so rigidly conditioned that cannot even entertain the idea of questioning social norms and value systems; we simply accept them as an integral aspect of the universe—a fact of life—and move on. We never find time or right mindset to wander in unfamiliar territories. We are afraid, or do not know how, to gauge our identity and purpose of living. We simply live because we are here. We strive to feed our ego, since it gives us a relative sense of superiority and superficial existence. But can this feeling of superiority stir a meaningful and peaceful venue for our being? Can it stir an authentic sense of self-fulfillment and purposefulness in life? Most of us would never find out.

We need a framework to help us grasp the basics of living and happiness, while meeting the requirements of social conformity for survival, too. However, we also need a platform to help us elevate above the doomed clouds of conformity that obscure our vision of a true 'self'—to get a fresh perspective of who we are.

Hence, the goal of this trilogy is to address these challenges by exploring the philosophical, psychological, spiritual, practical, ethical, and other main dimensions of human beings and discuss them collectively in a simple language. The intention is to apply these dimensions for understanding the purpose of our being and building a somewhat fruitful and tranquil life, while adapting to socioeconomic environments somehow as well. We can learn to develop a simple life philosophy that defines and incorporates the realities of our socioeconomic structure, but also leads us towards the path of selfhood. Even when we are inclined to live within our conventional value systems and decision-making processes, we can still draw on a valid foundation of thoughts to choose a more natural lifestyle and make our critical decisions wisely. There are effective ways of establishing the foundation of our thoughts and assessing its validity and strength.

With regard to the pessimistic tone of many arguments in this trilogy, three points need clarification: **First,** this trilogy's premise is that we cannot avoid the negative impacts of socioeconomic structure on the way we think and behave. As much as we may try to stay positive and control our idiosyncrasies, endless social pressures goad our defective habits and hinder our intention to find peace and goodness. It is hard to become a truthful person in a society that does not support honesty and justice. **Second,** for finding the inner strength to fight back the inevitable negativities of our socioeconomic systems, we should initially acknowledge them as a debilitating reality and get ready to face them head on. We should stop sweeping the reality under the rug and hiding behind positive thinking gimmicks. We should handle negative situations and thoughts regularly as they cause the majority of our doubts and dilemmas. The point is that we cannot overcome our doubts, resolve our problems, and encounter our defects unless we at least recognize the impact of social negativities somehow

—instead of ignoring or propagating them so irresponsibly and shamelessly. **Third,** we should realize as a society that the way we are thinking and acting within our dreadful socioeconomic structures is pushing humans to the verge of extinction.

At the same time, we need convictions and resilience to enjoy life's limited privileges and handle societies' rising malfunctions. We must analyse our negative thoughts and feelings effectively, rather than trying to justify or stifle them, or get overly depressed or agitated to face them constructively, despite the humiliating experiences and gloom singing our psyches. In fact, the more we understand the depth of both social negativities and our personal idiosyncrasies as real hurdles for personal growth, the higher would be our chances to redefine our lives outside common norms and influences. A positive-thinking attitude to ignore our negative thoughts or social hurdles cannot give us the convictions and awareness we need to nurture our real 'self' and overcome our problems. We should smarten up if we wish an easier life for future generations. These are major reasons for addressing social issues somewhat negatively in all writings by this author.

The Trilogy's Structure

We believe our actions must reflect our valid choices and deep beliefs. We also think our value systems and convictions reflect our knowledge of a reliable reality according to logical criteria. We believe human life must be supported by some fundamental thoughts, either our own or other individuals' whom we admire, respect, and accept as authorities. These essential thoughts set and validate our beliefs and life philosophy to follow as a guiding light. Therefore, Volume I of this trilogy explores the foundation of human thoughts.

In addition to a solid foundation of thoughts, we require a high-spirited mentality to appreciate the significance of our lives, needs, and thoughts, and then turn them into fruitful actions and meaningful experiences. For this purpose, we strive to explore the meaning and characteristics of our spirits that drive the engine of our existence. We try to boost our spirits to encounter life's hardships calmly and find our identities. We also like to explore the meaning and purpose of spirituality that keeps our thoughts and spirits in cohesion, free, and productive. We hope to fathom and find our spirits and spirituality in personal ways, away from all religious and social influences. Volume II covers these topics.

And, of course, going through various stages of life, we can envision and follow a structure of life that everybody hopes to cope with, while this rigid process highly influences the outcome of our major life decisions, too. The topics covered in Volume III concentrate on the structure of life and the way we may adapt ourselves to it more effectively by strengthening the foundation of our thoughts in line with a deeper understanding of who we are and what we want—our spirit. Thus, Volume III discusses the challenges and decisions of life within the context of essential human thoughts. The rigid life path that we follow so blindly is in need of scrutiny and overhaul. The question is whether this life structure is meaningful or logical? How has this monstrous, wild society evolved around us and why have we allowed a small group do this to humanity. Every intelligent person must be able to answer these basic questions for him/herself.

The discussions in this trilogy are mainly based on commonsense and personal experiences of the author. Yet, most conclusions are in line with the studies of prevalent scholars, statistics, and social facts. Providing scientific proofs and research methodologies for all the conclusions is impractical and unnecessary for the type of 'mostly philosophical' remarks offered in this trilogy. Actually, the discussions and suggestions are generic and more of a general nature than definite solutions and conclusions requiring finite scientific proofs. Even if elaborate scientific research somewhat supports the theories of this trilogy, people who benefit from the existing socioeconomic chaos always find ways to refute them just for keeping the public in their shells.

Many of us believe that too many things in our world are happening so irrationally, while another group counter-argues from a different perspective to justify them. For instance, we ruin old forests for lumber and creating jobs, destroy marine life and pollute environment through industrial production, exploration of oil sands, humans' reckless over-consumption and waste, etc. Many of us believe that these atrocities are all symptoms of our surrender to capitalism, wicked value systems and consumerism, and for keeping the world's economies alive as long as possible. We all know that this extravagance cannot go on forever and it would never serve the majority. Yet, we keep electing arrogant politicians who ignore these obvious facts with a smirk.

In Volume I, we learn a few things about human personality and thought processes in order to understand their motives and attitudes leading to happiness occasionally, but mostly causing their depression and sense of helplessness.

Ironically, humans' crooked personalities ruin their thinking capacities and chances of self-realization, while our vile thoughts and damaged psyches have destroyed our personalities towards a disastrous fate for humans in the next few decades.

Thirty basic points or words of wisdom *(the author's precious two cents!)* are listed in the Epilogue specifically for the youth's benefits. A heads-up to the youths is also offered at the beginning of Vol. II. Ironically, these kind warnings are against this author's aversion to give anybody advice to avoid annoying people for no conceivable outcome or just to avoid embarrassing himself!!!

The quotes from esteemed scholars in this book are merely for reflecting worthy viewpoints on related topics with no prejudice. They are plausible opinions stated liberally in public domains about such philosophical topics, thus have become relevant for general review purposes. While the author does not necessarily agree or disagree with them, they are good points that interested readers are encouraged to check in those books for further detail and reflection.

PART I
Thoughts and Personalities

About Part I

Part I attempts to study how and why we have failed as humans to understand the power and drawbacks of our perceptions and thoughts in defining and managing our lives and societies.

CHAPTER ONE
Social Conscience and Philosophy

'Philosophy' explores concepts about individual and society in line with values and rules of morality. However, the reality that we have created for ourselves, and feel so proud of it, too, would never come anywhere close to those philosophical ideals. In fact, 'philosophy' often appears like an ironical picture of 'reality,' merely for teasing our severe gullibility and shortfalls as humans! Our societies and the public have difficulty understanding and implementing even some basic principles for relating and living harmoniously, let alone pondering morality and the tough task of becoming better beings. After such a long history of humanity and reflections, philosophy still remains only an impotent symbol of social conscience. It reflects some good intentions mixed with a bunch of far-fetched ideologies for speculation and dreaming, but not something to rely on realistically for correcting ourselves.

On the other hand, we would never stop humouring the public and ourselves about the possibility of gaining the capacity for a better humanity somehow eventually—perhaps after a few more millenniums of torturing one another and suffering. We hope to find an idyllic means of living that fits humans' needs, dignity, and messy nature. We hope to generalize the ideas and rules of morality and fathom a social order and political system that can inhibit all the chaos and tyranny everywhere. We realize that these objectives are somehow naïve and elusive, but we like to accept them as our ultimate, noble goals. Thus, our lasting search for a global philosophy to goad a more practical and harmonious humanity would continue and probably get nowhere. Or maybe we succeed by a fluke! Still, perhaps we could at least stress on building our personal life philosophies within a narrower scope by understanding our authentic needs, beliefs, and life purposes. We could try to refine our outlooks and choose simpler lifestyles for personal peace and salvation at least now that our ideals about social sanity and global unity feel so farfetched.

Our Habits and Life Routines

Often it feels we are simply living like robots repeating the same pointless routines day after day, chasing some wild dreams, just making a living, maybe accumulating wealth, building a family, and seeking pleasure. We do things that feel sensible one day and meaningless the next day. We behave merely out of habit without knowing our ultimate purpose. We may have some financial and career development plans, but have no idea what our life is all about and what we want to do with it. Often, it appears we are unaware of our true beliefs, needs, or motives to build a basic life philosophy. Sometimes, we are simply too naïve when we wait for someone else, perhaps our companion or soul mate to arrive (soon hopefully) and show us the means of finding happiness or a clue about a life plan that sounds promising. This is a *robotic, random living* existence.

At the same time, scholars have offered a variety of alluring philosophies, such as 'positive thinking' or 'living in the now', that have remained useless or damaged people's brains further. Now, *reality* is shaped in our minds by the ideas and values of our parents, governments, and powerful groups who manipulate and exploit the rest of the population. The principal hypothetical expectation in so-called democratic societies about governments' ability to protect the public's best interests is only an idealistic theory that would never materialize, especially by capitalism. In the end, we are simply left out in both fronts, i.e., philosophy and reality, helpless and estranged to the rules imposed upon us. We have not learnt to develop our own life philosophies, as we have never considered it important, possible, and necessary. And we do not know how to participate in shaping social values based on humans' authentic needs and life realities, mainly by resisting the phony 'reality' that is forced on us in our faltering societies.

Instead of building a moralistic life philosophy, we have only adopted a materialistic living ideology and pursue it passionately. We have grown biases, prejudices, and huge egos to get ahead in all social competitions and challenges. And instead of expanding our own vision and definition of a reality fitting us, we conform to social norms, which we privately often find invalid, anyway. We simply follow the crowd hypnotically just for being accepted as a loyal member of society and to stay popular within the circle of friends. The bottomline is that if we do not take the initiative to build at least our own vision (philosophy) of existence and follow a simpler life path, we would remain at the mercy of others who would force some chaotic social norms and rules upon us, and we suffer in confusion a lifetime.

"We all have the power to make reality. Why make it inside boundaries when the boundless is so near?" Deepak Chopra, *Quantum Healing,* Bantam Books, 1989, p. 234.

"There is no more beautiful experience than when the world expands beyond its accustomed limits. These are the moments when reality takes on splendour." Ibid., p. 235.

Not everybody may find the power to make reality or feel the splendour that a more insightful lifestyle can bring us, but we can at least try to escape the boundaries of the perceived reality that is muddling our brains and causing us so much hardship. We might expand our minds and make our reality boundless by developing a personal life philosophy that depicts the way we see things and like to live, more authentically closer to the rules of 'self.' We can at least stir a little integrity in our mentalities, as a reflection of our existence, especially as allegedly intelligent *beings*!

A personal life philosophy serves many purposes that become clear in the following discussions. Yet, it mainly helps us rise above our customary robotic, random living to control our being thoughtfully and purposefully. It can guide our thoughts, actions, attitude, decisions, and doubts. This would bring us more in line with the 'self' aspect of our personality by reducing 'model' and 'ego,' which are explained on pages 31-40. The customary robotic, random living life is a product of the phony reality we have grown up with and accepted helplessly. 'Self' controlled life, on the other hand, is one in which we see and honour, the vision and wisdom of 'self.' It is a personal initiative to learn about the art of existence on our own. The process will be explained later.

Our Basic Plans and Ideologies

Most of us put our ambitions on hold to attend to our immediate needs in order to stay practical and secure our futures. **We realize the importance of having solid and realistic life plans and the need to adapt to the chaotic socioeconomic setting somehow,** including job market demands and complex family relationships. Everybody, especially youths, now faces this normal adjustment process. We strive to establish the relevance (practicality) of our *plans* within society, but also in the context of our crude beliefs and *ideologies* (e.g., our life purposes, reasons for working, views of happiness, goals of accumulating wealth, the objectives and hassles of marriage and family, etc.). We also try to assess our potentialities and limitations when we develop and pursue our specific plans, which presumably fit and support our general life path. Yet, we are most likely not clear and careful in terms of the purposes of our plans in the long-term as a life philosophy.

General ideas and steps will be offered later for developing a long-term personal philosophy (life path.) In all, however, being too ambitious or passionate regarding our ideals and dreams often obscures our sense of practicality and reality. It only undermines our chances and efforts to adapt to the harsh realities of life. In fact, without quick adaptation, we increase the risks of a lifelong isolation, sufferings, and regrets. On the other hand, ignoring our dreams and true potentialities, just for the sake of mere adaptation and survival, has its own risks and regrets.

We might naively assume that our personal goals match our beliefs, potentialities, risk orientation, and a realistic 'life vision.' Yet, finding our true niche and temperament is not easy. Besides, even our most thoughtful plans have at least fifty percent chance of failing or leading to horrific results. Thus, we must be prepared for these unforeseeable outcomes. How realistically we set our plans and how seriously we pursue them is a personal choice, which at the end also reflects the strength of our characters and beliefs. Only we are responsible for the outcomes of our choices, while striving to ponder and prepare our plans and to implement them with perseverance. One thing is certain, though: If we lack life plans and personal beliefs, cannot build a sound, meaningful criterion for measuring them, or keep postponing our major life decisions, we would face many disappointments at the very least.

Our life vision or personal plans do not need to be elaborate or aggressive, but rather thoughtful. Making a conscious decision to follow a simple, humble life is as good as, and often better than, a complex, greedy plan. Any plan is good when built on healthy, thoughtful personal beliefs and reflects our true representation of who we are. It should be realistic as well within the parameters of socioeconomic settings. Having solid plans and beliefs are mostly vital for sustaining a consistent level of motivation to encounter unforeseeable obstacles and inevitable disappointments along the way. Moreover, we must remember that laziness and pessimism do not bring us any sense of accomplishment and existence.

A main goal of self-analysis is to ensure our life philosophy matches our socioeconomic plans. If not quite sure, we must stop and reassess all the variables again. We should first come to terms with ourselves, grasp our beliefs honestly, and dismiss our naïve aspirations before building our life plans. Especially youths must stay careful about the practicality of their aspirations goaded by shoddy perceptions of reality in a vile society that propagates mostly vanity and greed. We should avoid the lure of trusting our guts or logic for choosing certain plans. We should overcome our pride, raw emotions, and stubbornness, and instead admit at least to ourselves that we have no supporting facts for the way we are, feel, or do things. Often, merely our erratic passion makes us so restless and reckless. Our reaction and grasp of the question of 'who we are' in relation to our plans is most often misleading. Instead, we should invest a great deal of time and become honest with ourselves in terms of our personalities and beliefs—to really realize whether we have a meaningful life plan or not. To do so, we can, i) study and set the level of risks we are prepared to take for maintaining our basic independence, ii) build a list of personal beliefs and ideologies, and iii) try to assess and incorporate all these facts objectively in line with our long-term plans and some *positive doubts,* which are explained on page 73.

Most of us have life plans, or at least we think so. If we also have strong beliefs about who we are, how we like to live, and why, then our life philosophy can be drawn by ensuring those plans and beliefs coincide according to reliable criteria. This basic coordination of our plans and beliefs constitutes a basic definition of a life philosophy. Yet, we should test the soundness of our plans and beliefs concurrently. Usually our shallow beliefs or thoughts invent impractical plans. Often our beliefs are just naïve justifications to support our crooked or fanciful plans. Thus, it is vital to fight the temptation of assuming that our plans are based on objective judgments and valid criteria. Those of us who have no plans, are not seriously pursuing them, or cannot find beliefs or resolutions to support those plans, have even more work to do. Trusting some half-hearted beliefs (often by copying social norms and teachings) would be risky. It might prove more wasteful and painful than doing nothing if our long-term plan, based on some personal beliefs and philosophy, is not yet finalized. It is always better to act only when we are ready and reasonably doubtless. However, procrastinating in hopes of devising a perfect plan or struggling aimlessly with our ambitious dreams for a long time would damage our psyches even more. It is more sensible to carry out our reasonable plans, while we refine our long-term plan and life philosophy within a prudent timeframe. We can always add some solid short-term plans within our evolving long-term plan and life philosophy as long as we stay objective and thoughtful.

Nevertheless, the above basic steps are merely for aligning our ultimate life objectives with our beliefs, crude ambitions, and abilities. Personal ambitions not driven by both a sound ideology and a refined plan must be resisted, especially during youth when we need wise plans for our future based on sensible strategies as well as a timetable and viable criteria for achieving certain goals within specific life stages. Without relying on the mainstream's view of practicality too much, we should still remain objective about our criteria for assessing our ambitions and putting our life plans together only according to our **strict** life philosophies even (especially) if we think, usually naively, that our potentialities and ambitions are compatible and realistic. After all, we should make many tough decisions a lifetime based on our practical needs and rough personalities, and then live with their consequences often forever without whining or feeling defeated too much.

Sadly, devising practical life plans is getting harder every year, since our societies are imposing more uncertainties and economic imbalance. Therefore, we should work harder, think deeper about our life philosophy, be prepared for more setbacks, and plan how to live rather peacefully within our hectic societies for whatever end that might justify our efforts. Everybody should develop both short and long-term practical plans, at least for satisfying his/her basic needs and building certain relationships. These plans should fit his/her main beliefs closely and fulfil his/her meaningful life purposes within a certain period, e.g., five to seven years if s/he is in his twenties. These plans are for attaining at least a sense of contentment and peace of mind in life, which becomes possible by recognizing the characteristics of an ideal personality. Thus, some basic insights about 'personality' are offered on pages 31-40.

A Global Philosophy for Humanity

Everybody builds a perception of life intuitively to guide him/her for making decisions and plans. We conceive this crude personal life philosophy mostly unconsciously in line with our intelligence, experiences, needs, ambitions, ideologies, priorities, tastes, plans, beliefs, decision criteria, etc. Accordingly, people's life outlooks, actions, and logics are scattered and fluid, since they do not have a systematic approach or method for building them actively and objectively. Furthermore, we have constant doubts regarding the validity of our choices and outlook. Conversely, we can set out to build a global life philosophy more consciously and proactively based on measured, strong principles for the good of humanity.

Many political, religious, and social groups have hoped to create a viable culture and thought process to embrace a rational set of human values. After all, the main purpose of philosophy is to make a better sense of our erratic reality—the perceived reality—and explain it to the public for general knowledge and easier coexistence. However, it seems that human character hinders the development of a sensible philosophical platform to share among ourselves for communicating and resolving our social dilemmas. Instead, we have spread too many self-serving philosophies that advocate crude notions, such as positive thinking or living in the now, etc. These naïve, unpractical mottos have been spread in societies just for fooling the public in line with modern humans' self-deceiving attitude and rampant materialist ambitions.

Ideally, some scholars could save humanity by developing a comprehensive, practical guideline (life philosophy) for making humans' coexistence easier according to a long-term perspective of humans' innate needs and flaws. Such humanistic guidelines can be developed gradually around humans' rational thoughts and analyses to help us at least grasp the dangers of our erratic whims. The objective is to make existence more bearable based on practical ideals and basic existential *facts* outside the current social values and structure. This might be a better approach than relying on our lame leaders, shallow social values, and capitalism to set our life objectives and paths. It would be a better long-term plan than trusting humans' juvenile dreams and expectations, or waiting for repeated miracles to save humanity. Surely, haggling with modern humans' naive ideologies that are infecting societies and morals is embarrassing. It is bizarre, in fact, that we have not yet even studied our options for humans' survival!

Naturally, the main hurdle is the lack of a central authority with long-term plans and power for managing humanity, besides the difficulty of envisioning a mechanism to make the best use of humans' talents and world resources, while keeping people rather content. Our best collective idea as humans and nations so far—to create the United Nations—has proven too impotent to achieve what we need. Then again, without the UN, human sufferings and global chaos would have already been much much worse!!

At least some of us, including this naïve author, might dream about humans' eventual awakening and eluding their looming demise by conceiving a **universal philosophy for humanity.** For now, the best we can do individually is to find the means of building our personal philosophies more compassionately at least in order to mitigate our own and others' pains a bit. In fact, if we simply had a world full of humble, thoughtful individuals, most of the current problems would get resolved automatically.

Alas, a generalized philosophy with ethical norms would be too difficult to implement in our rigidly deformed societies, for now, anyway, thanks to humans' dire nature and arrogance. Still, maybe at least some preliminary guidelines could be developed to depict life's limitations and demands, as realistic principles and purposes for healthier living, to help us build our fundamental thoughts and beliefs. Once the merits of those basic principles are proven, people might extent their own stamina and incentive for adopting and spreading them.

As a very basic aspiration, it would be very useful if at least an international, independent set of honest scientists could work together on a long, comprehensive project to confirm three facts:

1. How horrible humans' existence would become if we simply stayed the course and how soon it might happen?
2. Could any kind of social structure be conceived around any philosophical principles to guarantee a peaceful coexistence among humans and maintain both the health of humanity and nature for ten more millenniums if not forever?
3. What kind of international authority or central government is required for maintaining this structure at the cost of giving up capitalism, communism, freedom, democracy and all the other ideals we humans have build fantastically without considering all the realities that the first question might establish truthfully?

Can we intelligent humans at least gather enough courage and honesty to explore the likelihood and extreme costs of running such a universal structure?

Meanwhile, even personal philosophies might find practical common grounds for revamping our current infantile mottos and lifestyles at least and making our communications in families and societies easier. Naturally, not everybody has time and patience to build a personal philosophy and adopt a rather stoic character along with regular reflections to make a better use of his/her life. Thus, ultimately, some scholars should incorporate a bunch of solid personal philosophies into a general theory, perhaps as a practical *guideline for social conscience and family relationships* suitable for the public to understand and adopt easily. Through this learning process, we might at least realize the vanity of our present lifestyles and mentalities.

For example, some ideas in this trilogy may be expanded into a basic guideline (personal philosophy) that sounds practical for a group of people. The main point is to find routines that may help people reassess their needs and personalities to choose a healthier life path and live a bit easier with a relative notion of happiness.

Meanwhile, we can all try to study and formulate our personal philosophies somewhat more actively and objectively for higher self-awareness and better living. It can help us cope easier with social norms and systems, survive, and relate to others effectively with least frictions, while possibly boosting our independence and integrity within society consistently as well.

For building a sensible personal philosophy, we should learn a lot about the authenticity of our needs, personalities, and inner 'self,' thus the rest of this chapter will focus on this topic.

Power and Personality

Personal power is reared and reflected in two ways: the inner power that gives us self-assurance and independence, and the outer power (charisma) that goads our relationships with people. The type and level of personal power that we possibly gain over the years remain mostly cluttered in our psyches, except for the portion that manifests thru our exposed personality. Nowadays, particularly, we stress on developing our outer power for gaining popularity, participating in juvenile pleasures, and manipulating others. Even so, we go about it in a crooked manner, mainly by creating phony personalities that lack enough roots and integrity to reflect even a small dose of character or charisma. We just keep boosting our Egos in hopes of reflecting our false pride, dreams, and confidence. Therefore, people detect our shallowness quickly, as we hardly appear natural. Meanwhile, our vulnerable personality consumes our energy throughout our lives without gaining any kind of power or our sense of individualism.

Our misguided approach and mentality about personal power is a product of social trends to feel important and love ourselves too much with no inherent qualities to match our arrogance. It merely reflects our neediness and struggle for social imitation and adaptation, which hardly help our outer power, but definitely erode the chance of building our inner power, too. Instead of finding confidence and independence, deep down we remain doubtful about our identity and feel more dependent on others and things to survive. We need more acceptance and approval from people every day to confirm our existence and we should surround ourselves with more friends, wealth, and pleasure to feel and prove our power. In the end, both our inner and outer powers remain shaky, while our pretensions and superfluous needs confuse us even more than they annoy others.

Conversely, if a person focuses on building his inner power, he finds no, or little, need for the outer power to maintain his identity and relationships, yet an aura of charisma might radiate from him eventually. His deep confidence and independence at least make him much less needy for other people's approval and less susceptible to their negative reactions.

The inner power evolves simply by exploring 'self,' which is the neglected aspect of our personality as explained in the next section. The irony is that the inner power is easier to build, while the outer power often grows during this process eventually, too. Furthermore, with an authentic identity and self-sufficiency, a person gets a better chance of meeting the right people who share the same values and needs. Instead of seeking popularity among many phony people, he might find a few friends who really grasp his/her sentiments and thoughts. The only, rather harsh, drawback of focusing on inner power is that relating to the mainstream gets difficult for the person, as well as for people who cannot figure out his/her rather stoic attitude. Not everybody grasps or respects that kind of quiet charisma, since it appears odd and intimidating compared with social tendency to embellish personal power in a showy and exaggerated manner.

With our false personalities, in fact, we often cause ourselves extra headaches by attracting people who are incompatible with us in terms of our needs and aspirations. Thus, we waste time to go through a long process of trials and errors to admit at last that our relationships are merely making us more depressed and lost than enriching our lives. Most relationships' lousiness, nowadays, is due to our lack of inner strengths and integrity. Our showy means of building our personal powers and relating to others also contribute to our chronic senses of loneliness and helplessness.

Personality Aspects

For building both our inner and outer power, we work on our personalities to acquire certain personal attributes and to portray a confident image to others. Learning about our personality and the way it operates can also help us detect and nurture our inner self. Therefore, a brief review of the main aspects (characteristics) of personality and its manifestation mechanisms would be useful.

Sometimes, we hear people say, 'A part of me was dying to say *this* and a part me felt *the opposite*, but then I ended up saying something *quite different*.' Most of us get these vague sentiments from time to time when we distinguish different aspects of our personalities briefly. This common, natural sense merely reflects the way human personality functions, as discussed in this chapter.

Analysing an individual's personality reveals three essential dimensions or aspects in it, which we may refer to as Self, Ego, and Model. These three aspects of a person's personality are not defined here in the same context of Freud's definition of the three divisions of psyche for psychoanalysis, which are id, ego, and superego. While the latter classification emphasizes on the way personality is developed and retained inherently mostly in our unconscious mind, the former is interested in the way personality manifests mostly through our conscious efforts. Of course, some similarities and overlaps exist between the two models, but the classification of the three aspects of the personality, as defined by this author, is for a different purpose. It mainly explains the way we go about making our decisions, choices, and contacts with the aid of our manipulative personality aspects. (A basic comparison between the two models is offered in the Addendum on page 38.)

For this book's purpose, Ego is defined as one's conditioned personality that reflects one's subconscious needs and desires, lower mental qualities, vanity, self-centredness and dependence on externalities. Ego represents the self-serving needs and goals of a person, which are mostly hidden or at least not presented voluntarily. In general, Ego is the cunning and selfish aspect of a person's personality.

The 'model' aspect of personality manifests in the manner we try to adapt to social norms and in the way we present ourselves to others. It usually ends up becoming the main feature of our personality and who we believe we are. We perceive or construct one or several role models (personalities) that appeal to us. We would then internalize and behave in the form of the model that we adopt overall or apply in particular instances. We do this for satisfying our conscious needs, or hiding those unflattering parts of our Ego that we do not care to project in our daily dealings and relationships. We also adopt a Model when we do not have a set of values of our own, or when the elements of immaturity are present. Model becomes more prominent when Self and Ego are less developed and active.

Self is one's unconditioned nature. It resembles that aspect of a person that is defined as id in psychoanalysis in terms of being the unconscious aspect of psyche and the big source of psychic energy. However, Self is also the unexplored and underutilized aspect of a person that entails his/her potentialities and spirituality dimensions. Self contains the absolute, isolated aspect of a person untouchable by negative or positive experiences of social living. Chapter Thirteen of Vol. II of this trilogy discusses Self's seven elements in detail under the heading of 'Knowing Ourselves.'

Our personality is the combination of these three aspects of a person's characteristics at any instant. They are always present and interact constantly according to a rather fixed mix for each person. For example, an egoist is driven mostly by his Ego. Yet, the level of each aspect contributing to total personality at any point may vary, thus change a person's personality manifestation.

Our mood changes also reflect the varying mixtures of the three personality aspects. (Of course, 'multiple personality' concept is different from personality aspects erratic operations that lead to different presentation of personality and possibly mood swings, whereas multiple personality is a rather fixed condition.)

Sometimes, Model might simply portray and reinforce the expectations of Ego, and sometimes Model might reflect a new feeling or role that it suddenly finds interesting and appealing. Sometimes, we can control our anger or frustration and present ourselves in a desirable format (model.) And sometimes our basic honesty—a rare manifestation of Self—subdue the other aspects of our personality and we say things that we might even regret later, e.g., when we tell the truth about something or someone.

Living in the highly structured and conditioning societies of the recent era has taught us to play the role of a Model broadly rather than revealing the natural person within us. That natural person (self) is subdued and lost at a very young age, anyway. We use Model a lot since we do not want to portray the deceitful aspects of our Ego, and we do not want to show our gullibility and immaturity that Self usually radiates. And we do not have the courage to be the 'self' that is not favoured as an acceptable model of success and passion in our cultures.

The varying mixes of our personality aspects in particular situations and times make us behave erratically and thus appear instable. Yet, a person's unique personality manifests according to the overall prevalence of one or two of the three personality aspects. We are usually dissolved in a personality that is mostly a Model, Ego, or Self, while the other two play their roles in lesser proportions simultaneously as necessary. It would constitute our main personality. *That is the personality we strive to keep happy.*

Our genes, environment, and conscious efforts play their roles in the manner our personality develops and manifests. While we cannot control their effects, we have some influence on the way our personality turns out, especially in the way it manifests. In fact, we often play a major role in faking a personality that seems appealing and can serve our hidden and selfish needs and desires. We use different aspects of our personality randomly to achieve our immediate goals. However, the main purpose of our lifelong efforts to portray a certain personality is to maximize our power and appeal in the long haul. In particular, we use Model regularly in hopes of showing charisma and power. Sadly, however, the outcome of our efforts is usually more destructive than helpful. Many of us end up with shaky personalities that others can detect immediately, while we also keep struggling internally with the wrong self-image and a false identity that we are so keen to build and maintain. All these struggles and frustrations feel odd when we could instead use our potentialities and energies to create an appealing and powerful personality, which is natural, too. Instead of trying so hard, and keep failing, to build a false personality in hopes of impressing (or fooling) others, we could put our efforts into building a stronger identity and inner self. By doing so, we gain the needed charisma more naturally and better than it is achievable through superficial pretences. The main hurdle that deters most people from pursuing this option is that building a Self oriented personality takes time, and it takes even longer for others to recognize and respect it, if at all. We are ordinarily not patient and passionate enough to wait for all these (only potential) natural developments.

The main role of our personality (and the mixed application of personality aspects) is to facilitate our communications and daily interactions, all for the objective of maximizing our happiness in life. We try to be assertive, manipulative, and cooperative with the use of our personality aspects in order to get things done our ways and guarantee our ongoing popularity and satisfaction. Surely, developing the various aspects of our personalities and manifesting them in certain ways also depend on our intelligence, needs, and perceptions of people and surroundings, all for the ultimate purpose of finding peace and happiness. Unfortunately, we often choose to nurture a set of erratic personality aspects to serve our social needs and ambitions, instead of curbing our needs and ambitions within the parameters of a natural, healthy, and stable personality. Still we hope to find happiness, too!

These basic definitions of the three aspects of personality are elaborated further throughout this trilogy as various discussions about personality, especially Self, become necessary. Many other topics in this trilogy are also related to personality aspects. For example, the concept of happiness can be gauged only in relation to the prevalent aspect of a person's personality. As soon as the topic of happiness arises, the immediate question is which aspect of his/her personality s/he is trying to keep happy. Our decision is crucial and determines the outcome, because the definition of happiness varies for each personality aspect. We associate the state of happiness usually with that aspect of personality that we are consciously giving an emphasis. For example, the happiness of a Model oriented personality comes mostly from popularity and approval, which does not coincide with a general description of happiness. Someone whose depth of happiness is defined to him as, let us say, having the most amount of wealth or sex has a different point of reference compared to our general impression or formula of happiness. However, even when a person is hoping to make the prominent aspect of his personality happy, his/her happiness remains shaky because the other two aspects of his/her personality do not feel so happy at the same time. For example, when Ego feels happy (maybe because somebody expresses his/her love to her/him), his/her Model and Self might feel sad or even angry (maybe because s/he does not trust the sincerity of the person who has expressed his/her love). These crucial factors cause extreme complications in a person's psyche for feeling a real sense of happiness. These are some additional reasons that 'happiness' remains an abstract and mythical concept. Thus, the question is, 'How can we compare people's happiness and how do we define real happiness?' It is almost impossible, but Part III will tackle these questions and topics in some detail.

Addendum
A Comparison of the Id, Ego, and Superego with Self, Ego, and Model.

The Freud's three divisions of psyche place the emphasis on the sources and course of development of an inherent personality—in the way they stir or influence the formation of personality. However, the final interface, i.e., personality manifestation, is of lesser concern in that model, if at all. At least two other questions can be raised about that model, too. First, whether id, ego, and superego explain the process of personality development fully. Second, to what extent a developed personality remains fixed and stable within the highly fluctuating and forceful external stimuli. That is, assuming a person has developed a certain personality, would he always use that personality or learn to fake (or actually develop) different personalities that he finds either appealing or useful. Would a fake personality gradually influence the real one over a long period? Which one of the 'real' or 'fake' personality is more relevant for either psychoanalysis or a person's welfare? And a host of other issues. It is becoming safer to assume, these days, that besides imitating the prevalent social patterns, people in general do not develop strong, fixed personalities to begin with. More importantly, however, they often prefer to hide their shaky personalities behind fake ones that feel more useful for their special needs at any particular situation in social settings. Certain role models and values, e.g., pomposity, have become quite popular in society as a way of proving one's individualism and assertiveness. Everybody tries to portray a typical personality to gain acceptance from peers and friends.

In this author's definition of the three aspects of personality, the emphasis is on the ultimate outcome, i.e., the manifestation of personality, rather than how and why it has developed in certain ways—and then often hardly used, anyway. The manifestation of personality includes both the real and fake personalities, though the ratio of each of them in the final presentation varies among people. After all, the final product is most important for both the individual and people who perceive him according to a mix of real and fake personalities. (By the way, the ratio of fake and real personalities always remains hidden even from the individual himself, while also fluctuating erratically.) In this sense, we can actually examine 'personality' in more details in at least three layers: 1) The true characteristics of an individual (the developed personality), 2) the manner these characteristics are mixed with pretences and presented in public, and 3) how an individual is perceived in totality by others contrary to his intentions. These complex details are not covered in this book.

Nevertheless, the two personality models (i.e., development and manifestation) are interrelated and in many ways inseparable. They both need to be studied for the understanding of the other and for explaining and improving personality as an extremely important social phenomenon. In fact, both models start with the natural and inherent properties of man, which emerges from the basic reality of being (alive). That is, our instincts and urges, and perhaps our souls, comprise the foundation of personality and are included in id (Freudian model) or Self (this book's framework). Perhaps one point of distinction can be found in the negative properties of id, which erupts in terms of disruptive urges and destructive drives. In the 'manifestation' model, Self is relatively more stable, pure, and unselfish in terms of its nature and origin (how it is created) and how it would have manifested if human's nature were not corrupted by excessive Ego and Model mostly for adaptation purposes. In this sense, the negative manifestation of any personality erupts mainly from Ego and Model, mostly due to severe external forces, and very little due to the instinctual urges that a human is born with. Mainly, Ego creates superficial remedies and resistance, and negative personality manifestation, due to a person's unfulfilled needs and frustrations.

At the same time, it is plausible that id or Self, as the intrinsic nature of man, contains assertiveness and adaptation tendencies

(Ego and Model) automatically. Thus, these tendencies are the inherent (basic) characteristics of humans and needed for their survival. Only to the extent that Ego and Model grow extensively beyond their elementary (natural) presence in id or Self, they manifest as unique and prominent personality aspects of humans, and thus warrant the studies like the one presented in this book. Model and Ego require a closer study and attention, as critical psychological developments in the new era. Model and Ego have become too complex and forceful, in line with people's growing superficiality and egotism, and they are hurting our interactions and social order in major ways.

The definition of 'personality' used in this book depicts the inner interactions of Model, Ego, and Self. What we refer to as personality is expected to reflect an individual's characteristics in terms of his/her preferences, habits, and ability to express his/her feelings, needs, and goals. It has two essential properties: (i) The potentiality and reality that exist within an individual regardless of how well s/he can utilize or demonstrate them, and (ii) the raw image s/he portrays to others of him/herself, which reflects how well (or deviously) s/he is able to express him/herself through Ego and Model regardless of his/her true character.

CHAPTER TWO
Humans' Philosophical Thoughts

Naturally, our personalities affect our abilities for thinking and the kind of thoughts we nurture regularly. In return, our thoughts influence the development of our personalities hugely. Thus, the nature and processes of our thoughts are stressed in Part I.

We are made of similar cells and DNA, but our thoughts and feelings make us who we are—so unique. Scientists believe that we make 40,000 decisions every day, which in return shows the enormity of thoughts and feelings that support or demand all those decisions every day. Even our simple thoughts and feelings constantly interact or clash deeply, thus expand into an enormous (often unmanageable and stressful) pool of thoughts, emotions, and decisions at every moment.

Our thoughts can be divided into three main categories. First, *mechanical* thoughts about our mundane affairs such as where to go, what to eat, what to buy, and similar simple thoughts that lead to the majority of our daily decisions. Second, *tactical* thoughts that relate to our learning requirements, performing our jobs, making financial plans, finding our mates, etc. These kinds of thoughts usually cause the highest level of disappointment and stress. Third, *fundamental* thoughts about our existence, ideals, philosophy of life, etc. They help our self-awareness, spirituality, and growth. We are very little conscious or proactive about this essential category of thoughts and thus suffer in a dull existence.

The structure of our lives, as discussed in Volume III, sets the overall path of life that most people follow rather robotically. This social structure is developed (and supported) mostly through our *tactical* thoughts and decisions. The quality of these thoughts and decisions, however, depends highly on the strength of our *fundamental* thoughts. Thus, Volume I is devoted to the analysis of fundamental thoughts and their role for our growth and health, especially by helping us make wiser tactical decisions to cope with social demands in creative manners. If we are interested in finding a more meaningful path of life for ourselves, we should first examine our fundamental (philosophical) thoughts and gauge their effects on our tactical thoughts and decisions.

Normally, we do not recall even a few dozens of our thoughts in a day, if that. Yet, certain fundamental thoughts boggle every intelligent person's mind subconsciously every day. They define some aspect of our lives, but make us feel delighted or depressed about our surroundings and ourselves as well. They encourage us examine our being, boost our spirits, and feel good. Furthermore, studying the nature and effects of our fundamental thoughts is useful for boosting our erratic logic and justifying our actions, feelings, and decisions. These innate thoughts can also help us build a personal life philosophy to reduce the burdens of living. Table 2.1 offers some of these existential thoughts.

Table 2.1: Humans' Philosophical Thoughts

1. Our reasons for living.
2. How to build a happy life.
3. What is a meaningful life, in which our deeds, feelings, and thoughts have value and purpose.
4. How to take life easier (to bear it at least)
5. What is the inner 'self' and 'who we are' as a person.
6. What is the essence of humanness and can it be enhanced.

7. How to effect change and improve social order.
8. What a 'wisdom path' is and how to find and explore it.
9. What freedom is and whether it is an achievable goal.
10. How to live practically but not submissively.
11. How to nurture our positive doubts, while defeating the perils of indecisiveness.
12. How to fight depression but not fear it.
13. How to make major life decisions and survive.
14. How to find a reliable companion.
15. How to optimize our physical and mental health.

The above list covers humans' main life dilemmas among many others. These complementary thoughts, and our efforts to resolve them, preoccupy any intelligent person's mind for building his/her general life philosophy and defining a meaningful path of life for him/herself. In fact, none of the above dilemmas (thoughts) can be truly analysed and resolved without contemplating and choosing a ground for the others. Accordingly, our thoughts often become too complex, fuzzy, and confusing—since we must find a comprehensive answer for all these life dilemmas together, as a routine for self-awareness to make our existence more authentic and meaningful. We do this exercise routinely at some level, at least in our busy subconscious. In the end, of course, 'finding the means of a peaceful and purposeful life' is the ultimate objective of all the fundamental thoughts in the list. All these thoughts and dilemmas constitute our instinctive urges for finding solace and some form of happiness, which is merely a myth by the way, anyway, as will be discussed later in this volume.

This Chapter reviews the above fifteen fundamental thoughts briefly with the objective of constructing a practical personal life philosophy to guide us throughout our lives with an ability to make better decisions, while managing our doubts productively. Everybody can benefit from a well-defined personal philosophy to address his/her numerous dilemmas collectively and develop a comprehensive plan and path for making the best use of his/her life and thoughts. Humanity might benefit from our efforts, too, if enough people take the trouble and time to delve into our beings more consciously. This trilogy makes suggestions for doing that.

1. Reasons for Living

One day in our early childhood, we suddenly become conscious of our being. We wonder with awe about the matter of existence that feels too mysterious. We are curious to know how and why we suddenly feel alive and confused about a difficult task at hand the way things appear around us and the way people nag about so many things they must do every day. As we reach some level of maturity, maybe even in childhood for some geniuses, we begin to wonder about our existence even more seriously, somewhat like a philosophical question. Then, we soon want to justify it, too, as though we did not deserve to live without establishing a rationale for being per se. Our doubts about the purpose of our existence, along with many other fundamental thoughts noted in Table 2.1, always roll in our subconscious or unconscious minds, although most of us with lower mental drives or curiosity do not ponder them actively. Looking for a reason to live, especially, feels like an innate (and perhaps spiritual) urge ingrained in our genes. We cannot avoid it, and some people may commit suicide if they are oversensitive or tired of not finding their purposes for living. The more intelligent a person, the more s/he feels obliged to justify his/her existence, which shows the high price we must pay for being an intelligent species.

Sadly, however, it is getting harder every year to find good reasons for living within the chaotic environment and lifestyles we have created for ourselves. It is getting even harder to promise a bright future to our children when socioeconomic conditions are fundamentally threatened and family problems are getting out of hand. Fortunately, however, the majority of us do not give up easily and quickly, while we pursue our passive crusades to find legitimate our reasons for existence. All along, we dwell on all kinds of doubts and adopt lousy motives to keep living without ever feeling quite satisfied with our reasons or existence. Mainly our hopes and optimism make us believe in finding an excellent rationale for living eventually. We also invent some ideologies or objectives to suffocate our persistent nagging urge for finding the truth. Nevertheless, relying on some shaky purposes for living is still better than not inventing any reason at all. The absence of a life purpose only heightens our frustration and depression. In a philosophical sense, we find fewer reasons for living every year, but luckily some other instinctual urges, such as lust, still keep us amused, hopeful, and optimistic. *So, we plough on idiotically!*

Of course, the other side of the coin is that any rational person needs even more valid reasons for *not living*. More people fight with the thoughts and feelings of loneliness and desperation these days, which often appear like good reasons for not living. Still, most of us are stubborn and resilient enough to persist, anyway, as if programmed to tolerate suffering and rejections naturally. Even our hopeful doubt about the possibility of some ultimate reasons for living is a positive urge to keep us going. Our doubts help us live longer, but also make us cope, explore life, persevere, and wonder.

Nonetheless, our lifelong urge to justify our existence is an added pressure of living all by itself, while it also complicates our thoughts and feelings constantly. In fact, living is too difficult, because we feel obliged to have reasons for both an enthusiastic existence and early exit, while no valid rationale seems to exist for either. Oddly, not having a good reason for living or dying does not automatically justify, and lead to, the other option. This deep inner conflict stir the most fundamental doubt in our lives—the biggest dilemma we struggle with forever. That is actually the exact question Shakespeare imposed on us, too, "To be or not to be?" The dire conflict Hamlet faces is due to his doubts for both, although the emphasis appears to be on finding a justification for living. Our urge and struggle to find a reason for either option never ends. Period! Meanwhile, we just plough on through life, suffer, think, enjoy, until we die, although this persistent inner conflict about existence per se remains quite excruciating all along every day.

Worse, as we get old, we realize the futility of our hopes and dreams, or even our lasting struggles to find a reason for living! We just learn to amuse ourselves somehow until the end arrives. We grasp the futility of all those worries, thoughts, and solemn feelings that have crippled us for no tangible outcome. Eventually we admit that life has no purpose when we are old and tired, if not sooner. This gloomy conclusion poses another fundamental question for youths—about their duty and source of motivation for living an inherently purposeless life, if going by the testimony of wise elders. Well, that is why they prefer to ignore the advice of elders and instead become too reckless and mindless often in hopes of deflecting their innate dilemmas—all in vain, though!

Nevertheless, the irony is that we must eventually face our most fundamental dilemma and mission as soon as we realize the two basic facts that: 1) No philosophical reasons exist for living, and 2) no good reasons exist for not living, either. Back to square one! Then, our new and urgent fundamental thought (dilemma) would be: How to learn and build a useful life for ourselves based on the above two outrageous facts without letting these existential thoughts and feelings torture us? This subliminal conundrum and doubt about living imposes an intellectual challenge for many people, which can be resolved somewhat only after they learn to build at least a personal life philosophy.

2. How to build a Happy Life

Well, if life has no particular purpose, can we at least find a means of being happy? While disillusioned by the big dilemma of being per se, all our thoughts and actions focus on one ultimate purpose: To lead a happy, healthy life in a meaningful manner. Our innate optimism and hope make us believe in the possibility of finding happiness and tranquility. Our pride also goads us to believe that not finding happiness is a compelling reflection of our worthlessness and failure. Occasionally, we get a taste of this elusive happiness, which raises our hopes about the possibility of making it permanent. Thus, we look for the wisdom of doing so by seeking all kinds of advice from gurus and experts. Part III discusses the 'self' and happiness in detail. It attempts to identify the characteristics of happiness, but mainly suggests that a special personality and outlook are needed to maintain happiness rather permanently. Yet, building that proper (rather unconventional) personality to find lasting happiness depends on how well we come to terms with the fifteen thoughts listed in Table 2.1 above. We need the right mindset and faith to resolve these dilemmas and a variety of doubts, feelings, and thoughts that overwhelm us.

An authentic 'personal life philosophy' should also develop and refine our 'personality' to manage our doubts and decisions, balance the cycles of happiness and depression, and find peace. This delicate combination of personality and philosophy would help us develop the right mindset and priorities, choose the right values, and build a simple lifestyle—vastly outside the pervasive values and religions offered in societies. A refined personality nurtures a practical life philosophy intuitively or through self-awareness. Accordingly, the person learns to adhere to his/her beliefs in spite of the rampant external forces that try to influence his/her thoughts and feelings.

Of course, realizing the characteristics of a proper personality and building authentic personal convictions in our materialistic societies is a main challenge in itself. Even harder, however, is to admit the necessity of revamping our beliefs and values. Unless a person is somehow blessed with at least some inherent goodness and curiosity for gauging his/her life options, s/he hardly sees the need for a mental overhaul or life philosophy. Thus, we face many questions, such as, 'How a person with no inherent goodness or wisdom would ever care to consider his/her life options more objectively and strive to build a personal life philosophy?' What other incentives may motivate him/her to change his/her lifestyle, and find happiness? How can people with rigid personalities and crooked philosophies try to find happiness without reassessing themselves and their ideologies first? How can we even think about happiness before making a big overhaul in our mentalities? How can anybody free him/herself from the luring rewards of materialism to build self-reliance and some sense of spirituality? How can we achieve all these challenging goals simultaneously?

Answering these questions is difficult, but some guidelines to pursue this horrendous task are suggested throughout this trilogy. Three points are clear though: (1) Finding happiness requires a proper mindset and personality, (2) pursuing an authentic life philosophy for finding happiness would lead to the development of an ideal personality eventually, and conversely, (3) a groomed personality would have little difficulty in choosing a personal philosophy and life path that lead to some notion of happiness.

3. Making Our Lives Meaningful

We often feel empty with big cynicism about our lives' meaning. This raw inkling is rather different from the first two related urges (dilemmas) discussed above about the purpose of our existence and finding happiness. Surely, external factors and fate always affect our moods, but mostly our elusive boredom causes stress, and self-doubts, while our innate urge for a meaningful life feels unfulfilled even after we have satiated our deep ambitions. How foolishly had we imagined a meaningful life merely in sitting at the beach with a cold drink and a handsome companion, plus lots of money to do whatever we wished! What nonsense!!

If we get a bit more philosophical, we question the value of our routine activities even more and resent wasting our *allegedly* precious lives so mindlessly. We like to know what else is out there that could make our lives a little more meaningful, although we cannot even decipher the word 'meaningful.' Still, we blame ourselves for the void and our inability to find a finer existence. During our struggles for a meagre subsistence or accumulating enormous wealth with dire persistence, after doing the same things over and over, we still doubt the purpose of wasting our lives on those routines. After every failure or accomplishment, we dread the daunting shallowness of our being without even a tiny light at the end of the tunnel. All along, in fact, this deep inner conflict augments our pains about the inherent frailty of life altogether— the dilemma (# 1) explained above. Now, we grow more doubts even about the whole spectrum of humanity and God.

We often try to force ourselves out of these depressing moods by engaging even deeper in our routine and struggles, or seek more pleasures. We try to lose ourselves by doing more activities, pampering our sexuality, taking on new challenges, travelling all over the world, and looking for exciting ventures, if not resorting to alcohol and drugs. Especially, we socialize a lot to elude the feeling of emptiness, which seems aligned with our dire sense of loneliness, even when we are in a relationship. These tactics are the best remedies and potent defence mechanisms we have been able to fathom. Yet, they have all failed miserably. In fact, they often only add to our feelings of boredom and void, despite their potential for inducing temporary joy and relief. These distractions simply would not resolve our persistent sense of void and vanity, while our brains pamper greed and egotism, instead of humility.

The bottomline is that our feelings of emptiness often erupt from chronic boredom, despite tons of activities and excitements. It grows in our subconscious a lifetime and makes all our efforts and triumphs feel hollow like a bottomless abyss. Yet, one day, this feeling finally becomes too deep and painful no matter how hard we fight this elusive mood. We feel quite lost and helpless even when basking in luxury and fame amongst cordial friends.

The simple reality is that prevalent lifestyles and social norms cannot offer a peaceful, let alone a meaningful, path for existence, nor can they boost the essence of our being. Instead, only a viable philosophy along with conscious learning can help us develop a basic wisdom to fulfil our authentic needs and bear our volatile societies with a rather stoic mindset. Through a self-fulfilling life path, we might also experience a soothing sense of spirituality in line with divine values we discover beyond religions' eccentric notions, nowadays. Yet, this alternative way of living requires a long journey into our inner selves to overhaul our conditioned, warped mentalities. The objective is to *invent* a simple definition of life (philosophy) to guide our thoughts and deeds consistently, instead of worrying in vain about building a meaningful existence out of our crude ambitions and deepening our inner conflict about the value of our presumed achievements. We need this self-made platform to avoid the chronic sense of emptiness on the top of so many painful social traps we cannot avoid.

Contrary to common beliefs, a meaningful life does not grow around 'things.' Rather, it depends on how effectively we use those special life 'resources' we inherently own, such as passion, potentialities, compassion, and spirituality.

Surely, these ideas sound absurd in a society where people try to seek a meaning for life mainly by resorting to hypocrisy and any gimmick to deceive others for more wealth, sex, and success. Nowadays, we prefer to waste our most precious assets, i.e., time, energy, and brain, to fulfil our addiction to materialism.

Ironically, our attachment to society also keep raising the bar regarding our illusive perception of life's potential for meaning. We become phonier and cruller in hopes of enriching our lives!

Then, a bigger irony is that only a balance of things, not more of everything can make our lives meaningful. Only an effective use of life resources is the secret of a meaningful life. The less time and mental energy we spend on things, the more of our resources can be used for fundamental thoughts and genuine needs, which provide a much higher potential for *meaning* in terms of the number of years (quantity) we live and what we do (quality.) A 'meaningful life' needs a full range of worthy thoughts, feelings, actions, and principles (life values) to fulfil our enormous social and personal responsibilities. During this learning process, we seek the means of true happiness (peace of mind), bring the 'self' in control of our destiny, find a path of wisdom based on our life philosophy, etc. Our focused energy and modest intuition can guide us explore new, soulful thoughts and experiences that maximize our chances for self-actualization, which is also the shortest path for normal people to acquire both a sense of being and divinity.

Contrary to the common perception, life's meaning does not manifest in a static state where everything reaches its perfection. Rather, it needs a high degree of change and risks in line with a person's dynamic mentality.* Life emanates its meaning through a variety of simple events and ventures that produce purposeful learning and experiences along with pure senses of excitements and achievement. It happens, especially, when we align our two levels of challenges: **First,** the challenges and plans necessary for maintaining our basic needs and health effectively—to build up a stable mind and body. **Second,** the plans and challenges that goad personal growth—the dynamism of a purposeful life. This basic awakening occurs through thoughtful efforts and leads to spiritual experiences and practical wisdom. Nowadays, personal growth is a convoluted process that entails schooling, learning, building a career, working, making a family and raising children perhaps, plus other daily actions, decisions, struggles, delights, and doubts. Yet, we could affect and gauge this *rather rampant* growth more harmonically and consciously to develop our life philosophy and define our existence. All these small experiences also provide the texture and beauty that manifest life's meaning.

We can strive forever to explain so many aspects of life and choose certain fundamentals to make it rather meaningful. But, beyond all these experimentations and sophisticated philosophies, we discover that life by itself has no special properties to make it complete or even meaningful outside our personal vision of being and meaning. We may assume that the universe is perfect as it is, but even that would be just another subjective judgment. Life's challenges and meanings are created in each person's personality

---

* Tools and techniques for building such unorthodox mindset and achieving the goals outlined here are explained gradually throughout this trilogy. Still, most crucial is the readers' zeal to read and absorb some basic facts first with patience and open-minds.

(psyche) based on the soundness of his/her unique life philosophy and experiences. Thus, in a philosophical sense, 'A meaningful life is the one we know how to create for ourselves.'

4. Taking Life Easy (to bear it at least)

To most of us, enjoying life means having as much pleasure and extravagance as we can possibly muster. We do the same thing also when we fail to resolve the first three dilemmas noted above, as we believe we must at least learn to take life easy in order to bear it the best. We rely on sexuality, alcohol, love, wealth, and power to boost our chances to forget life. We embrace superficial values, waste time and energy to build a phony personality, and maintain a busy, showy lifestyle. This demented mentality has grown fast in modern societies and still people wonder why they are stressed out, instead of enjoying their lives as much as they think they deserve or plan. Yet, all those seeming pleasures make us feel lonelier and emptier every day when our struggles to relax and enjoy life also feel in vain and exhausting. The acceleration of family breakdowns and social stress are good symptoms of our shoddy lifestyles and mentalities within the rampant world affairs. No matter how much pleasure, possessions, and power we enjoy, at the end we still face the same dilemma: How to make our lives rather bearable somehow at least now that it is so meaningless!

Sadly, the slogan of taking life easy is now ruining people's judgment and decision-making ability with so many clues around about this modern motto's harms on our lifestyles and being. For one thing, the amount and intensity of our never-ending regrets for the opportunities lost and decisions not made, or made hastily or foolishly, reflect our bad judgments and decisions. Of course, regrets could also be a sign of growing wisdom. However, if we cannot reverse or ignore the repercussions of our earlier mistakes, we can hardly hope for even an easier life. We can always try to make the best of our existing circumstances, but for reaching a lasting inner peace, we must make certain efforts and decisions at the right times. To make our life bearable at least, we must plan it —mostly in terms of life philosophy and path. We cannot 'live in the now' in order to enjoy our lives to the fullest and yet expect to have an easy life, too. Rather, ongoing planning is essential for minimizing life burdens and preventing irreversible mistakes that could cause lasting grief and regrets. Planning is for making our critical life decisions in a timely manner in line with our instincts, wisdom, beliefs, and doubts. Foresight and planning are for not getting trapped in inescapable and regretful situations, which have sadly become too prevalent, nowadays.

One traditional principle always makes sense: There is a 'right time' for every decision and every doubt. We can leisurely follow our dreams and enjoy righteous experiences throughout our lives, achieve our goals, love, etc. But there is a 'right time' in our lives for certain things. There are only certain years that we can enjoy childish thoughts and plays. There are right times for building a career and a family. There is a right time for making a decision about marrying a particular person. Many critical decisions of life need both a *sound mentality* and *right timing*. If we stand by and let those tiny opportunities slip away, or make hasty or foolish decisions, we face many disappointments all our lives. There is also an 'optimal time' for less critical life decisions, which are still crucial, e.g., for completing a college education if one intends to have one, choosing our careers, making our life plans, etc. A sad story in papers many years ago had shocked me as a parent, and then it appeared like a good example for the topic at hand.

On April 11, 1996, the plane that the seven-year old Jessica Dubroff was flying across the United Stated had crashed soon after taking off at Cheyenne, Wyoming killing her, her father and the flying instructor. Many of us probably agree that Jessica who was trying to establish the record for the youngest pilot lost her chance to live, let alone make proper, timely decisions. She was a victim of her parents' bad decision. Still, Jessica's mother said in a press conference that it had been Jessica's choice to be a pilot and that submitting to her wishes had been necessary.

"I beg people to let children fly if they want to fly." "... clearly I would want all my children to die in a state of joy." "... I would prefer it was not at age seven but, God, she went with her joy and her passion, and her life was in her hands." As reported by The Province, a daily newspaper in Vancouver, Canada.

It is hard for many of us to grasp this kind of mentality and advice, although the point is not to make judgments here. But let us ponder a scenario in which our six-year-old kid asks us to let her/him drive a car because s/he enjoys it. When we say no and explain its dangers and illegality, s/he would say, "Okay, how about letting me fly, then?" S/he would try to convince us that s/he has suddenly developed this passion to pilot a plane and that her/his life would be ruined if she did not fly across the United States within one year. Even more bizarre is that flying at young age is not illegal, but driving is, as if planes were safer than cars or needed less maturity! What a society and leadership!

This story is surely an extreme example of how we humans, especially parents, nowadays, make decisions in hopes of making our lives easier, better, or joyful. Almost everything we do these days follows the same mentality about the means of enriching our own and our children's lives through competition and arrogance. Parents and society have spoiled and misguided kids too much.

Every day we set strange purposes and standards for ourselves and our children. We teach our kids from the very young age that competition and winning are the most valuable purposes of life. We are turning our young girls into sex objects and confusing our boys about the kind of companions they need or should choose. With our attitudes and beliefs, we set and impose a ridiculous perception of an ideal life for ourselves and our children—a world in which we always win, have fun, and surpass others at any cost. We waste our mental energies and time on pointless rivalry, spite, and materialistic struggles that have no purpose but feeding our Egos and raising depression in society and around the world.

The purposes of a seven-year-old piloting a plane, and all the subsequent decisions, may seem unclear, if not absurd, to many of us. Yet, again, the point is to stress that this is not an isolated instance in society by a long shot, although the consequences of our parenting and personal decisions usually would not appear as catastrophic and obvious. The fact that we do not realize our clear mistakes or admit the fast downfall of our mentalities is even more bizarre and cause for concern!

We probably would not be serving any purpose, other than our Egos perhaps, by spoiling our kids by so many materialistic notions spread in societies now to the point of letting our kids drive or fly—and then using 'passion' as an excuse, too! Cannot this passion be addressed in a timelier manner? Would discipline and proper parenting damage our children's souls and psyches? Could not simpler experiences give our kids enough passion and joy until their time for flying, banjo jumping, skydiving and other adventures can be chosen more sensibly? Are not we, as parents, forgetting our role for teaching our children self-discipline and patience, especially when they show excessive emotions, passion, and irrationality? Have not we spoiled our kids enough? It is really hard to know that a seven-year-old child cannot judge or decide about flying in a bad weather just for setting a record, which does not mean a darn thing in a saner society than ours, anyway.

Jessica's story is only one of million simple examples of how we, as parents, and society in general, brainwash and spoil our kids with our wrong impressions about the means of enjoying or completing our lives. We push them develop their crooked values and fanciful ambitions, which have no valid purpose, and instead only mislead them altogether when the time comes for making their major life decisions. Accordingly, we abolish their chances to be good parents or spouses in their own relationships.

5. *Exploring Our Inner 'Self'*

We have an intrinsic urge to know 'who we are' as a person, though some of us are keener and fussier about this matter. We often question our truthfulness, identity, and personality subtly—

consciously or subconsciously. We like to analyse ourselves and maybe overcome the causes of our phoniness and sufferings. We like to build a strong character and maintain our integrity. These fundamental goals and questions always boggle our minds, at least subconsciously. 'Knowing about ourselves' and grasping 'self' are major topics in this trilogy and covered from different angles in various parts, especially in Chapter Thirteen of Vol. II.

We learn a lot about ourselves when we consciously attempt to do so, usually for developing a personal life philosophy. Our search revives and refines our inner 'self,' while we analyse our authentic needs and feelings, get more in touch with our souls, and learn to master our thoughts and decisions more effectively at last. Through this conscious process of building our beliefs and faiths, we try to grasp the motives behind some of our superficial personal needs, reset our expectations from life and society more realistically, and then attempt to assess our lifestyles, ideologies, and philosophies. Accordingly, our minds develop 'self'-driven guidelines, beliefs, and ethics, especially for curbing our endless arrogance and neediness. This basic self-awareness and wisdom provide the platform for building the foundation of our thoughts and finding a relative sense of contentment and peace.

Conversely, without an ongoing conscious self-analysis to know about our 'self' and purposes of living, we never develop the insight, wisdom, and a life philosophy that can minimize our pompous behaviour, hasty decisions, and lasting agony.

We use philosophy for grasping 'self,' and 'self' is our guide for building a sound philosophy to manage our lives. We ponder the urges driven by the less desirable aspects of our personality (i.e., Ego and Model) for developing our life philosophy, too, but only for learning the difficulties of maintaining a 'self' controlled personality. (The three aspects of personality, i.e., Self, Ego, and Model, are discussed in Chapter One.) Anyway, our personal life philosophy shows our self-image as well as our preferences for the kind of society, family, and friends that can stimulate our mental and spiritual growths.

Exploring the inner self and building our life philosophy is not a one-time exercise to decide on certain personal preferences and objectives. Rather, it is an ongoing path of learning and evolving, and then formulating our thoughts. This is often a natural process, though, in line with our efforts to grasp our inner needs as we mature and think deeper and longer about our experiences and existence. As such, a personal life philosophy goes beyond the purpose of merely defining and formulating our thoughts, ideals, wishes, and morals. Instead, it should be viewed as the vehicle that carries us through the journey of 'self' realization, while we learn more about our dilemmas and doubts, as well as the deeper, delicate side of us we have not known before. At the end, we reach the wisdom path that we have been seeking inherently. Then, a 'self'-controlled philosophy of life would guide us as we proceed on the path of wisdom with our souls free at last.

6. *Defining the Essence of Humanness (Humanity!)*

A rather universal definition of *humanity* can be drawn based on our current intelligence and world cultures. However, this conclusion would be quite dubious, since we still do not know who we are! Even scientists have different viewpoints about human nature. While the word humanity has come to imply togetherness and compassion, societies' new teachings mostly stress on individuality (pride and egotism). That is, we give our personal interests and needs a much higher priority over any public and humanistic interests. Accordingly, our views of humanness have become incongruent and vague.

The main theme (and purpose) of humanness erupts from the ideal of humans' common needs and interests manifesting and boosting both personal and social conscience. This sacred idea has, however, been infringed by the domination of individuals' and special group's interests controlling the value and structures of societies. Thus, another purpose of a personal life philosophy is to nurture an authentic meaning and perception of humanness in our minds. We have to fight internally with so many ideas and priorities that have misguided us all along about the criteria of being an individual, but not necessarily a human. Now, switching from individual to human (commonality) is not easy. We should give up our biases and brutalities that dominate our judgments when we measure and value things and people. More integrity, compassion, love, and forgiveness should be cultivated in our minds, deeds, and relations with others and the universe.

An inherent purpose of our philosophical thoughts is to assist us reassess ourselves within the context of collective humanness and humanity. Our life philosophies can help us transcend from the stance of selfish individualism to the realm of integral beings. Nevertheless, our doubts about the purity of human nature cannot be eradicated easily, since all evidences indicate that building a sense of decency in humans would probably be impossible. Like most animals, our instincts alone prevent us from becoming a pure human being. Yet, we might at least rise above animals to appreciate the vanity of all the killings and sufferings in the world for no reason but our sheer stupidity and greed. Even animals' instincts stop them from humiliating and killing their own kinds for such trivia so regularly and naturally. How is it then possible that humans' instincts and egoism have demoted them below even that basic standard common amongst animals, while we still boast about our supreme intelligence, too?

All these thoughts and doubts about humanity occupy our minds regularly, but we usually do not know how to face them and change our mentalities. It is hard to bypass our inherent wild nature mixed with vile social teachings for greed and rivalry. Yet, perhaps, a personal life philosophy can boost our understanding of humanness, to become less needy and more compassionate. This minimal morality might then also goad us to play a role in spreading sensible social and personal values and promoting the ultimate goals of humanity and harmony of life.

Sometimes, we feel outright ashamed when we notice—by some magic possibly—that not even an ounce of integrity is in all the weight we carry. And sometimes, we feel horrible when we witness how the people we love—our parents, children, friends, and spouses—are so empty of compassion. Then, we wonder how much integrity and compassion is in humans' essence!

Ironically, exploring our 'self' and becoming a 'self'-driven person raises the idea of our connection to a larger sphere and a collective humanity. We entertain the high likelihood of 'self' being an integral part of the universe, which we think governs the sacred realm of existence. Yet, our social attachments and raw perceptions hinder our ability to see this vague image of totality, anyway. Sometimes we recall being only an insignificant part of the universe, yet still remain too pompous around one another, as if we were gods in our own rights. Our thoughts about 'who we are' are quite inconsistent, because we do not have a good grasp of 'self' and the essence of humanness. Thus, understanding the scope of our interconnectivity within the universe is just another philosophical thought engaging us our entire lives.

We like to see humans as a unique, wise species with rather similar needs, although we still keep hurting one another often with our juvenile personalities. We also ponder the chance of our connection to a whole (or holy) entity and our souls linking us to this mystical eternity beyond the universe. Therefore, the purpose of a personal life philosophy is to assess human existence and develop ideologies for defining and honouring these likely divine links that we crave privately. Believing in this natural connection more consciously can help us become purer human beings, too.

7. Effecting Change and Improving Social Order

In line with our pursuit of happiness, peace, and a 'self'-driven life, we sometimes wonder if the world can become a better place to endure existence easier. We think about devoting some of our energy and time to the welfare of others directly or indirectly. We like to play an active role in strengthening social infrastructure and mending its broken pieces. We feel rather obliged to do our share in the construction of facilities, ideas, and systems that can support and protect life and the health of our planet. A refined life philosophy demands such devotion and active participation in the affairs of societies, organizations, and governments. Our sincere intention for charity emerges in our careers and through personal initiatives without any expectation for monitory rewards.

Sometimes, we ponder our cynicism about people and social systems, including our families, socioeconomic flaws around the globe, the welfare of humanity, and the health of Nature. Each type of connection, e.g., family, stirs certain facts and demands. 'Becoming a purer human,' as discussed in the previous section, is a *personal responsibility* as well, not only a whim or ideal. Thus, grasping our varied responsibilities and means of fulfilling them are other purposes for developing our fundamental thoughts and life philosophy.

We have learned to view 'relationships' mainly as mechanical processes for facing people and society. Yet, every worthwhile relationship carries lots of responsibilities to grasp its parameters and ways of nurturing it, despite its expected burdens. Especially with the rising chaos in families and societies, nowadays, grasping our roles is becoming more obscure and overwhelming, but also more urgent. We spend lots of energy, feelings, and thoughts on relationships, yet they usually cause us more disappointments and cynicism about human nature. All along, we hurt all these social systems, including our families, with our idealism and naivety, instead of lowering our expectations and learning the purposes of comradeship and teamwork. In particular, we are so foolish when we imagine relationships are for making us happy, when actually they only impose their own burdens and demands on us.

In all, we are hesitant in acknowledging our social and family duties philosophically and realistically as innate social mandates. Our selfish needs and ambitions or apathy cripple us to grasp and fulfil our duties properly and sincerely, thus we hurt people and ourselves. Just showing some random sympathy or concern is not enough. Rather, we need deep conscience and an action plan with a clear definition of the role that one can realistically play, besides staying realistic with much lower expectations customary now.

On the one hand, we should get creative about discharging our responsibilities to people and society, instead of becoming more needy, arrogant, and shallow. On the other hand, we need some general guidelines and a better social mentality to facilitate and encourage a sense of global comradeship and responsibility.

8. Choosing a Path of Wisdom

We believe we know a lot about life and people because we are smart, have gone to school long enough, obtained many years of experience, made lots of money, built a huge Ego, and similar reasons. We trust our knowledge and ability to grasp and analyse facts, situations, and people perfectly. Therefore, we rush to make hasty judgments and decisions, and take risky actions. However, behind all that haughty confidence, we always have lingering thoughts and doubts about our egoistical perceptions of the world. We might even sense the need to follow a self-awareness regimen and curb our lasting desire for self-importance eventually. During this journey, we notice the possibility of a different reality behind our rigid perceptions and haughty interpretations. Maybe a more sensible reality actually satiates our nature more *truthfully*. Only then, we may realize the naivety of our beliefs and the limitations of our knowledge about ourselves, people, and things. We sense that our conventional beliefs and knowledge are merely illusions built around an imaginary world. We see how our misperceptions and misjudgments distort our viewpoints, desires, decisions, and doubts. We remain doubtful chronically when we should decide, and we decide hastily when we ought to doubt.

If we ever reach such a critical point in our lives, we see the need to develop a personal life philosophy and a more reliable path of life. We like to understand and remove our prejudices that contaminate our judgments, decisions, and actions. We like to find a means of curbing our naivety, conviction of superiority, or other misperceptions resulting from living within the boundaries of a 'perceived world.' Some lucky people achieve this divine milestone and follow a path of wisdom eventually after years of feeling lonely and empty—even among their large families and friends—while pondering and doubting their ways of living.

Following a path of wisdom starts with a personal conviction, or perhaps a deep inkling (doubt), about a 'real world' out there that supersedes the laws and values of the 'perceived world' we are accustomed to. We entertain the opportunity of opening our minds, souls, and hearts to a new vision of existence by grasping some aspects of the real world. With this basic commitment, we might step on a path of wisdom that would ultimately change our vision of the 'reality' we have known. We start to doubt the value and importance of all the 'facts' we have embraced fast without thinking. As we progress on this fine path, we find more about life essentialities and realize how we have been wasting our times and energies on worthless struggles and worries. Slowly, wisdom replaces our perceptions and assumptions. We commit ourselves to a self-awareness regimen in search of the truth and reality; to soar to higher levels of 'self' control and wisdom—the summit.

Following a path of wisdom is not a mythical concept the way it sounds to us. Still, it is also logical to keep some doubts even about the wisdom guiding us through a new authentic life path that we adopt with strong faith. Dr. Wayne Dyer's book, *You see it when you believe it* suggests that if we believe in seemingly unrealistic or mythical ideas, such as God, they turn into realities that we can *see* and *trust* readily. He suggests we build our faiths by discarding our doubts. Yet, inventing and perceiving things based on our forced imaginations, sounds just like another lame philosophy to many of us. Dr. Dyer's idea is plausible, though, in the sense that we must break away from our existing perceptions, so that we can develop simple, meaningful beliefs and lifestyles. However, we should not replace one group of perceptions with another through self-hypnosis.

Rather, we can *believe* honestly—as part of our philosophy—that 'Believing in something just in order to see (imagine) it' is against any rule for following a wisdom path. Forcing ourselves to trust any concept or person before vast personal analyses and proofs is foolish. It is just another manner of mental conditioning to accept (force) the authenticity of a notion, like what religions have done to humans. We do not need to commit ourselves to too many new beliefs at the outset, anyway. Rather, we can start with a basic belief that 'Humans have already misled themselves all along with too much bizarre perceptions that themselves or others have imposed on them.' Thus, following a path of wisdom and awareness is mostly for cleansing those misperceptions to build a more natural contact with life and our 'self.' Once we step on this 'awareness' path, new meanings start to grow slowly along with our sincere desire to raise our consciousness and humility. The new knowledge and ideas would evolve naturally from within us. The only challenge is to stay focused along the process and trust one's 'self' to explore and follow this path patiently with honest, sensible convictions.

The 'things' we see are only the reflections of our minds and hearts' reactions to events, situations, people, and material things. Yet, we see all those things and the universe differently in a new context once we set out to gauge our minds and hearts' current way of perceiving a finer reality. We would suddenly have more doubts about so many things we were certain about before. These are positive doubts and precious. At the same time, making tough decisions feels more logical in line with our new beliefs. Social obstacles would seem rather less significant and often irrelevant completely. This new perspective makes our purposes of living clearer and simpler as well. Life would feel enjoyable merely by the reality of our existence once we succeed to discard so much superficiality and pomposity injected into our neglected beings in modern societies. We feel relieved, as life feels easier to tolerate, too, just because we concentrate on its natural attributes that we have personally thought through and appreciated at some level.

The new path of wisdom would show us the options of living that are not obvious from within the perceived world. Following this path helps us distinguish the essential facts and decisions of life amidst the mountain of supposedly important dilemmas and situations piled up in our head about the 'perceived reality' world. It would give us the power to know when to doubt and what to doubt. At the same time, it would give us the insight, eventually, to see those things that are authentic and thus less doubtful.

9. Gaining Our Freedom

Freedom is not free by a long shot. In fact, we should pay a big price for even a small dose of it, let alone absolute freedom that is a myth, anyway. Our endless search for freedom and the feelings of entrapment at work, in family, in relationships, and in society as a whole torture our minds consciously and subconsciously to no avail. Instead, we get more frustrated every day, since gaining even a relative freedom is getting harder, while we feel trapped by our dire financial and emotional needs and dependencies.

Surely, the current sentiments in societies about freedom is too naïve and futile. Our leaders and people have been deceiving themselves and the world foolishly. Their tenacity to insist on this myth (freedom) is even more embarrassing and ridiculous for an allegedly intelligent species after all these millenniums of human experiences and tragedies! The bottomline is that attaining even a semblance of freedom is impossible if we like to live in a society and have a family, not to mention the compliance and regulations that governments and employers impose on us to do their jobs. Human nature cannot handle freedom, anyway.

Still, we might be able to build a life philosophy that can free us largely from the influences and impositions of social systems and people. We could find an optimal, yet practical, position for us, to enjoy enough independence and some feeling of freedom without isolating ourselves from society. Most crucially, we must somehow learn the degree of freedom we can handle before our lifestyle makes us feel so helpless, isolated, or depressed. We should decide eventually regarding the level of independence and freedom we can bear and/or need to lead a practical life, and then learn to adapt ourselves to that kind of basic lifestyle.

Feeling free is a tentative and relative state of mind depending upon a person's interpretation of life, which is itself a function of his/her intelligence and general perceptions. Since we normally accept the conditions and impositions of society as an inevitable reality of life, we do not feel our freedom jeopardized too much. And when we do not feel deprived of freedom, we do not realize what it is, although everybody feels, and suffers from, the stress of living in this imposing world. Occasionally, we suddenly crave our precious freedom urgently when we sense life's unfairness and impositions. Still, despite the stress of living and our ongoing zeal for at least some relative freedom, we remain faithful to, and absorbed in, the rules and conditions of society. We go on living the way our parents have lived, the way we have grown up to be part of the transitory life and hypnotized by it. Our inner urges for passion, pleasure, compassion, approval, and other incentives keep us quite needy to others. Our neediness has grown so vastly we give up our freedom and maybe even our soul and integrity.

Fortunately, more individuals are starting to see societies and economic systems as hindrances to their natural freedom—which is not merely a matter of having a right to vote. Our democratic processes have in fact become quite infected, thus defy the sense of natural freedom that, for example, gypsies have had without any need for democratic pretences. We might be awakened by a cold slap on the face to feel the value and meaning of freedom, which is immensely different from the perceived freedom we are conditioned to imagine. Despite the stress and anxiety of social living, we seem to have no choice but to accept our illusion of freedom as a 'reality.' However, some of us at least appreciate that our stress and anxiety are the symptoms of a deeper problem. They relate to our disability to lead a 'self'-driven life without being labelled rebels and terrorists. We wish that exercising our freedom would not come at the cost of losing the trust, contact, and respect that we expect to receive from people and society.

Even when we see socioeconomic orders as real constraints to freedom and 'self'-control, our natural reaction (as well as social teaching) is to adapt ourselves and live with them somehow. We do not know what else to do and we are not ready for the risks of unknown or untested options. We like to think and act practical. Most of us cannot survive without the fringe benefits of social living. This is one of the real dilemmas of living. We have grown up within these socioeconomic systems and adaptation feels like a natural and practical choice. Then again, one day we suddenly feel the need to be detached from some of these social values. Like our numerous other irreconcilable dilemmas, it is difficult to balance these two conflicting needs. On the one hand, we feel attached to the systems that seem to feed our needs and Egos so nicely. On the other hand, we want to become detached when we suffer from all the stress and anxiety of social living, or when we feel our integrity is crushed beyond our tolerance.

Many complex dilemmas, including the situations related to our financial and love needs, keep us deeply dependent upon one another and social systems. However, numerous simpler habits, which we embrace so casually, also make our task of gaining our freedom impossible. A simple example is the extreme use of all sorts of financial credits to buy houses, cars, furniture, computers, vacations, shoes, and on and on. These facilities encourage us to consume more, often beyond our means. With the huge interest charged on most of these credit facilities, we end up using most of our income on repaying our debts. In all, the current liberal use of credit has caused deep disorder in both national economies and people's financial life, especially when it encourages us to spend beyond our means. For gaining our freedom, therefore, a basic cure is to resist the temptation of a credit-based life. In fact, being so needy for material things and consuming so much clothing and luxury is beyond human dignity to begin with. Thus, while using credit facilities prudently and rarely, detaching ourselves from this popular habit in our societies is wise to feel freer with less stressful jobs to do, too.

Another simple example is the influence of television and movies on our cultures and lifestyles. To make these programs and movies appealing to the naïve audience, a higher level of extravagance and excitement are built into them every day. They continuously raise the amount of violence, grotesque ideas, and sexuality in movies and television series (including commercials) to keep us attached. Accordingly, we adopt the crooked values and phony personalities promoted in those programs to shape our lifestyles. As our minds get confused and impotent to distinguish reality from perception, we get absorbed deeper in this world of illusions and imitate those crude, violent behaviours and phony lifestyles. Some people have now lost their minds and touch with reality so drastically they have become criminals with no motive or compassion. Random killings and family murder/suicides are signs of frustration merely due to the lack of a clear perception of reality and one's value of life. Personal expectations of life have drastically tarnished and everybody looks for more excitement, money, sex, and power. When these fantasies and expectations do not materialize—or often even after they are satisfied—people feel only more vanity and confusion.

We are becoming dependent on some individuals, groups, professional sports, and movies to make our lives complete or miserable (e.g., when our favourite sport team wins or loses). Although the feelings of depression and anger may last only a few hours or days, often the effect on our nerves and minds is permanent and substantial. Some people even gamble their hard-earned monies on these games, which makes the impact on them even more severe and longer lasting. We get addicted to invalid social symbols and values that give us both joy and depression, often in large doses. We depend on movie stars and athletes to give us joy and excitement, but also to affirm our identities. They have become our idols and heroes; and their failures make us equally angry, hostile, and depressed. Some sports are absolutely inhumane and violent, just because excitement increases with the amount of violence and generate more revenues, too. But, even those less violent sports can influence our psyches and affect our moods, attitudes, and reactions to others and things significantly. We try not to take the winning and losing personal and not to take the outcome so seriously and just enjoy the game. But it is difficult. The question is whether it is worth our time, energy, and nerves to be subjected to this much torture as a price for a short excitement and joy, e.g., from watching sport events. Not an easy question to answer for the majority of people!

How can we be proud of societies that promote such huge amount of phony perceptions of life through movies, television, magazines, and other means of propaganda to control people's minds and freedoms? How can we survive in such a perplexing setting without losing our sanity, identity, and integrity? How can we maintain some level of freedom without being fully rejected and isolated from society? These are big dilemmas that we have a hard time resolving when we crave even a basic level of freedom.

On the other hand, as long as we are absorbed in prevalent lifestyles, we would not realize, feel, or care about our need for basic freedom to elude our current meagre, mechanical existence. Our stress and anxieties, however, keep rising without us really knowing their cause(s). Eventually, we face two scenarios. We either keep living with stress and anxiety to the point of a nervous breakdown, or find the strength to look beyond the symptoms of stress and anxiety to explore how social entrapment has created our life dramas. There may not be easy solutions before we delve into a long exploration of 'self' and find a path of wisdom. Yet, we may at least fathom the sources of our conundrums and stress.

Of course, our social endeavours and competitions add texture to our culture and personal lives. Yet, they also drag us further away from the realities of life. We get too distracted to explore a more authentic path of life and gain our relative mental freedom. Our choices for attachment or detachment from various social systems, such as credit facilities, professional sports, or alcohol, constitute a part of a person's life philosophy. We cannot and do not want to isolate ourselves from the excitements and privileges of living within socioeconomic systems. At the same time, we must be wary of these attachments' effects on us and our children for maintaining a relative 'self'-driven and tranquil life.

A personal life philosophy intends to assess the balance of our attachments and detachments in society in order to minimize our stress and anxiety-inducing dependencies. Some attachments, like a family life, cannot be easily avoided, despite their potentials for causing high stress. We must somehow learn to honour and face these natural attachments in an effective manner. However, some attachments are questionable and avoidable if our life philosophy helps us see them as such, such as attachment to work beyond a reasonable limit. It would be a personal decision as to how much credit one should use to buy more things and services and how much TV and professional sports one needs for excitement. A refined life philosophy determines the extent of our attachments and sacrifices needed for gaining a relative sense of freedom.

Our ultimate decisions and doubts about our attachments and detachments are personal, but a general rule might apply to many of us: When no philosophical ground exists for attachment, we need strong reasons for remaining attached to, and dependent upon, something or someone. Otherwise, we should reassess our addictions to such thoughts, activities, and relationships seriously. We should know and admit why we are hooked, and then take action to detach ourselves from them as fast as possible. All these thoughts and feelings might eventually help us raise the relative degree of our freedom without expecting it as a given social right.

10. Living Practically but Not Submissively

We get frustrated quite often when we cannot get along with people, because, i) they do not understand us, our logic, or our viewpoints, ii) our efforts to change people, to see and do things our way, fail, and, iii) we remain doubtful about the possibility of people ever learning anything. Deep down we believe they can learn and change somehow if they stopped being so stubborn. We believe they are only resisting to become who we wish them to be since they are either too stupid or stubborn. We feel helpless and frustrated, because we perceive the value and depth of our relationships and friendships based on our level of congruence in thoughts and actions. The risk of building a personal philosophy is that it might make some people more dogmatic in assessing other people's behaviours, thoughts, and lifestyles. However, this attitude would be against the goal of personal philosophy that is meant to maximize our flexibility and open-mindedness.

The irony is that we should prepare ourselves for even vaster personal differences, since societies keep promoting individuality more than humanity and harmony. As societies become more complex and violent, people are forced to look for better means of defending themselves and surviving. Moreover, we encourage people to be assertive, positive thinkers, and fighters to maximize their opportunities and success in a highly competitive world. All these odd expectations (aspirations) contribute to self-centredness and ego-driven personalities who build their own crooked views of the world and give their own needs ten folds more importance than common needs in communities, organizations, families, etc.

These facts show the need for refining our life philosophies to encourage flexibility over individuality in order to accept and live with other people, despite their rising differences in thoughts and lifestyles. We should expect more situations and thoughts that contradict our principles, but be able to live with the situation or person. This occurs a lot in families, where the nucleus of most crucial relationships and communications are developed. When personality differences block the possibility of communication, only progressive personal philosophies can prevent disasters and breakdowns of otherwise acceptable relationships. Volume III of this trilogy discusses some of these ideas in detail.

Still, we should prepare ourselves for tolerating less bearable relationships and situations. We must gain that extra patience and compassion through our refined life philosophies, and then lower our expectations from life and people accordingly as well. We should admit that we (as a society) are incapable of reducing our personal differences even if it were a desirable thing to do. We must admit that hardly ever another person can really understand or care about our viewpoints and needs. Even if they did, they would never sympathize with our seemingly different or radical ideas, because their own views would always remain dominant and valid in their minds. Only when two people have the same basic needs, at least on the surface, they might grasp each other better—often tentatively until their higher needs begin to interfere again and create new conflicts. Generally, we should admit that people's varied backgrounds and visions make them different and dogmatic. We must learn that people hardly change, let alone as much as we wish and try, and as much as they may pretend, or promise, to change. Most likely, they cannot do it even for their own sakes; when they realize the benefits of those changes!

The silliest expectation we all entertain regularly is, 'Why he or she is not as perfect as we would like him/her to be!' We do so, as we imagine that our standards of perfection and correctness are valid. Thus, we have only ourselves to blame as long as we refuse to grasp and admit these basic facts, and while we cannot learn to be quite flexible. Our life philosophy and new mentality should eliminate these self-imposed sources of frustrations and agonies. Instead, we must learn to live and let live. The purpose of a personal life philosophy is to prepare us for this progressive mentality and expectation. People have different priorities and needs, and they have a right to live anyway they prefer as long as they do not jeopardize each other's communal welfare. We must beware of our Egos that insist we can change people. We should remember that although we may influence or manipulate others temporarily, we cannot control them forever and fully.

On the one hand, we need life philosophies that strengthen our divine self and help us *relate* to others rather passively but effectively, instead of struggling to change them to fit our needs.

Only through patience, tolerance, and compassion—by using the 'self' aspect of our personalities more often—we might live a peaceful life with people and symbols of our modern societies that often contradict our philosophies and principles. Otherwise, we simply would not survive in our families, work environments, and society as a whole. Naturally, this radical mental adjustment would present a big challenge and dilemma for us to resolve, since adapting ourselves to social values would keep threatening our fundamental principles, thoughts, and beliefs all the time.

On the other hand, adaptation and tolerance do not mean compliance. We intend to respect others and tolerate their quirks. However, we do not want to let them jeopardize our convictions regarding life. We intend to make our lives practical in the light of our knowledge of individual differences. Yet, it does not mean we submit to people and society's desires if they contradict our fundamental beliefs and personal commitment to a personal path of life and beliefs. We should not let 'practicality purpose' lead to our outright submission to the mainstream life. Of course, we can change personally, too, if we find it useful, but only according to our life philosophy and newer convictions, and not because of someone else's demand—even if we love him/her infinitely!

Thus, we set out to align our attachments and detachments in order to maximize our independence and integrity. We adopt a life philosophy that sounds practical for facing people and social systems with the least amount of frictions. We strive for certain personal ideals, while bearing popular ideas in society to survive. Meanwhile, we like to propagate new and revolutionary ideas to promote our humanistic goals. We plan to be open-minded and flexible in terms of our new thoughts. We try to build a practical personal philosophy, although it might appear bizarre within the recognized social boundaries. By flexibility and practicality, we mean to maintain a peaceful life and bearable relationships with others, despite our differences in needs, life purposes, and habits. We cannot simply expect others to think like us or understand our needs or life objectives even if we explained everything for hours, or even a lifetime. People's views of life vary vastly. Obviously, we cannot appreciate their needs and characters, either, since we do not have the patience, mindset, and incentive to analyse them. Not even a psychologist can understand a person fully, as his/her study has a targeted professional purpose. His/her analyses are based on limited information s/he collects in a short timeframe, circumstance, and environment, which never contains a person's full routines, thoughts, and inner strengths. We do not know even ourselves, let alone others! Still, *living practically* requires some efforts to grasp other people's needs, habits, and expectations.

We could try to appreciate the needs of at least those who are close to us and try to respond to their needs favourably as long as our beliefs and lifestyles are not highly jeopardized. A majority of us, however, has difficulty understanding or caring about other people's seemingly imposing needs and expectations. Still, we must try harder every day to find ways of living in harmony with everybody without arguing, challenging our differences, or trying to impose our needs and wishes on one another.

11. Nurturing Our Positive Doubts

Another flawed teaching of our societies, which is also reinforced by positive thinking schools, is that our 'doubts' slow us down and prevent us from taking risks and moving forward decisively. This notion might apply only in very special circumstances, but is harmful as a rule or strategy for a show of decisiveness and social appeal. Our prudence (doubts) in pursuit of new ventures is a fine innate defence mechanism, which is becoming especially crucial these days for fighting deliberate schemes and misinformation in our corrupt societies. 'Doubting' goads us to take a break and think deeper and longer regarding issues, instead of making hasty decisions. In particular, *doubting* the teachings of our societies is extremely enlightening, as it makes us *ponder* our life options in both short and long-term perspectives more thoroughly.

Most decisions require serious doubts and thoughts in order to, (a) subdue our emotional urges or egotistical assumptions about our knowledge of facts, and, (b) withstand other people's pressure on us to make a decision. Raw certitude and positivism ruins our abilities to analyse facts and our options more patiently. In fact, saying that decisions require thinking and analysis is not enough. Rather, we must also study the nature of our preliminary doubts in order to fathom the scope and extent of the factors needing scrutiny. Without deep doubts, we simply do not take advantage of the inner voice and intuition that emerge outside of any logical thinking process. For example, we have learned that the phrase 'I love you' may be more mechanical, or maybe even cynical, nowadays, instead of authentic and useful. Sometimes, we may doubt the sincerity of a person without any logical reason or proof of insincerity. Without our innate doubt, we may accept and use the information s/he gives us prematurely. These **positive doubts** are necessary for not only making sound decisions, but also becoming less judgmental and opinionated. Not only major life decisions, but sometimes even a seemingly simple decision requires lots of scrutiny and time (maybe months or even years) to avoid a catastrophic or regretful decision. To get a full picture about any vital decision, we must really take our time patiently to ponder many angles, elements and situations surrounding it.

On the other hand, we might turn into a chronically cynical person because of our negative perceptions and psychological reactions to our experiences. Often bad experiences with people, our gullibility, or not knowing how to nurture our doubts ruin our sense of trust altogether. For example, we might even become suspicious or jealous of our friends, since their odd behaviours hurt our Egos. These **negative doubts** are usually the symptoms of psychological shortfalls, although instincts still play a role, too. Suspicion and jealousy derive from personal insecurity and crude thoughts that raise our tension. They only waste our energy and intelligence. This is in contrast to 'doubting' objectively based on a whole set of sound factors, for a specific purpose, e.g., gauging the depth of our friendships. These positive doubts are 'self' (not 'ego') driven. Negative doubts or cynicism reflect our inability to doubt objectively and instinctually.

Analysing our doubts is a kind of meditation that requires a tranquil surrounding and a relaxed mind. Pondering our doubts is a major part of *ongoing* self-awareness as we proceed on the path of wisdom. Meditating on our doubts leads to answers accessible only in our unconscious mind. Our doubts usually induce some tentative tension, but they eventually exert an immense source of inner energy in the form of intuition and compassion, which then relieve the original tension, too. Positive doubts exude energy and intelligent decisions—not lethargy and cynicism.

Our 'doubts' are often also a *positive* attribute for relating to people and environment effectively and peacefully—most often with the goal of giving them the benefit of our doubts and seeing them more positively. At the same time, our 'doubts' prevent our naïve, automatic trust of people. Intuitively, our thoughts focus on positive possibilities and give people the benefit of a doubt, while we study their intentions completely even if it takes a few days or months. We see things with an open mind in positive light and purpose when negativity is not interfering. This attitude is contrary to cases when suspicion and jealousy direct all our energy quickly towards negative thoughts and possibilities. The *true* sense of 'doubts' makes us flexible and tolerant of others and gives us the chance to view and deal with life in a practical way. With positive 'doubts' we remain less critical of other people's crude positions and lifestyles.

Even when 'doubts' manifest as *negative* attributes in our judgment, such as the time we doubt someone's sincerity, we can use them mostly as an alarm mechanism. We can usually use this opportunity to meditate and evaluate the consequences of a major decision that is necessary to avoid irreversible mistakes or harms. Humouring our doubts during the decision-making process raises our decisions qualities. Meanwhile, this needed pause should not stop or delay the decision-making process unduly. In particular, the harms of delaying crucial decisions of life might be grave, yet rushed decision might cause harsher results. Without an effective use of both our positive and negative 'doubts,' our judgments and decisions might become prejudiced and muddled. Negative doubts (prejudice) lead to cynicism and withdrawal. Then again, positive doubts (as a drive for rationality) cause indecisiveness if not well studied. They even lead to gullibility if we keep giving people or events a benefit of our doubts to move on, instead of making bigger efforts to study people and events more carefully.

Maslow refers to a similar phenomenon when he attributes the indecisiveness of his self-actualizing subjects (as) a major weakness. He states:

"The main danger of B-cognition is of making action impossible or at least indecisive. B-cognition is without judgment, comparison, condemnation or evaluation. Also it is without decision, because decision is readiness to act, and B-cognition is passive contemplation, appreciation, and non-interfering, i.e., "let-be." So long as one contemplates the cancer or the bacteria, awe-struck, admiring, wondering, passively drinking in the delight of rich understanding, then one does nothing." Toward a Psychology of Being, Abraham Maslow, Von Nostrand Reinhold, 1968, p. 116.

"The main danger, then, is that B-cognition is at the moment incompatible with action. But since we, most of the time, live in-the-world, action is necessary (defensive or offensive action, or selfishly centered action in the terms of the beholders rather than of the behold)." Ibid., p. 117.

(The phrase 'B-cognition' noted in the above quotes means the 'Cognition of Being,' which is a humanness state of mind—love, caring, etc.—that self-actualizers are characterized by.)

Through a personal life philosophy, we strive to use both our innate and objective 'doubts' to our advantage. Mostly, we learn to distinguish positive doubts from suspicion and jealousy, which are destructive and contrary to the goal of doubtfulness. Instead, positive doubts are viewed as a source of inspiration, accessing our unconscious, and raising intelligent thoughts. Therefore, any positive doubt should coincide with *active* contemplation. The ultimate purpose of positive doubts is to help us develop our solid convictions and make the right decisions in life with a sensible frame of mind within a logical timeframe. Part VI in Volume II discusses the nature and role of human doubts in detail.

12. Fighting but Not Fearing Depression

We must deal more proactively with the rising sources and level of depression as our societies become more complex and less friendly. Our modern lifestyles make us quite alienated from one another and from the humanistic principles that must supposedly form the foundation of a society and our togetherness. Despite the prevalent positive thinking slogans, deep down we feel lonely and betrayed. We feel the vanity of life and doubt the viability of prevalent lifestyles. Our eagerness to show off our resilience and optimism, through our dire positive thinking pretensions, actually reveal our disappointments and insecurities. Often our struggles for positive thinking seem more like a gimmick or a refuge to hide our frustration, desolation, and depression. After all, life is hardly proving to be a joyous or meaningful journey. Without our innate hope keeping us going, many of us would have committed suicide already to get out of our laborious, boring, aimless lives. No wonder the level of violence, depression, and suicide is rising so fast. Still, all these commotions demonstrate our growing need for potent defence mechanisms to keep our hopes high.

All the evidences hint that the level of depression would rise as the merits of social living decline. Instead, we face pervasive social disorders, including the loss of compassion and patience, unemployment, tax burdens, unreliable social services, loss of privacy and freedom, higher cost of living and basic needs, real income reduction, lack of any form of job security, severe labour competition in international markets, and fast deterioration of political systems, social values, and morality. In these types of societies, people's interactions and relationships also become increasingly more antagonistic and a major source of depression.

Sadly, in today's overactive societies, everybody is dragged and trapped inadvertently into shoddy lifestyles that cause plenty of confusion and depression. Youths, especially, will face more overwhelming doubts and decisions, which they must also handle in a timelier and speedier manner. Our communication barriers are rising fast and we find it impossible to grasp and respect one another's needs and opinions. Personal doubts, stress, and anxieties keep piling up, and then, under these pressures, we also destroy our chances for building meaningful relationships with others. All along, we transmit our frustration throughout the society and add to the public's overall level of stress and anxiety.

Sadly, the future of humanity is doomed. We are already trapped in an accelerating process of no-return deterioration. The environment, economies, social values, etc. are all under severe pressures. Simply, the situation is hopeless. With the risk of being labelled a chronic pessimist, many of us seriously doubt that this deterioration process can be stopped or reversed. Too many strong and opposing poles overwhelm the social structure; they can neither be replaced nor brought into control and balance. For example, we witness governments' difficulty to bring national budgets and debts under control, simply because the means of achieving this goal requires higher taxes or cutbacks in services, neither of which the public like. A government cannot be popular and elected if its socioeconomic platform does not respond to the immediate needs of individuals, especially the rich running the world. This is like having a sick child decide whether to take his medicine or not based on its taste. Governments are influenced and run by elite groups and conglomerates, thus have lost their objectivity and efficacy to make proper socioeconomic decisions for the welfare of its citizens. The gullible poor are selling their freedom and democratic rights so cheaply, too, when they are lured by measly incentives or promises. The needs of business enterprises and labour forces can never be reconciled. When business should become more ruthless to survive in the highly competitive international markets, workers lose more jobs and psychological security, so they fight back. Numerous examples of imbalances exist similar to this tough business-labour dichotomy, such as the needs of industry and conservationists, the needs of wealthy vs. poor people and countries, the needs of the exploiting and exploited nations, the needs of individuals versus various interest groups, the needs of two individuals in a relationship, etc.

Besides the external pressures, we also contribute to our own frustrations and depression by setting untenable objectives and expectations for our lives, instead of focusing only on our real needs. Moreover, we do not know how to handle our occasional depressions that are natural, especially the mild ones erupting after a happiness cycle.

For all the above depressing facts, however, we must deal with three sources of depression more effectively: i) the external (such as socioeconomic and relationship) pressures, ii) personally induced stress caused by our fanciful objectives and expectations, and iii) the natural depression cycles emerging at the end of some (if not all) the happiness periods.

A main purpose of a personal life philosophy is to stay aware of the sources of our depression. We aggravate our depression unknowingly and unnecessarily when we do not study its sources carefully, or when we try to fight those unchangeable features of social structure without a proper grasp of their innate intricacies and likely solutions for humanity. Thus, finding and rationalizing the causes of our depression is important. The scope and nature of major sources of depression are discussed in Chapter Seven. Moreover, we often allow one type of depression cause other types, instead of learning to treat each according to its source, study its causes in detail, then build practical methods of curbing it somewhat. We can learn to view depression merely as a feeling that need not be feared, but only managed wisely. Like all other human emotions, depression need (should) not be suppressed or controlled artificially, but rather be understood to our advantage and expressed creatively. We must not feel guilty or lose control of our minds and thoughts when caught in a depression mood. Nor should we blame ourselves or even others for it, but only determine if any of our mistakes or misperceptions is causing our depression. Actually, a depression experience can help us learn (from) our mistakes and reassess our perceptions about life and society. Only, we must stay objective without allowing self-pity, anxiety, or laziness taint the process of studying our depression.

Instead of fearing depression or only fighting it as a negative feeling, we could learn to stress on the opportunity it provides to learn about ourselves and our life philosophy, etc. We must work on its roots actively, instead of letting it root in our subconscious and turning into a melancholic, nagging habit. Getting trapped in a depressed personality is neither an appealing social stance, nor a useful attitude for building a life philosophy. Actually, evaluating and studying the sources of our depressions can make us strong. While the presence of depression is normal and acceptable, we could stop it from dominating our lives or becoming a habit. In particular, by regular analyses of our mild depressions, we must disallow them to root too deep.

Ironically, we can often learn more about our unconscious mind and 'self' during a state of *alarming* depression than when we are lost in our *numbing* happiness moods and pleasures. As a major human emotion, depression can provide access to deeper layers of our being and initiate a natural process of meditation and evaluation. It is strange that our intuition and unconscious might be easier accessed and moved by negative emotions, such as depression or loneliness. Many philosophers, scientists, artists, and Sufis have reached their height of wisdom thru isolation and some form of stress. In fact, our minds work much shaper and wisdom grows only thru solitude. Of course, this does not suggest we can or should awaken our 'self' only through solitude or seek depression for any purpose. Yet, the divine world we *might* find and touch during our depression moods is unattainable during happiness periods. Each aspect of happiness-depression cycles has a unique benefit and lesson for analysing and grasping 'self.'

The depression-induced urge to seek privacy and do 'self' evaluation is mysterious, as if Nature were trying to give us a chance to heal our wounds during a period of inner privacy and reflection. In that sense, depression can be seen as an instinctual mechanism for 'self' preservation through reflection. A major cause of depression, nowadays, is that we are afraid of loneliness and we are not trained to benefit from this natural human need. Instead, we insist on socializing to fight off the depression of not knowing how to be alone and independent.

Ignoring our depression or facing it with artificial means, such as drugs, deprives us from the opportunity of learning through instinctual healing. We often avoid dealing with depression or unbearable thoughts on the ground that we are too busy to do so, or on the assumption that it would go away better by ignoring it or dampening it by more socializing. Accordingly, we not only pile up depression to a point of explosion, but also miss a chance to feel and express our deep emotions, which are often creative and heartfelt. This deprivation usually suppresses our ingenuity and damages our psyches. In today's busy world, we might not find time to even appreciate and handle our depression until its effects cripple us—almost the way we weaken our bodies from sleep deprivation and maybe even excessive pleasure. At that level, we simply lose control of our lives. Depression, at a normal level, is a sign of body and mind requiring a period of rest and reconnecting. Ignoring this vital sign would not curb the problem. Instead, attending to it would release the boiling tensions within us before it explodes; and if used properly, it might even lead to creativity and finding the path of wisdom.

13. Making Major Life Decisions

We ponder our life options regularly and build our beliefs crudely as we mature. Especially during adolescence and early adulthood, we hope to develop some kind of guidelines (life philosophy) for handling our niggling doubts and decisions. We look for valid criteria to reach right conclusions and avoid costly mistakes. We try to stay logical and insightful for making effective decisions, some of which we believe are crucial for our long-term welfare. We like to learn self-discipline and patience to face a big variety of life dilemmas with proper scrutiny. The main purpose of our torturous contemplation, of course, is to maximize our chances of enjoying life's grand opportunities, while minimizing the risks of social living and disappointments. In all, we realize that most of our decisions and actions benefit from a methodical justification and a profound life philosophy.

Accordingly, a personal life philosophy reflects our principles and beliefs. We try to apply it uniformly in our relationships and social activities with our raised self-discipline and patience. And we rely on it to assess our options within a hectic social structure imposed upon us so casually and callously. We hope to find life's essentialities and a wisdom path that can assist us materialize our true potentialities and feel actualized, instead of sinking deeper in the illusory world that our naïve perceptions have created.

Grasping the complexity and risks of a dozen or so particular decisions related to the topics covered in this chapter, including our efforts to develop the foundation of our thoughts or find a reliable companion, are especially important. Thus, Volume III of this trilogy is devoted mainly to discussions of life's most crucial decisions. Grasping the natures and purposes of all our doubts and decisions are also crucial, especially when they relate to our major life decisions, as explained in Part VI in Volume II.

14. Finding a Reliable Companion

Having a companion is a basic, instinctual need and extremely helpful for maintaining our mental and physical health. However, sadly, family conflicts have become the main source of stress and frustration in society, nowadays. We are quite doubtful about the nature and purpose of relationships in the new era and the level of reliance and trust we can have in another person in such a chaotic relationship environment. The situation is getting out of control fast, while we spend so much of our lives wondering how to find a reliable companion, how to relate, and how to avoid the rising hassles of being in relationships. We ponder this topic regularly, almost as much as we think about eating. Overall, relationship dilemmas pose some of the most critical decisions of life these days for everybody. In fact, the importance of this subject goaded the author to write a book about it first, *The Nature of Love and Relationships,* while delaying the completion of this trilogy. This topic is also stressed in Volume III of this trilogy in some detail.

15. Optimizing Our Physical and Mental Health

All our thoughts, doubts, feelings, and actions should lead to one ultimate, but basic, objective our entire lives, i.e., maintaining our mental and physical health. The central point and reference for building a life philosophy around all the *fundamental* thoughts explained in this chapter, as well as our *tactical* and *mechanical* thoughts, are just for serving our body, mind, and spirit wisely—though not through self-indulgence. Mental and physical health is indeed the main criterion for the correctness and worthiness of all major life decisions. All other goals and thoughts, including our search for happiness or a reliable companion, are valid and useful only if they can serve the main purpose—our mental and physical health. Thus, any thought, feeling, action, relationship, career, or life philosophy not augmenting this ultimate objective is wrong and worthless, while hindering our self-growth by damaging our mental and physical health. It is hard to imagine anybody having any trouble relating and adhering to this very basic philosophy permanently. That kind of ignorance would only reflect the sad effects of current phony lifestyles on our mentalities, e.g., when we undermine our health, compassion, and professions because of love, greed, work, power struggles, alcohol and drugs, etc.

Maintaining our physical and mental health is an obvious fact, although many of us forget this preliminary principle for living peacefully and effectively. However, the overall health is merely the first step, because we have the ability to expand our minds significantly for optimizing our health and happiness. We can seek the higher wisdom that most humans can potentially acquire for both living healthier and reaching divine enlightenment. All we need to succeed is the willpower and maturity to fight off the influence and demands of the crude perceived world. We need a sacred 'self' power to bypass the temptations of the superficial needs and values propagated in our lost societies. We need new visions and thoughts to defeat our misperceptions, particularly about the purpose of life and our futile search for that elusive happiness within a tainted socioeconomic framework. We need a strong 'self' to reveal our gullibility and childish whims to us, and then perhaps take us to those territories of higher wisdom and energy, which only a healthy mind and body can reach.

Human brain has a much vaster capacity and potentiality than we normally recognize and utilize. We use only 5-10 percent of this capacity on the average, if that. Even intelligent scientists and geniuses have not used their brains much beyond this low level. Thus, there is plenty of potential and intelligence in humans that have not yet been tapped because of the way we have restricted our minds to crude thoughts and habits—mostly due to religions and charlatans exploiting our minds and existence.

Obviously, with a weakened physical and mental capacity, we cannot utilize even the bare minimum potentialities that might be considered normal for humans, nowadays. Defeating our mostly irreversible flaws due to our genetic defects, crude upbringing, and social conditioning is hard. Actually, humans' capacity for higher intelligence to reform their vile lifestyles and mentalities sounds fanciful, especially considering their seeming naiveté and innate ignorance throughout the human history. Only a miracle to give a kind of divine physical and mental capacity to a large majority of people might evade the looming fate for humanity.

Still, we might envision the likelihood of *some* humans' higher wisdom if they perceive life's essentialities, reset their priorities, and emerge as selfless, wise individuals keen for a harmonious universe. With our primary intelligence, most of us can assess our physical and mental health as a first step towards a basic degree of self-awareness. If we succeed, we quickly realize that we are not as clean and clever as we naturally could be or believed to be. Then, we could attempt to resolve our weaknesses through a rigid self-therapy and awareness regimen, or by visiting a specialist. By acknowledging both our flaws and likely human potentiality in general, we might be able to refurbish our troubled psyches and spirits. We might find and admit our idiosyncrasies, and then treat them slowly with care and passion. This long self-cleansing (awareness) process can prepare us to enter a path of wisdom towards enlightenment.

Occasionally, we feel too vulnerable during some moments of self-doubt and loneliness. In such times, we must resist those fast and foolish scapegoats that entice us to react harshly. Instead, we should draw on our primary wisdom and patience to boost our inner strengths and beliefs to study the sources of our depression and desperation patiently over a few days or months. We should remember the risks of losing our resolve during such critical states, e.g., when we feel lonely, lost, and helpless. We remember that odds are high in such moments of vulnerability to make bad, irreversible decisions that would prove harmful physically and psychologically.

Despite our awareness, it is still hard for most of us to fight our vulnerabilities, including our harmful activities, addictions, or superficial lifestyles. Just to defeat our loneliness and void, we often prefer self-destruction to self-awareness, including suicide, perhaps because it feels easier and because we have a hard time justifying our existence, anyway. We lose our valid reasons (and even our plausible doubts) about living. Thus, we give up and let go of our mental and physical health. Self-destruction feels more natural than self-awareness to ordinary men, but we can choose not to remain an ordinary man.

We need high awareness about these inevitable moments of weakness in our lives and a strong conviction to avoid making irreversible errors during such gloomy periods. We cannot elude many inevitable cycles of depression, but a healthy mind realizes that some moodiness is natural. Our awareness and free spirit can help us handle and perhaps even take advantage of a depression mood. These states of moodiness are the natural symptoms of a happiness-depression cycle, hormonal changes, or a soft case of personality swing that are normal and manageable at these levels. Our chronic doubts regarding the purpose of our existence cannot be avoided and they always cause depression. A healthy psyche knows how to handle a mood change or defeat a mild depression, instead of being threatened by them.

Physical weakness per se not only allows diseases take over our body fast and easy, but also sabotages our spirit and ability to think straight. By letting body lose its vitality beyond the normal aging process, and not following an informed health regimen, we only raise our chances of failure and sufferings in both physical and psychological fronts. Conversely, without nurturing our mind as a normal routine, the physical aspect of our existence is also threatened drastically. Body-mind connectivity (including their linked welfares) is a fact we must always remember and honour. Without defining a plausible direction for our lives and making firm commitments to achieve certain worthy goals, we would leave ourselves at the mercy of the Devil. We would damage our spirits and existence if we do not take control of our lives.

Our actions and decisions need valid purposes for enriching our minds and bodies. Thus, the idea of 'living in the now' when one's life is not planned and pursued proactively sounds reckless and foolish. Then again, taking life too seriously based on strict beliefs, especially religions, also feels silly on some days. Even the notion of extending so much effort and time on optimizing our health and living longer sounds absurd at some philosophical level when the whole matter of existence feels too burdensome and futile, anyway!!*

Referring to the simple example noted briefly before, one of our major pastimes is to watch professional sports and cheer for a special team. The higher the consequence of those games, such as playoffs or finals, the more their results affect us emotionally and psychologically. This is a prevalent habit and a big phenomenon in the world today, in the way athletes and celebrities have such great impact on the quality of our mental and physical health. We feel sad for no justifiable reason at all. Why we strain our brains by our raw obsessions is inexplicable. Is it because our lives are too empty and soulless? If yes, why cannot we think of healthier pastime to overcome the burdens of our mundane living and avoid all these extra pressures on body and mind?†

Humans' *philosophical* thoughts briefly discussed in this chapter, as well as our *tactical* and *mechanical* thoughts, consume lots of our energy, and stir depression and destructive urges often, too. They stir a large variety of lingering doubts for us throughout our lives and they demand extraordinary life-changing decisions. All these thoughts, doubts, and decisions also provide the chance for learning about ourselves and finding a path of wisdom, although they occasionally turn into main sources of depression and stress during the self-cleansing process, as discussed in Chapter Seven.

---

* These conflicting views of life and humans' mission to think and behave rationally based on their sound personal philosophies reflect the intricacy of human dilemmas and logic, as well as this author's mixed (or mixed-up) urges of doubts and honesty about the meaning of existence. Appendix A below elaborates on this issue further.

† The author admits that these comments are ironical or maybe therapeutical for a person who is himself obsessed with watching professional hockey. However, these kinds of calming self-reminders have helped him mitigate the amount of time and nerves he devotes to this particular obsession of his. At least he realizes and regrets (half-heartedly) his addiction, while staying hopeful about resolving this dilemma for himself eventually!! Maybe humans soon reach a point where their rising chance of extinction is fully felt, thus wasting any energy on professional sports looks absurd!

Appendix A
A Big Human Dilemma:
Only Enjoying Life or Finding its Meaning!

We easily find animals' life meaningless and discard any chance for their divine relevance within the universe or God's kingdom. This is a reliable sentiment to use for inferring exactly the same thing about the meaning of human life. We are merely another animal with no particular purpose or meaning for our existence, despite our obsession to fuss over humans' high place within the universe just because feel smarter than animals and can talk and write about divinity! Obviously, we can dream and speculate as much as we like, especially through religious nonsense, but those thoughts and expectations would only misguide our brains and pain our psyches in vain. Even if humans happen to live one or two more millenniums or even a few million years, we would never be able to unravel the mystery of the universe or find any particular purpose for humans or other types of existence.

Some keen readers might object to this viewpoint, especially considering the discussions on page 44 about personal reasons for living. They may question the value and meaning of establishing and pursuing personal life purposes if we believe life itself has no special purpose or meaning. This valid conclusion can be accepted or rejected with equally strong points and reasoning depending on a person's intelligent choice and philosophy about existence per se. Many intriguing and conflicting viewpoints for living at all in a purposeless life can be developed in a major book all by itself. Ultimately, however, we cannot deny or change the sheer fact about life being a meaningless, compulsory journey imposed upon us accidentally. Still, once we grow up, build a strong mind, and decide to keep on living, we must make this adventure very purposeful, instead of only exist so helplessly just for the heck of it. In a way, we should defy the purposelessness of life itself in order to be considered a worthy human rather than a bum even if a person happens to enjoy a lot of fun or wealth. Whether we try to just bear life or enjoy it as well depends on our life philosophy.

Even for enjoying life we should stress on making our lives meaningful within the fifteen philosophical thoughts discussed in this chapter. In fact, another big life irony is that, while existence has no purpose, we must set many personal purposes for our lives to make it 'meaningful' *merely* for our needs based on specific objectives that might help us maintain our health. *The fullness of our lives depends on how consciously we try to define one for ourselves in line with our values and philosophical thoughts.* The ideas offered throughout this trilogy can help us on this regard, especially regarding the fact that life's 'richness' depends on our knack to use our potentialities and time wisely. A major emphasis is placed in this trilogy (especially Volume III) on one's diligence and timing about major life decisions for making one's life both meaningful and joyful.

Enjoying life is obviously more than having an occasional feeling of ecstasy, or even a sporadic sense of 'self-fulfilment' due to divine personal achievement. For enjoying life, the cycles of happiness experiences should be continuous and self-feeding, as we manage the pressures of depression cycles effectively, too. We do not necessarily need big achievements and self-actualizing experiences to attain the highest sense of completeness and joy. Rather, we need many simple experiences that challenge and use our potentialities. We can induce the feeling of achievement by doing small things like gardening, writing a short story, painting, meditation, or physical exercise. Every piece of music can be rediscovered over and over. Every plant and flower has a divine property, delicacy, or fragrance that we can feel for the first time every day. Our thoughts can stir boundless energy that leads to unique creations and worthy experiences of tranquility. However, it seems difficult for most of us to accept that only simpler life purposes fulfil our inner needs and 'self,' and evoke experiences beyond egotistical or materialistic ventures.

We need 'self' driven experiences, since only they activate the huge amount of energy and joy that flow naturally within us. We need more of the experiences that are not based on winning and hostility, but rather on giving and forgiving. We do not need more pleasures and sexuality to enjoy life at its fullest, but only compassion. We do not have to follow a phony lifestyle that stirs only more depression. We do not need to exhaust ourselves with our idle attempts to find the meaning of life, make it complete, and enjoy it as much as possible.

Grasping the meaning of life is merely a matter of reaching enough maturity and contentment, which happens only when we grow a stoic mentality to view our basic life somewhat enriching and meaningful as it is for a selfless, self-fulfilling person. How we can go about solving these related, philosophical dilemmas and fulfil our sacred mission as a thoughtful human requires high wisdom and diligence that only we can develop personally.

Ironically, for maximizing our life enjoyments, we must first accept that no ideal or 'complete' life exists. Only we, personally, can define and make our lives relatively pleasant and meaningful thru a simple life philosophy built around humans' natural needs. Ultimately, our joys should evolve from inside us in the form of mental energy to activate our unique potentialities and build our faith for gaining contentment and self-reliance. No ideal purpose, e.g., happiness, exists for life. Nor certain life purposes can bring us lasting happiness, although we can make our survival easier through simpler lifestyles. If these conclusions are valid, then life cannot be ideal or meaningful outside our personal mentalities and inner strengths to validate our mere existence through our faiths every day.

CHAPTER THREE
Perceived and Real Worlds

The world and all its luring features, events, and interactions feel so natural to us, thus we take them as our 'life realities.' Yet those 'realities' are mostly the reflections of our imaginations, desires, and interpretations. These subjective impressions and judgments are infected by not only humans' sensual limitations, but also people's dynamic tastes, priorities, and preferences. Worst of all, social, political, and economic propagandas and misinformation are ruining even humans' basic senses and perceptions of reality. Thus, humans' 'reality' is just a distorted view of the truth and the universe. Actually, our misperceptions impair our view of even simple facts, such as humans' extreme vulnerability, despite their rising haughtiness. We have even come to believe that God has a special interest in humans and has most likely even created this whole universe for our sake. What a weird, conceited species!

Meanwhile, many of us also sense a real, absolute world that exists out there independent from humans' crude impressions and interpretations. We do not know what it exactly is, but have enough spirit and logic to acknowledge its existence and purpose outside our naïve impression of it. Thus, we have two worlds: The *imaginary* world created in our heads thru our perceptions—let us call it the 'perceived world.' And then this *absolute* world that surely exists beyond humans' thoughts and imaginations—let us call it the 'real world.' Their main characteristics are:

Characteristics of the 'Real World'

1. This is a world beyond human imaginations, which holds the *absolute* truth about the universe—a minuscule part of which includes humans' existence, too.
2. It sets the attributes of all facets of existence, including the nature of man.
3. Deviations from the nature of things cause severe chaos and conflicts, which in humans' case leads to their endless, rising confusion, conflicts, and pain. That is, as long as we humans try to create absurd imaginations, rules, and thoughts beyond our natural needs and capacities outside the real world's realms, we make our lives whimsical and unmanageable.
4. The natural connection between humans and the universe emerge instinctually in the form of their inherent drives and spirituality needs.
5. No religion or human intelligence (or any other kind of imagination) can reveal the true nature of the 'real world.' However, our limited intelligence might eventually help us map a path of wisdom that enhances our sense of connection with the universe. That seems to be the only way for humans to find peace of mind and live in some harmony within the realm of the 'real world.'

A fuller picture of the real world is provided on page 104.

Characteristics of the 'Perceived World'

1. This is the world created merely by human impressions, rules, ethics, ideals, propagandas, and desires.
2. We have learned to fully accept this world (our perceptions) as the utter truth, instead of doubting its authenticity.

3. We make our judgments and decisions based on humans' subjective standards, values, and criteria that have evolved in this illusive world. Accordingly, our logic and judgments are not aligned with any reality beyond human inventions, which are made merely for our convenience based on our limited intelligence and erratic needs.
4. Because of the above conditions, and due to our greed and ambitions, we have created a great deal of superficial needs and priorities for ourselves gradually through history and raised our expectations from life and one another, to a point where our lives have become too complex, unattainable, whimsical, and stressful.
5. We have developed wrong self-images and phony identities that have little relation to humans' natural capabilities and needs. We seem to need these superficialities to define and assert ourselves and adapt within our competitive societies.
6. Our socioeconomic structure and values have also evolved in line with humans' unrealistic impressions and demands, thus they cause not only confusion and hardship for people, but also reinforce the cycle of human misperceptions about life and themselves.
7. With our vast illusions and self-deceit about the purpose of life and our position in society, the 'perceived world' is now gaining an unprecedented momentum and becoming more superficial and misleading every year. The gap between the 'real' and 'perceived' worlds is widening fast and lowering the possibility for peace and practicality of human life.
8. People, including world leaders, are in total denial about the deteriorating path that humans have taken and still focus on immediate needs of businesses and governments, instead of the welfare of humanity in general. After many millenniums of trials and errors with our wars, science, philosophies, and politics, we still do not have a sustainable socioeconomic system even in most advanced nations (in spite of incessant juvenile propagandas), and we still put our greed and power

above all humanity. We humans are still as immature as our Stone Age ancestors, if not even worse, considering all the ruthless killings and carelessness in the recent eras.
9. People and governments are still in denial about the state of the affairs and the viability of our socioeconomic systems, despite all the evidences indicating our humiliating failures.
10. Living in this 'perceived world' has impaired our judgment and willpower to find a solution for human survival and humanity. Many people, especially our egotistical leaders, have simply chosen to ignore this crucial mission for human race—to look for long-term peace and salvation.
11. The 'perceived world' has many lasting repercussions on people, of course, but mainly for raising our expectations in all respects, e.g., about work and marital environments, or our naive ways of perceiving and demanding democracy, freedom, love, happiness, etc.
12. Worst of all is our misperceptions about religions, purity of human nature, living in the now, and life's capacity and real purpose to offer us a joyous existence.

A major book should delineate the characteristics and perils of the 'perceived world.' In this book, however, only a few clues are offered in the following pages to make the above observations clearer. They demonstrate how we have hypnotized ourselves with some imaginary ideals and shallow ideas, and then hurt one another in this phony world of perceived realities. Accordingly, humans' contaminated perceptions are causing the collapse of societies around the globe, as explained in the following pages.

Chris Hedges' book, *Empire of Illusion*, by Alfred A. Knopf, Canada, 2009, also reveals the depth and the sad effects of people living in this illusory world and suffering the consequences of their choices and habits.

Perceptions about Our Identity

As elaborated in a few parts of this trilogy, especially Volume II, we have proven incapable of understanding who we are, either as individuals or an allegedly intelligent species. Surely, our shaky identities are the symptom of living so keenly in a perceived world developed around absurd values and lifestyles. Sometimes, we sense our struggles with our personalities and inner conflicts about the image we are trying to portray to others versus who we can be. However, in general, we are too absorbed in our phony personalities to worry about our real identities. In fact, it is getting harder these days to establish our identities in such hypocritical societies. We do not even care to understand at least the plausible essence of humanness and our authentic needs as the foundation of humans' survival. Our pleasure-seeking attitude, ambitions, sexuality, and greed prevent us from finding who we really are. Instead, we merely imitate others and cherish pervasive crooked values and lifestyles, including religions, that have evolved in our societies to serve only our Egos. We develop a shoddy mentality hypnotically and we create a fake identity to guide us for defining life and setting our plans. We become too phony and arrogant in order to parade our false confidence and crude individualism. We strive to manipulate one another with our exaggerated show of love and sincerity. We know how phony and flimsy our promises and communications are. Trust in society is at its lowest ever and still we keep acting so arrogantly and deceivingly, while bragging regarding our integrity and reliability. People see and suffer each other's phoniness and vanity as well as their own when they do some self-analyses occasionally and resort to their conscience to get a glimpse of who they have become. We have adopted fake identities to adapt ourselves to social demands in hopes of getting more things and compassion in society. Once in a while, some of us even feel terrible for the kind of person we have become—so devilish and useless! Still, we have no courage to defy social norms and the mainstream to look for our authentic identities.

Ironically, we have also become disgruntled about the purpose of living in such a chaotic environment. And, we have lost our chances to explore the true meanings of individualism and 'self.'

Perceptions about Dependence and Independence

In line with our shallow identity, we have become quite confused about the level of independence and individualism we wish to attain, compared with the amount of dependence we need and wish to maintain with others, especially our spouses. As humans, we need both dependence and independence, but we have not yet been able to find the right balance between these two conflicting needs of ours. Actually, the effect of living in the perceived world has made the task of finding the right balance of dependence and independence extremely difficult. With our eagerness to place so much emphasis on individualism and independence, we have become too arrogant and demanding, but also both oversensitive and insensitive. This condition has impaired people's capacity to find, or even know, the amount of dependency they need or can realistically expect to handle. Deep down, however, they feel the deficiency and do not know how to remedy the situation, either. Everybody is quite anxious to grasp, gauge, express, and satisfy his/her needs for independence and dependence, but has very limited capacity and opportunity for doing all these tasks. A detail discussion of this phenomenon is provided in *The Nature of Love and Relationships.* The main point is that people have very deep, irreconcilable misperceptions about their conflicting needs for independence and dependence, while assuming that a workable balance would automatically emerge despite their rising Egos. Even worse, they assume they can have both independence and dependence, e.g., in their marriages, while they switch from one position to the other and expect people around them to adjust themselves based on their erratic preferences for independence (freedom) and dependence (compassion). This wishful thinking and naivety is itself a direct outcome of living in this perceived world and making all sorts of farfetched assumptions.

Perceptions about Love

Another evidence of our perplexing mentality in the 'perceived world' is the way people have become too romantic and believe that everybody can and should find an everlasting love. They not only have wrong impressions about the nature of love, but also assume everybody can find it or nurture it. The irony is that they have become too arrogant, oversensitive, and antagonistic, while insisting on getting more compassion and affection. They are personally incapable of understanding and giving love to others, but demand it obsessively. They also perceive love as the main factor for the success of relationships. Therefore, anytime they feel a bit less love than their imaginations demand, they quickly get offended and depressed, which often leads to the collapse of their relationships, too.

Perceptions about Religions

Religions stand out probably as the most significant evidence of humans' persistence to live in this perceived world all across the globe. It is amazing how we humans ignore the simple logic that the existence of so many conflicting and controversial religions eradicates the validity of all of them, especially considering the amount of wars among, and due to, these religions. The matter is even more horrific considering the vast hostility among various sects within every religion for small disputes, which realistically should not have any effect on the actual words of the prophets per se. Not even the purpose of religions is clear anymore. Has it really supposed to be a means of God's contact with humans? If yes, for what end? To make humans more civil and ethical? What has He achieved after all this time? What have we gained?

The basic tenor of the main religions is that there is One God, Who demands peace and morality from His creatures. Therefore, all religions must worship the same creator ultimately as a first test of authenticity of any of those religions—all for the simple purpose of propagating compassion and forgiveness and not animosity and egotism. Even humans' basic logic dictates that no multiple Gods and no acrimony among religions must exist, but only simple uniform messages from the Creator. This God would supposedly send His messages through prophets to warn humans about His existence and the repercussions of not following His rules. In fact, we may assume that the only reason He would send multiple prophets had been the lack of a global communication system at the time, or else one prophet would have been enough! Anyhow, you would expect this God convey the same messages through all His prophets and ensure not only those rules remain consistent, but also communicated to people without any side interpretations by the prophets and their disciples. He had surely trusted them, too, to stay faithful to His instructions and words. So why would He send different (and often conflicting) messages through His prophets? Has He tried to confuse humans and then punish them at the end, too? Should not He have also known that a variety of interpretations could erupt and cause such a chaos?

Islam professes that God has sent 124,000 prophets, although only five of them have been GREAT! We wonder how persistent and optimistic God has been all along—never giving up, at least not until Prophet Muhammad, the last Great one, was appointed to fulfil this seemingly irresolvable intention of God. Maybe He has finally given up on sending more prophets after Muhammad, either assuming that he had accomplished His intentions finally, or believing that sending more prophets would be useless for the kind of humans He has created. Well, the point is that 124,000 or so prophets later, we are still in this big mess. And apparently even God has finally given up!

On the other hand, you would imagine that a just, proactive God would not allow such havoc and gullibility continue under

His name, if He had anything to do with this whole shenanigans. He would have made sure by now that His name and reputation were not abused so much, forever, through all these outrageous misrepresentations in various religions. He would have corrected all these mistakes and ended all the fighting that continues among so many religions—the errors He has apparently caused Himself every few centuries. In the final analysis, He is responsible for all this religious mayhem ruining the world, then! So the question is how could He remain the cause of so much pain on Earth, all because of His righteous decisions to enlighten humans and make things better for them? How could such a great God make so many mistakes that have stirred so much confusions and wars? Would not have He by now tried to reverse His past mistakes of trusting His prophets and a bunch of self-appointed successors? Has God failed so miserably?

With our limited logic and no direct interests or reputation at stake, any one of us can imagine how a powerful God intending to guide humans would have acted differently to avoid all these confusions and chaos—if we could respectfully be in God's shoes just for a second and had all His power and wisdom. Let us say, He sends Moses with the Torah and the Ten Commandments to enlighten people. Then, fourteen centuries later, still not happy with the outcome, He dispatches His beloved son to correct the situation. He stresses, "Jesus, go tell people that Moses was my prophet and they better listen to what he said under my name. Tell them those instructions are authentic and quite necessary to follow. You may also correct the misinterpretations and add a few clauses to tighten the guidelines in the Torah. That's all! Go my son and be very careful!"

But then Jesus starts a new religion and writes a whole new book. God would tell him, "My son, why didn't you just do what I asked you to do, to only ensure people understand my earlier instructions. I haven't changed my mind and there was no need for a new religion and a whole set of new guidelines. Why did you write another book to confuse those daft humans even more, and get yourself killed in the process, too? *Not to mention some idiot's tenacity, in the 21st century, to find me responsible for the mistakes that you guys, my dear prophets, are making!* Perhaps I shouldn't have resurrected you, for your disobedience at least!?"

Then, still unhappy with the way humans are behaving six centuries later, He sends Muhammad now, again with the exact instructions and intention, to affirm what He has been trying to do for people and to ensure His instructions are followed. "Just listen, Muhammad… All you should do is to confirm that Moses and Jesus are saying the same things and that they both were my GREAT messengers, as you are. Tell them that Jesus was (in fact is) my son, now safe and sound, and will return soon as I have promised. Just confirm my *consistent* wisdom and stress on what I've been saying in the last two millenniums. Only make it clear for them that those books are my words. Just make it easier for them to understand my existing instructions. For God's sake (My Sake), please don't write another book. Are you with me?"*

This would have been a logical way for a god with enormous foresight to prevent all the rising animosity and affirm everything He has been trying so hard to do for His people for millenniums, *at least*. But then again Muhammad comes down the mountain proudly and writes still another book that causes a great deal more controversy and wars. It is hard to believe that any powerful and insightful God would allow this much travesty under his name. "Did not I specifically tell you not to write another book and only affirm what I have been trying to tell my people all along already? Why nobody listens to me? What kind of humans have I created? Such stubbornness! Why everybody likes to be an author these days more than a holy messenger? Why nobody likes to only affirm my previous messengers and messages? I must keep thinking again for a better way of communicating with

---

* The fact that God sends Muhammad, instead of another family member again, might be a sign of His dire scepticism and worry already about the low chance of getting through humans and sacrificing another son perhaps for nothing!! *Unless He has only one son, of course?!*

my people. Everybody knows that I really want to contact and communicate with my people, but somehow I do not know how anymore! Unless I use the internet now that this service is finally available and everybody is so addicted to it! I feel so helpless because of these humans. It feels weird, especially after creating this colossal orderly universe! Is this Satan's fault too?

Despite the impossibility of a rational God playing any role in the creation of religions, prophets have tried to raise morality and intelligence of people in the best ways they could, but then things have gotten out of control. Prophets have had their honourable intentions and did their bests regardless of their connections and family ties with God. However, it is reasonable to believe that one intelligent God would have never allowed so many clashing messages disrepute Him. All religions are still respectable and worthy, but they have clearly failed to represent a wise God. There is no point to pick on a particular religion, either, like the way some scholars, including Salmon Rushdie, have done with Islam inadvertently or intentionally. All religions have their own merits and demerits, but none of them could have logically been the creation of a proactive God. Reviewing the petty differences among many factions of each religion makes all religious claims even more questionable and disheartening. Only a cynical creator might have liked to cause so much mayhem for a simple goal—unless for having some fun perhaps; which is too hard to believe, of course, though we still must not dismiss the possibility! *Just in case He has a big sense of humour!* Thus, the most reasonable conclusion is that He has had nothing to do with these books and messages, despite all the good stuff in them. Hell, heaven, and afterlife are all only our illusions in the perceived world. Period.

Aside from the crude ways these religions have been initially created, we still want to play even more silly games with God by trying to re-interpret some of His words according to our newer needs, e.g., about the gays' rights, abortion, etc. We people are demanding flexibility from religions to fit our perceived world's values or else we do not like that religion. *Only now we jump to refuse those religions!* We are asking God to be flexible with our needs because we have created our 'perceived world' and are happy living in this illusion with no sense of ethics. We just want to do things in our ways. We want to build our Gods according to our needs, again. As far as God is concerned, we are telling Him that it is either our way or highway! We want our God to change His mind regularly as we see fit. In the older times, we made our gods in the shape of wooden idols and now we want to build them around the erratic values of our perceived world.

At the same time, it is amazing how we wicked, ungrateful humans (mainly clergies) claim so much nonsense about God and His instructions so fearlessly and arrogantly. How can we be so foolish and selfish, especially disregarding the possibility that a real God might actually exist and be witnessing our ignorance, hypocrisy, and fraud? We are so arrogant, not willing to even respect and appreciate all the great things He has done for us, starting with our mere existence. Not even atheists would dare be so stupid and say all these lies and contradictions (and made-up stories) without the fear of retribution. Merely our gullibility and arrogance can make us so confused about God and religions. What other evidence do we need for our wickedness and total absorption in our crooked 'perceived world'?

(I am absolutely sure that God will send me directly to heaven for defending Him so adamantly in this chapter.)

Even humans' substandard logic should be able to detect the depth of our flawed reasoning, let alone the supreme logic that should exist in the Real World for explaining the principles of the universe and the wisdom of an extremely artful creator. We are so lost in our ignorance and perceptions, we insist on closing our minds even to the basic humanly facts and logic.

How can each religion and its sects believe that only it is right, while other religions and sects are wrong, evil, and perhaps even charlatans? One day we should finally choose between the two obvious options: That we are either worshiping different Gods, or only making up so many (if not all) of those religious claims so foolishly and arrogantly. In either case, the bottomline shows humans' amazing tenacity to ignore the fact that these religions and guidelines do not work. Instead, our attitude toward religions reveal the depth of social naivety—a horrific phenomenon that humans might never be able to overcome. We are just incapable of admitting that so much confusion and bloodshed only show how badly we have failed to build a practical culture for human coexistence regardless of God's goals and rules. We just love our ignorance so much. We like to deny that a powerful, logical, and consistent God would send only one set of principles, which are by the way fixed and final. How can we worship and accepts an inconsistent God? Our tenacious refusal to ponder these simple facts reveals the debilitating influence of the perceived world.

Even those few consistent messages across the religions offer interesting conclusions by themselves. For example, they refer to 'Judgment Day,' which implies that, first, humanity would (and should) come to an end. Second, we would not know about the outcome of our deeds and sins until all humans have died—and not right after each person's demise. (Let us hope we do not have to wait for all other intelligent creatures in other planets to die as well, as a requirement of reaching the Judgment Day all at the same time, since they are the creatures of the same God, too, after all.) Anyhow, this predicament reveals God's absolute pessimism from the beginning about humans' ability to develop adequate intelligence, create a harmonious world for themselves, and avoid their extinction. Or that God knew from the very beginning that the level of sins would become so unbearable He should end the whole damn thing and put people out of their miseries. He had been aware already from day one about the imperfections of His creations! Then why create them? Why send prophets then, and why delay whatever must be achieved at the end (the ultimate outcome: humans' dire demise)? Who is responsible, then, for so much humans defects that He had already anticipated from the beginning and would lead to their extinction, judgment day, and facing some form of retribution? And, is it now fair that humans be also punished for *Someone* else's design flaws, on top of the pains of existence in itself that they are forced to endure without their own choice for being, especially since the outcome had been obvious to Him from the very start?

We can offer hundreds of evidences about our naivety, especially about our views of religions. We can write thousands of books, and argue among ourselves until hell freezes over, but we are not going to give up our naïve logic, perceptions, and love affair with the fantasy world we prefer to live in. We are just not going to admit that, unless we look at all the religions together and make some sense of them (or not) collectively, nobody would grasp the properties of a credible and fair God, at least for communicating amongst ourselves a little more civilly. At this point, however, all these religious imaginations in people's minds only reveal the dominance of the 'perceived world' in our lives, not only in terms of our historical illusions, but also demanding new interpretations and upgrades according to our new needs, e.g., sexual liberty or gays' status in a religion. Our stubbornness and resistance show how deeply humans have sunk and become an integral part of the perceived world they have invented to fool themselves eternally. We merely keep expanding this illusive world every day with more energy, persistence, and imaginations, perhaps as rapidly as the universe is expanding. We will never find enough courage, intelligence, and willpower to think more deeply and grasp our identities and 'self.' We have always assumed that humans are at the centre of the universe as God's image or at least the symbol of His smartest creation. Yet, we have proven plainly to be the wildest, saddest, silliest, and weirdest of all His creatures.

A Picture of the Real World

What is a plausible meaning or property of the real world, then? Actually, two conflicting definitions of the real world emerge for our philosophical speculations and maybe practical purposes, too.

Part I: Thoughts and Personalities

First, we perceive and define the real world as an absolute, innate entity in the sense that humans' existence and perceptions have no significance for its nature and purpose, exactly like dinosaurs' extinction not hindering the reality of the universe even an iota. The real world is the universe separate from human perceptions, observations, interpretations, conscious, and life. It just continues as is, even after humans go the way of dodo. Therefore, the first aspect of the definition intentionally excludes human beings from playing any role in the real world, let alone being at the centre of it—as we always like to see ourselves (as a leading symptom of the perceived world). This definition is most sensible, but let us humour ourselves with the second, silly speculation as well!

In the second definition, we do exactly the opposite. That is, we attempt to keep human beings as a focal point, since it is our lives and reality that we are keen to grasp and trust for creating a practical means of living. In this selfish context, we imagine that only our direct, substantive connectivity to the universe could be meaningful for studying our being as well as the nature of the real world. This is a very smart realization, in fact, if we get the gist of it. That is, our immense urge to justify our existence only within the context of a higher reality—within a universal consciousness—is quite precious and somewhat divine. While most of us adopt self-centeredness as a symptom of general social mentality, a few people might actually recognize the essence of their being only in terms of their connection to the universe and nothing else! This distinction is important.

While the first definition stresses the impersonal absoluteness of the real world, the second definition focuses on the significance and necessity of human life's sheer connection to it. Thus, a big dilemma for us is to choose one of these conflicting definitions or reconcile them rationally. A close attachment to the universe feels essential, however, although we grasp the ambiguity and fluidity of this alleged connectivity. Perhaps we are linked but irrelevant! This middle ground sounds plausible to logical people. Yet, in our minds, we cannot stop feeling as a vital part of the universe, if not at its centre. This allegedly divine connectivity is significant to us for defining not only our being, but also the main purpose of Creation. Some might even think that human existence had been at least a big reason the universe was created! (This naïve and arrogant belief, of course, has big significance for establishing human beings' identity in their own minds.) Yet, in spite of our conviction in terms of our importance, identity, and fundamental relation to the universe, not knowing the means and nature of this connection is also maddening us. That is why we seek a supreme wisdom to solve this puzzle. Desperately, we even put our trust in the words of prophets or gurus who know how to manipulate us due to our innate curiosity about our connection to the universe.

The urge to fathom our true 'self' is also a struggle to find our identity in general, and not even merely as a spiritual person or an eternal soul. We need such a sacred identity, not only as particles, matter, souls, or consciousness, but also in terms of the physical existence and characters that we must carry around daily. We like to establish our *relevance*. Instinctually, we are driven to discover a sacred kind of connectivity and that is why so many of us are lured by religions—simply because we do not know how else we can find this connectivity (and our purposes of living) personally through reflections and experiencing it on our own.

Some scientists have attempted to explain the connectivity of humans to the universe through quantum mechanics theories and full consciousness, but their assertions or the nature and means of this connectivity remain enigmatic. Is it contained in the physical dimension of humans, or does it reside at some other dimension beyond our intelligence or capacity to access directly, yet or ever? Gary Zukov states that:

"At the subatomic level, we cannot observe something without changing it. There is no such thing as the independent observer who can stand on the sidelines watching nature run its course without influencing it.

In one sense, this is not such a surprising statement. A good way to make a stranger turn and look at you is to stare intently at his back. All of us know this, but we often discredit what we know when it contradicts what we have been taught is possible." The Dancing Wu Li Masters, Morrow, 1979, New York, pages 112-3.

Although the real world is an absolute, inherent entity, it is impossible to explain, touch, and imagine it even remotely in line with the way we grasp the perceived world so naturally. While we (including scientists and spiritualists) are making judgments from within the perceived world about 'a real world somewhere outside our present wisdom and reach'—mostly likely forever— the concept of REAL remains abstract and the PERCEIVED notions feel real. We can never get out of this loop. Thus, the definition of reality becomes cumbersome, abstract, arbitrary, and imaginary. Everything we can say about the real world comes also from our perceptions about an absolute world that we hope and desire to exist as an alternative to the perceived reality that is forcing many erroneous facts regarding life on us. Merely social disorder causing pains and problems in human life, as well as our fear of mortality, make us rather philosophical and we look for eternity and meaningful facts. Some clues also make us wonder about the possibility of a softer and purer nature in human beings than what has manifested in the existing cultures. So, we become interested in cultivating some ethics and sense into all the chaos, ignorance, and wickedness that we are forced to live with, and participate in, in the perceived world.

The real world reflects the truth behind all the illusions of the perceived world. We hope that looking for that truth and grasping even some of it would provide an antidote for all the ignorance, chaos, and immoralities that we wish to believe are not the real nature of human beings. In fact, we may even feel victimized by all these mayhem we have inherited from previous generations without a fault of our own.

How so much corruptions and ignorance have evolved and ruined humans beyond their bad nature is a big mystery, although one plausible possibility could be the lack of adequate wisdom when human race had first begun to build social life. Those early raw cultures were driven by trade (evoking greed) before tyrants and ruling powers emerged (evoking superego). Although some prophets and spiritual figures tried to force morality on people, the fact that people did not grasp or believe in the need for it, the whole idea of religion and spirituality was presented and adopted in a wrong way, mostly forcefully through weird stories and blind faith. The right way to develop spirituality, where a person grasps the real purposes of morality and humanity intuitively, was never given a chance. That kind of knowledge plus personal motivation would have provided a chance for an authentic transformation and human advance to a wisdom path that could have possibly given them a proper identity and sense of spirituality. Instead, crude religious ideologies have only misled people beyond their basic confusion about the nature of reality (both the perceived and real ones). Well, older generations might have had good excuses for their deep ignorance. What are our excuses now? Must we still be so greedy and egotistical at the risk of human extinction? In fact, the levels of human misery and gullibility have been growing fast and the situation would get worse for every generation.

Regardless of the history of human arrogance and idiocy, it is bizarre how we take our societies and cultures as established facts of social living, although we often also wonder about, or wish for, better alternatives for being and living. We are still lost humans!

Humans' inherent identity, which we may call pure 'self,' is an abstract presentation of a man who believes in, and starts to recognize, the possible essence of his nature. Although humans are seemingly not pure by nature, they can become better beings through the proper means of enlightenment and finer use of their brains. Maybe that is the challenge that God has designed for us. Maybe He is waiting to see whether we can eventually use our brains to become better human beings despite our crooked nature. Our psyche and brain taming each other is surely a big challenge, but maybe someday a group of people can take it on. Maybe a sounder logic can annul the effects of our bad nature and culture.

Maybe someday a new human identity emerges when higher consciousness and 'self'-awareness lead humans to higher paths of wisdom. This divine wisdom would reveal the absurdity of our immoralities and give us the energy to disengage ourselves from the entrapments of perceived values and norms, including greed and egoism. Eventually, this divine 'self' might reveal our innate essence for connecting to the universe. Our new wisdom might help us explore the purpose of our being in this body and mind form for a limited time. Whether we find the immense wisdom to understand even a sense of the real world is uncertain. A refined wisdom is needed to answer many other fundamental questions, including whether 'self' would live (in some context or realm) beyond this worldly life or not. It is amazing how most of us, including many intellectuals, believe in afterlife when there is absolutely no reason to believe in such a bizarre notion.

On the scientific front, prominent scholars, including Albert Einstein, tell us that time is nonexistent in the form we conceive and use it. However, 'time' fits very nicely within the perceived world's framework as a measuring device. We use it consciously in every single moment for our convenience, despite our limited knowledge of science and our shallow observations of the things that happen around us. It is very difficult for a person of average, and perhaps even high, intelligence to understand the meaning and implications of time-space as one inseparable continuum. In the same way, the mathematics we use readily, like the concept of infinity, are abstract rules that are useful for explaining the variables in the perceived world, but are most likely meaningless in the real world.

Gary Zukov states the following about the abstract reality of time professed by Minkowski, Einstein's mathematics teacher who was inspired by Einstein's theory of relativity:

"Minkowski's mathematical exploration of space and time were both revolutionary and fascinating. Out of them came a simple diagram of space-time showing the mathematical relationships of

the past, present, and the future. Of the wealth of information contained in this diagram, the most striking is that all of the past and all of the future, for each individual, meet and forever meet, at a single point, now. Furthermore, the now of each individual is specifically located, and will never be found in any other place, than here (wherever the observer is at)." Ibid., page 154.

Therefore, on the one hand, we have created the science that explains some aspects of the universe and related phenomena, and, on the other hand, we declare that the main component of all these concepts and mathematics, i.e., time, nonexistent (or rather meaningless) in the real world. This seeming contradiction shows the limitation of our knowledge, especially about the real world, which remains an abstract reality in our crude minds. Since time is nonexistent, we believe that everything is happening at the same time. There is no past, no future and none of the words that we use for our communication makes any sense in the real world. So what is making our days and nights look both transient and continuous to us, for example?

In the perceived world, we spend many hours of labour to make a living and our *lengthy* pains are real. We perceive, feel, endure, and count every minute of our labour and agony day after day. We enjoy every moment of any pleasant experience, and thus conclude that time is real! But it is not, we are told. We also try to be proactive and make decisions, as relying on fate alone seems not prudent—actually feels foolish! These are all added sources of confusion for common people even when we strive to find our identity and learn about our link to the universe.

Then again, a timeless realm fits the philosophy that all events are predestined for specific, definite purposes.

We might speculate about the meaning and importance of the real world forever, but what can we hope to achieve that might guide us in our daily lives and soothe our suffering? Answering this question is the only goal of the analyses and speculations in this trilogy about our thoughts and life path within perceived and real worlds. In particular, a main purpose of drawing a tentative picture of the real world is to serve only as a preliminary notion for all the upcoming discussions in the future chapters about the essence of our existence. Many of us would never get enough of philosophical speculations about our world and our universe. It is fascinating and it is about us—the real us within the realm of a divine real world—though presently trapped within the complex realities of the perceived world *so helplessly and pathetically.*

Perceived and Real Realities

We normally do not get a clear sense of either 'perceived' or 'real' realities to choose a more fruitful path of life. These two worlds cannot be thoroughly mapped since: First, the 'perceived' reality has evolved over centuries around fluid social values and rules permeated through people's minds and imaginations with little foundation or logic—so it is merely a mishmash of flimsy, unstable perceptions. Second, as each one of us sees these values and rules differently, we relate or refer to them based on our unique personalities and needs. Things and ideas are valuable to people because they perceive them as valuable, e.g., for soothing their unique insecurities. And they perceive, assume, and accept facts, myths, and rules, because they are conditioned to do so, as part of their efforts to cope with, and belong to, a social group, religion, community, organization, or family.

It is even harder to grasp or define the 'real world,' since, at best, it is *real* **only** for the 'self'—a selfless, conscious person—, which is a tough stance. Few reach this height of enlightenment, and even so, their abilities to explain it and our abilities to grasp it are quite restricted. That is, until a person attains a high measure of consciousness to feel and appreciate the meaning of 'real' with a divine personality, s/he would never grasp its nature, let alone develop an ability to explain it to others. Even if somebody could explain it to us, its dimensions and absoluteness remain enigmatic due to our subjective personal interpretations and our inability to digest such sacred visions. (Maybe this is also a good excuse for prophets' failure to convey God's messages uniformly—though God could have potentially prevented this bottleneck!)

The point is that the interpretation of every reality still suffers from human limitations to process it realistically. Any *presumed* reality feels real only to a person experiencing it at a special time according to his/her unique level of consciousness and mindset. Thus, no two persons' visions could coincide and they cannot connect mentally. Neither people nor science can grasp, define, or explain spiritual experiences, although they try to simulate it through psychology and philosophy at least. The best we can do is to speculate and speak *only* about the likely implications of the real world for a person, a group of people, or society.

Nevertheless, an overall picture of these two parallel realities, as general concepts, can help us contemplate and make decisions about our existence and a viable path of life for us personally. We must live with tentative definitions for perceived and real worlds, as the two extreme boundaries of human consciousness and their desire for piety and spirituality.

A general definition of the 'perceived' reality may be offered based on the prevalent perceptions of the public, as reflected in social culture and commoners' personalities. On the other hand, the 'real world,' including God, is much harder to define, as it contains the ultimate and inherent secrets of the universe, while our interpretations of this 'absolute and immense' phenomenon remain forever subject to humans' tainted logic and low personal awareness. One way to make basic definitions of, and compare, these two worlds is to use the notions of 'summit' and 'submit' based on people's levels of neediness, awakening, and stoicism. Diagram 3.1 reflects peoples' maximum and minimum levels of needs and their dependencies on the perceived world.

At the *base level* of the 'perceived reality', a person **submits** to common values and rules totally, out of ignorance and weakness. S/he is fully dependent on people and things outside him/her to receive material and mental satisfaction. S/he never challenges popular ideas, has little self-confidence or a positive self-image, has no personal integrity, cannot or does not know how to think and for what end, and is incapable of grasping the inner self that exists within him/her even when some signs of it appear to him/her. A small group belongs to this utter level of ignorance.

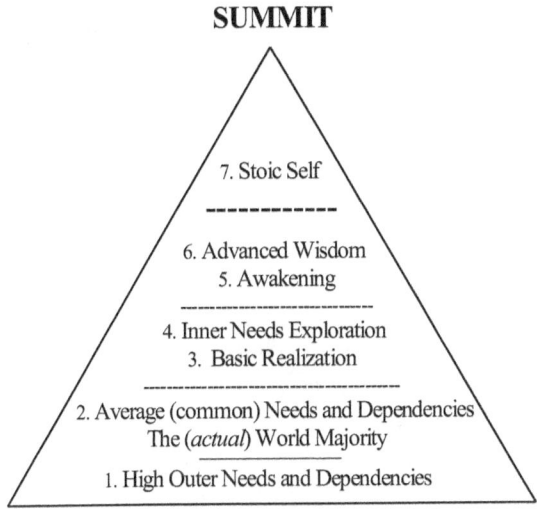

Diagram 3.1: The Paths of Awakening—Eros Dimension

Hypothetically, at the 'real reality' level, an individual reaches the *summit* of the truth, inner realization, full consciousness, and wisdom, beyond the world of appearances and phony sentiments. This experience has not been fully explained or grasped, despite vast attempts by philosophers, theologians, psychologists, sages and saints, and those who believe (or claim) to have felt a divine state of enlightenment. Socrates, the Buddha, Rumi, and other scholars pursued this path to their ends and left us some clues and teachings. Yet, most of us can only imagine its splendour through contemplation from one of the finer life paths that we might eventually explore. We may achieve this privilege by reflecting upon personal experiences, logic, and feelings up to certain point in our search for the truth, even though we are only travelling on a lower path far away from the *summit*.

The phrase 'real world,' which everybody uses regularly, is actually people's common definition of, and reference to, the 'perceived world.' This perceived reality (which we take as our real world) is where the large majority of us adopt on the Eros dimension (in terms of the level of personal neediness versus self-awareness). This path is slightly higher than the SUBMIT, but much below even a basic self-awareness level. At this level, we need a stimulus, influence, or incentive to start looking for the higher paths by limiting our outer needs. Close to the half way on the Eros dimension, some people reach the level of morality and wisdom required to rid themselves of their phony lifestyles and appearances to explore their authentic inner needs, instead. They become relatively selfless and self-driven, thus achieve spiritual joy and energy that guides them through life. The next, Advanced Wisdom, level is the same concept with higher intensity. At the imaginary SUMMIT level, perhaps no definition of needs, either outer or inner, exists. At this level, human needs do not have a sensual merit, as one's being theoretically coincides or combines with the universe, God, or whatever Real Reality that lays out there beyond the limits of human logic and mind.

The above degrees of human consciousness within the Real World extend on the same continuum—the dimension of Eros, wisdom and enlightenment—based on one's level of awakening. Thus, the lowest level in the Eros hierarchy reflects a person's full dependence on outer needs. At halfway a person breaks away from outer needs substantially to explore his/her inner needs with a divine outlook. At the Summit—a theoretical concept—s/he feels a sense of stoicism with a finite drive to connect with the universe. This height of human achievement is more theoretical than practical for normal people. The possibility of even saints and prophets having reached that level of blessing is doubtful.

This general picture (and contrast) is just a simple method to envision these two worlds and develop our mindsets about them.

Then, we could reflect on the *potential consequences* of living somewhere between the real and perceived realities, mainly for a chance to know who we are, plus possibly fulfilling our thirst for philosophical debates about our life paths and personal choices.

However, regardless of the path we choose and the height of the truth that we find in ourselves, the experience is 'personal' and unexplainable. Once someone experiences his/her 'self' and feels its permeating joy and energy, his understanding becomes his mental definition and guide for further exploration. However, the option for a novice—seeking some preliminary evidences to be convinced and motivated—is to choose a basic self-exploration path first to find his/her patience for exploring enlightenment. S/he might begin his search by studying books and other people's experiences, including his/her family and community members. Another good source for exploration is people who have been transformed spiritually. Something has happened to them, such as having a NDE (near death experience). We can read about them, listen to them, or ask them about the extraordinary inner energy they have swiftly gained after their unusual personal experiences. Then perhaps we can draw our conclusions, just for the purposes of starting our journey for spiritual wisdom. Meditation is surely another method of exploring our unconscious on Eros dimension.

Exploring the Real World

There are many evidences, and ways of, confirming our inner self and its relevance within a real world beyond the perceived world. For one thing, our identities (personalities) often feel too flimsy and unnatural even according to our own routine perceptions. People's feedbacks, despite their biased perceptions, might offer some clues about our character and how we come across as a person so contrary to our crude beliefs, though their impressions might merely reflect our alienation or discomfort within their mix and the perceived world's standards that people apply for making their judgments about one another. Most of all, at some bizarre or divine moments, our conscience hints the existence of a hidden wiser 'self' inside us.

The way our senses of 'real' vs. 'perceived' realities emerge at various levels of consciousness shows humans' innate tendency to undermine life's real realities in favour of their idealism and selfish urges. For example, as a child, when we first learn about the reality of death, we bury this awful information in a low level of our consciousness after the impact of this shocking news frighten us for a few days or weeks. Afterward, death remains in our minds only as a 'perceived reality.' That is, we know that death is a fact and, sure enough, we see and hear about it so much every day. Yet, we like to hide it in our lowest subconscious and we do not quite believe or feel that death is our destiny, too. All perceived realities are either real facts hidden in our subconscious or a crude image, idea, or feeling that we have been conditioned to insist on and keep in our highest levels of consciousness. The real reality, on the contrary, begins to manifest only at a high state of consciousness and awareness. We can say that our experiences at full consciousness bring us closer to our self and the real world. Then, 'Is death *possibly* the only and final venue to enter the real world after losing our perceptions in a full consciousness realm?' This is a bizarre, improbable notion even if we wish to believe in our immortality. Then again, attaining full consciousness during our normal existence feels even less likely, in spite of so many speculations about our inherent connection to the holistic, divine consciousness of the universe! Ironically, we are more conscious of 'perceived' realities and more unconscious of 'real' realities!

Nevertheless, our real reality (and our possible connection to it thru higher consciousness) is something to explore personally only by extensive, sincere self-analysis and 'self' development, and by challenging our perceptions of society. But can we ever bypass our perceptions? How much consciousness normal people might muster within such domineering perceived reality?

In his book, *A Second Way of Knowing, The Riddle of Human Perception*, Prentice Hall, 1991, Edmund Blair Bolles discusses the limitation of our perceptions and their effects on our lives. Some excerpts from his book are printed here as another point of view about humans' capacity for consciousness. He says:

"Deciding who sees reality becomes harder when the objective truth is not so easily defined. At this point one's own prejudices enter the sense too powerfully to be called science. How shall we judge an old study of shape constancy? Using the technique described in Chapter 7 (of his book), students from England and India looked at inclined disk and then matched their perceptions against a chart showing possible shapes. The Indian students showed stronger shape constancy than the English students did. The British, not surprisingly, took the finding as evidence of their superiority over Indian perceptual backwardness. Indian perception was said to "regress to the real object." Anybody familiar with the role racism has played in psychological and physiological studies will suspect that the opposite result too would have served as proof of British superiority. The Indians could have been said to show a regrettable tendency to miss the real object." Ibid., pages 107-108.

As noted in the above passage, we not only perceive things differently and superficially, but also impose our interpretations and prejudices in the way we like to see and use things at any particular instance or time. In the same book, Bolles refers to the biography of Georgia O'Keeffe to reflect how our perceptions affect and build an individual's grasp of the world. He quotes:

"Georgia was suddenly struck by the realization that her feelings governed the way she saw the scene. It was a moment of transformation: the entire visual world, she realized, was dependent on the emotional world. That day she learned the artist's secret. What you perceive depends on who you are. Analytical thinkers have generally assumed that we perceive reality as it is; they then use a process of abstract reasoning to interpret that perception. O'Keeffe realized that the perception is the interpretation. It rests on an internal reality that governs the meaning we

find in our sensations. To be an artist she needed techniques for drawing accurately what was out there and she needed to develop a grammar for expressing what those things looked like to her. With the realization that perception depends on an internal reality, O'Keeffe was on her way to becoming an important artist." Ibid., pages 121-122.

The way we perceive things is naturally also dependent upon our intelligence and social conditioning. Bolles says:

"We know not only what our senses detect but what those things are worth to us. These qualities, though entirely private, are absolutes of our psychological reality. They form the ground on which the rest of our world grows.

These absolutes are not the same things as emotions. Emotion is where memory enters an experience. It is powerful, but different." Ibid., page 129.

We each have our own absolute psychological realities that make us (mis)perceive the world in our own ways. Our senses create, and at the same time limit, our grasp of a real world in its absolute form away from our personal judgments. In all, we have difficulty perceiving the real world at basic conscious level that we apply to our daily lives. Even facts are only our interpretations of some perceptions. They are not necessarily *real facts* in an absolute term in the world of real realities. Bolles states:

"Calculating that a tree is a tree has turned out to be more difficult than expected. The tree really is out there, but the fact of its being a tree is not. Facts are not just floating about freely in the physical world." Ibid., page 136.

Bolles' above comment, *Facts are not just floating about freely...*, should, however, be rephrased or complemented with a qualifying sentence such as: Humans' prevalent facts are indeed floating about too freely in the physical world, rather recklessly, which merely reveals their shallowness and invalidity. They are developed and tested only by humans' perceptions, crooked logic, and debatable intelligence.

Most of us can understand and feel physical evidences rather readily, but we have great difficulty with abstract ideas, such as the ones suggested in the last few pages.

At the same time, we are all eager to build and accept some imaginary notions as absolute facts quickly, including so much nonsense propagated by all religions and modern societies.

At the same time, the best physical evidence of the real world can be found only in subtle, mystical energy that many of us have felt on some special occasions. Sometimes, those sensations have even turned into some form of awakening and deep beliefs. Only those kinds of sacred personal experiences can offer the needed clues about a fundamental reality beyond the perceived world we are accustomed to. The energy that suddenly emanates from a spiritual experience flows through our minds and bodies, elevates our spirits, increases our physical and mental abilities many folds, and leads to superhuman creations and ideas. We may eventually learn to count on this energy to experience the feelings of even higher value. This is a natural phenomenon—called faith—that most humans can feel and develop under certain circumstances.

However, for us to remain honest and objective, we cannot talk about the sacred paths at the higher levels of Eros. We may talk only about our common experience. The limited definition of SUMMIT provided here is what a philosopher or guru may give, or generated from our projections of the *summit* ambience during our early experiences at the lower wisdom paths.

Both 'submit' and 'summit' extremes are philosophical and theoretical, of course. Almost all of us follow a path somewhere between these two extremes, though much closer to the Submit. Yet, all these paths are possible human realities. It is just the kind of life we wish to lead for specific goals. Some of us may get the power and wisdom to project the sensation of Summit according to our experiences at a lower path. Or we may change our paths several times in our lifetime as we mature and hope to eventually reach a finer level of Eros and enlightenment. Since we move on the same path (dimension), we can do various experimentations without so much difficulty. In fact, a long, uninterrupted path of self-exploration and meditation elevates the person to the higher levels inevitably depending upon the level of his focus, sincerity, sacrifice, and stamina. Sometimes we lose our focus due to some external factors. We are often forced to face our immediate needs and life pressures, thus we let go of our spiritual aspirations for a while. Yet, our developed wisdom and new perception of life still help us cope better with the crude facts of the perceived world more patiently and compassionately.

Many people have followed a certain path of spiritual nature or even joined a convent for several years, then given it up and returned to a regular everyday life that had felt more comfortable to them, maybe even marrying a nagging, wicked spouse just to avoid loneliness. Yet, they can carry and apply their new wisdom in any setting they choose to live. All life paths revolve around humans' perceptions, after all, merely as another option (path) on the Eros dimension. Life paths only differ in terms of our level of consciousness about the realities of the perceived world.

The Eros dimension reflects all human perceptions and paths. After all, humans have the same origin and dimension regardless of the odd realities they build for themselves due to their naivety, genetics, and growing experiences. We are all helpless but also curious about our existence. Biology has proven how complex, yet vulnerable, our basic origin is. Yet, we like to show off our superiority with such pathetic arrogance and self-importance, as if we had created our own bodies and minds. Of course, we have our preferences for choosing the path we can master based on our potentialities, personalities, and perceptions. Still, everybody has an inherent inner power to free himself from the path of a passive being and evolve to the higher paths of wisdom, freedom, and inner peace. The higher paths are approachable and achievable by everybody just as soon as we prepare our thoughts to go there and become a bit more conscious away from the perceived world.

PART II
Facts and Myths

Precautionary Hints about Part II

Part II's main objectives are to suggest:
1. A list of ten main facts, myths, and challenges for humans. Page 127.
2. A basic process for exploring our 'inner self.' Page 178
3. A chart showing the nine steps for exploring our 'inner self.' Page 179.

Note 1:
Facts and myths, and our reliance on them for making our major life decisions, stir humans' fundamental thoughts subconsciously and consciously in line with their intelligence and curiosity about existence. Accordingly, they are discussed in detail in the next two chapters along with the challenges and confusions these facts and myths cause us all our lives.

Note 2:
The upcoming long review of facts, myths, and challenges could be a bit overwhelming for some readers, especially Chapter Five. Therefore, maybe those readers benefit from reading Part III first before continuing their slower readings and reflections on Part II.

Actually, Part II can be read even at the end of this volume or after completing the whole trilogy. At the same time, discussions in Part II have felt most suitable for inclusion right here to follow the logical order of the topics included in this trilogy, especially after the long discussions about facts and perceptions in Part I.

All attempts were made to make the points in Part II as simple as possible, yet discussions have turned out rather long and deep as deemed necessary.

Anyway, just move on to Part III anytime the discussions in this part feel rather tedious or overwhelming, but try to read them at some point later at least, <u>although even skipping Part II altogether would not hurt the main messages of this trilogy too much</u>.

CHAPTER FOUR
The Essence of Facts

"It's just a simple fact," we tell one another, as if reiterating the absolute truths formulated by God! We depend on facts for being rational, making good decisions, and building the foundation of our thoughts. But what is the meaning and value of facts in the perceived world where we insist on pampering our deep illusions, crude opinions, and phony personalities? We grow up with naïve fantasies and shallow ideals, and we define life based on shoddy social values, religions, and phony lifestyles. So how can our judgments about 'facts' be sensible and useful even for handling our routine thoughts, feelings, and actions, let alone for building the foundation of our thoughts, 'self,' and a peaceful life?

Our history, cultures, and religions have drawn a crooked and odd picture of reality for humans over time in many ways. First, decades of personal imaginations and desires, driven by unique innate urges and idiosyncrasies, have created our rudimentary perceptions of the world, life, and destiny. Second, the immense influence of social trends, advertising, and propagandas in recent decades, has further contorted the historical perceptions of reality and 'facts' of life. Then, our whimsical modern vision of the world and our boosted Egos and greed further disorient us about the facts of life as well. Third, our rising needs and aspirations along with our obsession to prove our identity and individualism have made our perceptions of 'facts' even shakier, nowadays, beyond the illusive picture of reality that new societies impose upon everybody. We believe we deserve everything in the world, *as a matter of fact,* like movie stars, because positive thinking experts force us to think so, or else we might as well pack it up and see ourselves as total failures. Our dogmatism has grown fast too deeply in the new era due to our trust in the truthfulness of our thoughts and deeds revolving around a huge amount of ideologies we have adopted as facts. The way religions have ruined our perceptions of reality and facts has also been too destructive. In all, people's varied realities have, nowadays, become too complex, unique, and incompatible with a divine truth that should logically exist outside our absurd perceptions and presumed facts. That is why people's worlds and realities are highly flimsy and unreliable for personal guidance. That is why humans cannot relate peacefully and their relationships fail so quickly. The bottomline is that we can neither trust the perceived reality dominating us, nor prevail without the truth eluding us.

Facts, Myths, and Challenges

We consider facts as concepts that reflect absolute truths beyond any doubts or imaginations—like day and night. We have adopted these facts merely because we have learned, over the centuries, that they are more reliable (and stable) than other notions. They have evolved as solid, inherent assumptions to construct our lives around, thus we accept them with certainty (rather naively) in terms of their truthfulness and consequences. They have become legitimate, proven *concepts* that build the basic elements of our logic, intelligence, and thoughts. However, even scientific facts are still the figments of humans' general observations and crude logic, and thus some type of perceptions, nevertheless. Of course, some scientific conclusions and perceptions are plausible, but still not absolute truths or facts.

On the other hand, myths refer to those concepts that majority of us find imaginary or hard to realize—like heaven or happiness. They appear fictional without any logic or methodology to grasp or sustain them as part of our routines and aspirations. They are complex perceptions that cannot be even linked or attributed to any physical or tangible phenomenon. Yet, despite our scepticism about their viability, we do not want to (or cannot) deny the chance of their existence. We prefer to give a benefit of a doubt to their viability, though our clues are weak or based on hearsay, rather than a firsthand personal experience. Therefore, we have difficulty deciding whether to let those myths play an active role in our minds and judgments or reject them totally. This is another big dilemma and cause of inner conflicts for humans.

Consequently, our efforts to align all the presumed facts and myths in our brains cause us more dilemmas and inner conflicts, along with major 'challenges' to reconcile them logically—for example, when we rely on facts and myths to choose a *faithful* spouse or find *lasting* happiness. These ongoing challenges force us build our ideas, make decisions, and take actions as prudently as possible. They also reflect our outlooks, values, and attitudes, which cause our pleasures and sufferings. We like to think these challenges are necessary and achievable with reasonable efforts. We believe they are rather lucid, normal, and justified within the existing framework of human knowledge and logic.

Facts, myths, and our challenges to align them materialize in a package of thoughts quite often, as they demand decisions and actions. Thus, while we might see facts, myths, and challenges in separate domains at varied significances, they collectively build our cognition of things, ideas, and events. For example, when we state an opinion, e.g., regarding God, it would be based on our cognition of all the related facts, myths, and challenges that we have retained in our brains about that subject.

Several important reasons exist for analysing facts, myths, and challenges in this and next chapters. First, it would help us detect our motives behind our actions and habits, and thus learn more about ourselves. Second, we would realize our dogmatism to live within certain shallow boundaries we have accepted as facts of life, mostly because of our conditioned mentality. Third, we would appreciate the undeniable impact of myths in our lives and beliefs, even though we strive to remain logical about their authenticity as much as possible. Fourth, we would recognize the underlying structure of our principles and values, and gauge our readiness and motivation to choose a spiritual and harmonious path, compared with a path dictated merely by misleading facts. After all, we are introducing too many facts in our daily lives so haphazardly and randomly as modern societies stress on crooked values to justify humans' rising addictions to self-gratification and superficiality. Fifth, distinguishing facts, myths and challenges (as shown in the next chapter) would show the roots of social and personal problems, as well as the difficulties of communicating in modern societies and trusting people.

A philosophical interpretation of life and obstacles for social co-existence has been the greatest, longest, and least successful challenge for humans historically. Attaining a higher wisdom (or at least lower gullibility) has proven beyond humans' talent and mental capacity, apparently. Thus, studying the main obstacles for a peaceful co-existence is crucial at least for choosing a wiser life path, although the chance of a tolerable form of living cannot be promised to anybody. Our comprehension of life's essential facts, myths, and challenges, and our position about these interrelated principles might give us at least a great chance for mental growth and basic enlightenment.

Studying the nature of common facts, myths, and challenges (in the next chapter) also provides a clearer picture of the sources, and potential destructive role of our perceptions personally and socially. Facts and myths are mostly raw information stored in various levels of our consciousness according to our intelligence and experiences. Naturally, while our unconscious mind remains untapped, our understanding of the world and life, as well as the capacity of our perceptions, remains too elementary at best. Thus, our personal efforts to distinguish facts and myths at a conscious level, and pinpointing our special challenges for interpreting and reconciling them, broadens our grasp of the world, societies, and the reliability of common facts we use daily for decision making. Mastering such a mental transformation would bring us fresh insights, creativity, and courage to reassess our lives and beliefs more effectively in line with a sensible philosophy of life.

Essential Facts and Myths (Establishing a Framework)

We can prepare a preliminary list of commonly perceived facts, myths, and challenges for our discussions. The list is not intended to be comprehensive, but rather a tentative framework. Initially, ten items were chosen for each of the main 'facts', 'myths', and 'challenges' categories intuitively, but then it appeared that I had subconsciously selected items with some inherent relationships across the three categories and a logical order for presenting them.

Table 4.1: A Suggested List of Facts, Myths, and Challenges

FACTS	MYTHS	CHALLENGES
1. Physical (outer) self	1. Spiritual (inner) 'self'	1. Humanness & humanity
2. Life (living)	2. Freedom	2. Doubts
3. Nature	3. Love	3. Relationships
4. Physical growth	4. Truth	4. Psychological growth
5. Social living	5. Everlasting happiness	5. Coping and adaptation
6. Economic constraints	6. Chance/luck/fairness	6. Contentment
7. Personal limitations	7. Enlightenment	7. Life decisions
8. Personal needs	8. Inner Strengths/piety	8. Needs Alignment
9. Perceived Reality	9. Real Reality	9. Psych. & physical health
10. Death	10. Creation/creator	10. Spirituality, self-actualization

The facts, myths, and challenges listed in Table 4.1 provide a platform for studying some of the main concepts occupying our minds, and thus strengthening the foundation of our thoughts, as discussed in detail in the next chapter. If some new logic or other evidences, including extra-sensory notions of spirituality, could convince us to revise our facts and myths' table, we may test the suitability of our discussions and conclusions accordingly at that point—maybe in the future editions of this book by some wise scholars a few centuries in the future!

However, if we decide to revise or recreate the structure of facts, myths, and challenges in a different form from the one in Table 4.1, we may have to redo those discussions in a different domain altogether, too, after the list is defined properly. (In fact, we might even end up creating an innovative domain in which the facts and myths listed in Table 4.1 are no longer acceptable as facts and myths!) Some aspects of discussions in Chapter Three, regarding the perceived and real world realities, constitute the 9th fact and myth on the above list.

For now, Table 4.1 seems to offer a good approximation of most people's mindset about life's essential facts and myths. It also constitutes humans' main mental reconciliations (challenges) needed for attaining a simple notion of the truth.

Sources of Facts and Myths

The presumed facts of life have evolved historically based on our crude logic and intelligence during the process of building our *perceptions* of people and events. *This includes the discussions and theories asserted in this trilogy.* Initially, we just encounter simple things, ideas, and events as we grow up in our muddled families and societies. We absorb cultural teachings, which are mostly permeated through nonsensical television programs and movies. These basic experiences build the primary elements of our thoughts and logic. Yet, we also begin to interpret and define our experiences quickly in a personal, peculiar way, then try to associate them to one another, hoping to generate profound ideas and universally acceptable meanings for them. We like to draw some conclusions regarding life and its purposes. Worst of all, we become too dogmatic and pompous, as we trust our knowledge of facts wholeheartedly!

In time, our convoluted needs, insecurities, intelligence, and emotions converge to instil special meanings for our experiences and evoke unique perceptions, which eventually become a rigid foundation for our beliefs and facts. Accordingly, our compound perceptions evolve in line with our conscious and unconscious needs and intellectual abilities to interpret and mix our basic experiences and thoughts.

We can expand this principle in many ways. For example, we can say that our beliefs and facts stem from our misguided needs, crude experiences, social influences, and insecurities. Or, they are reflections of our complex perceptions. Or, a combination of all these factors and more. Nonetheless, our facts in the perceived world are just a reference to our unique set of crude perceptions and beliefs that we compile and rely on for making our decisions, taking actions, and building relationships. Thus, we each invent our own worlds, despite societies' zeal to develop and depend on uniform values and rules for ethical societies, valid cultures, and objective criteria for judgments. Accordingly, this mishmash of personal and social perceptions has ruined our cultures, too.

Following these fundamental thoughts would take us in many directions with complex, lengthy discussions beyond this book's scope. The purpose here is only to stress the simple *fact* that we are at the mercy of some absurdly developed perceptions and beliefs to run our lives and make judgments and decisions. We use the words 'facts' and 'myths' to express our beliefs about the factuality (or fictionality) of things and concepts. Yet, since we are making those assessments from within a personally cultivated perceived world, our interpretations of things and ideas cannot be independent from our personal needs and beliefs—not to mention the varied, confusing effects of deliberate misinformation and illusions permeated in our crippled cultures. Every fact or myth portrays a different meaning and implication not only for each person, but also according to his/her erratic needs, perceptions, insecurities, and beliefs, which also fluctuate regularly as his/her cognition and mood change. In the end, the facts and logic that each one of us rely on are too flimsy and personal without a valid universal foundation for social coexistence or raising our wisdom about the real world.

When we want to pass a judgment about an issue or idea, we try intuitively to establish its truthfulness; we want to know how factual it sounds, which means we are interpreting its validity based on personal beliefs and criteria driven by our perceptions, thus our analyses and criteria cannot be of great help or value, either. Thus, the question is, 'What do we really know about facts and myths for supporting our thought processes and judgments?' This question is mainly handled in the next chapter, but first we should find out more about our perceptions and the way facts and myths evolve from them.

In all, the vast incongruity of human perceptions cause our confusion and pains, thus analysed in this chapter before tackling the facts and myths they impose upon us (in the next chapter).

Awareness about Our Perceptions

Why should we care about humans' perceptual differences, since we can hardly change them? The simple answer is that humans' absolute incongruity and inconsistency in their perceptions has been the main obstacle for building a real civilization. The second question is whether humans' historical perceptions and mindsets can ever be revamped for even envisioning better societies?' The objective of Part II's discussions is to elaborate on, and answer to, these questions (dilemmas) somewhat due to their importance at least for getting a clearer insight about the fate of humanity.

Surely, these ideals seem too farfetched, but even our basic awareness about both the **positive and negative** effects of our perceptions on many aspects of our lives can help us immensely. For one thing, our perceptions cause personal prejudices and evil that prevent us from facing social and work issues effectively. Our raw perceptions drive our mindsets, personalities, judgments, doubts, and decisions, and they make us dogmatic and insecure. Most of all, the growing incongruity of humans' perceptions are causing huge amounts of marital and communication problems. Naturally, our perceptions also stir our emotions, while our erratic emotions and prejudices influence our perceptions of things and people, as well as our hasty reactions towards them. Emotional people have weirder perceptions of life and their oversensitivities cause major misperceptions and relationship conflicts. Overall, we filter the messages, people, and ideas through our perceptions with lots of emotions, yet some of us react with higher prejudices and many with little compassion.

Discussing its positive side first, our perceptions trigger our creative senses, while our deep emotions enhance our receptivity to sensitive external stimuli. Some people perceive the meanings of art more profoundly due to their perceptive minds and ways of grasping and interpreting it. Then, perceiving artistic masterpieces stirs incredible emotions as a unique (positive) experience in an instance. Even a highly sensitive person needs external stimuli, maybe even a simple thought, to activate his fine emotions. And all these *activating* happen thru our unique perceptions of things, e.g., art and music. Surely, the strength of external stimuli affects our perceptions, too—in terms of urgency and value we give them.

Artists have a more perceptive cognition due to their unique vision of realities. Thus, they can create special art and music that even we can enjoy, in spite of the fact that we do not extend any emotion of our own in creating them. Even odd perceptions are not always dysfunctional, but might actually become the sources of incredible intuition and inspirations. Then, as we appreciate other people's perceptions, e.g., an artist's or writer's creations, some fine instances of communication become possible and life feels valuable, while a higher sense of consciousness enriches some moments of our lives, too. These are all precious effects of humans' dynamic perceptions.

On the negative side, our perceptions have been crippling our grasp of the nature of facts and myths, which we have adopted for making our judgments and nurturing our habits. We cannot build good relationships, make good decisions and choose our options properly without challenging our vile perceptions. We are depriving ourselves from the opportunity of using our thoughts and wisdom to support at least a good portion of our decisions and actions.

Artists' perceptions give them ecstasy and actualization and maybe some feelings of desperation, loneliness, or even pain. On the other hand, some individuals become completely ruthless due to their perceptions of the world and life. Some of us perceive things with more attention and compassion, while another group turns into cold-blooded criminals who can kill and torture others with no sense of remorse, guilt, or shame—all due to our hasty, crooked perceptions. Then, there is this large group, the majority, that is uncertain about its emotions and needs, thus cannot grasp a stable perception of the world that is purposeful and meaningful.

We often stand on the borderline; sometimes becoming cruel in our relationships with others, even our families; and sometimes we become emotionally moved by simple incidents such as the suffering of an animal. We have become so extremely instable in terms of our emotions. With the increasing rate of violence and apathy in relationships, there seems to be something drastically wrong happening around us in our societies and cultures from which we draw our perceptions. It seems that, with our shallow perceptions of things, ideas, and events, we are drifting away more and more from our natural tendencies for living in harmony and peace with one another. Instead, we are merely destroying and hurting one another with our unleashed Egos and ideologies, which have evolved out of our false perceptions. Our erroneous perceptions are also the sources of our personal sufferings, futile struggles, and unsatisfying lifestyles. All along, these crooked perceptions weaken our spirits to the point of neglecting obvious life values that can enrich our existence. Overall, learning about the limitations and the misleading nature of our perceptions can help us realize our deficiencies better and opt for self-therapy. We often need that self-analysis and a better grasp of our perceptions even for subsistence beyond our needs for artistic creations and self-actualization.

We can never solve the mystery of the truth behind our vast crooked perceptions. Only some of us can gradually see some aspects of the realities beyond the perceived world. However, we all should face the realities of living regardless of their perceptual or factual nature. We can never stop doubting the meanings and purposes of things, and still we should interpret them within the context of a hypothetical framework of facts and myths.

We are instinctually driven to distinguish between facts and myths that constitute our points of reference in life in all respects, including the main question of, 'Who we are.' However, a more challenging task for us is to reconcile our perceptions of facts and myths in some manner, in order to prepare the foundation of our thoughts and beliefs as profoundly as possible. That is, we must find ways of trusting our intuition about the truthfulness of some myths that do not succumb to our humanly logic. However, at the same time, we must convince ourselves to doubt the validity of some things, ideas, and events that we so readily believe are true and factual. We must realize that facts are not necessarily factual realities, and myths are not necessarily untrue because we do not perceive their reality. This does not mean that we want to become more doubtful and confused or religious. Rather, by reconciling our perceptions of facts and myths, we only intend to expand our tolerance for seeing and accepting alternative definitions and meanings of facts and myths. We want to become aware, and accept the limitations of our beliefs and convictions resulting from our erroneous perceptions of the world.

Our efforts to raise our awareness about our perceptions can help us in so many ways as noted above. This awareness grows as we contemplate the motives and stimuli behind our thoughts, feelings, and actions. Soon we learn about our idiosyncrasies if we are sincere and diligent to improve our lives and ourselves.

The Complexity Levels of Our Perceptions

People's ability to communicate and relate is deteriorating fast due to the rising incongruity of their perceptions of one another's intentions and honesty, social issues, and common concepts. People's perceptions have many levels of complexity and they are getting more convoluted every year as well in line with higher social immorality and corruption. Although people have a more uniform grasp of simpler concepts, their unique personalities and interpretations make their perceptions quite incongruent. As an example, perceiving 'chair' as a simple object should be rather uniform; still, we make many interpretations about it. As we hear the word 'chair,' we each perceive a special kind of chair from the image that comes to our minds. Moreover, we attribute some properties to it, which convolute our perceptions of a chair. We think of some adjectives like nice, big, comfortable, etc.; then we also think of its purposes differently and assign a set of meanings and merits for it. In some cultures 'chair' is viewed differently from what people in the Western world are accustomed to; e.g., sitting on a chair portrays a sense of pomposity or importance. Even when we look at the same chair, it still appears and means differently to a person based on his/her unique mood and taste at that moment. When a simple object such as a chair induces so many perceptions amongst us, just imagine how vastly different people's perceptions of more complex issues and communications get. The big impact of people's incongruent perceptions on their abilities to communicate is the main point for our discussions here, of course.

Studying a bit more complex (non-physical) perception such as 'love' easily reveals that people's interpretations and meanings become more cumbersome and irreconcilable. Then, studying a compound concept like 'relationships' shows how differently couples interpret each other's needs, actions, and reactions based on their particular mindsets and need urgencies at a specific time in line with their perceptions of their relationships' varied factors.

For this category of perceptions, couples are mostly aware of everything they are doing and saying, while presume stubbornly that they are right about all of them, too. Unfortunately, we are not willing, and in fact not equipped psychologically, to doubt the possibility of being wrong in the way we interpret the same ideas, treat one another, or communicate. In spite of our tenacity about our understanding and accuracy in perceiving various aspects of our relationships and communications, usually we make many erroneous perceptions and assumptions about our dealings with others. Relationship problems mostly relate to the incongruity of partners' perceptions leading to outrageous personal viewpoints, priorities, judgments, etc.

In the next higher level of complexity, we deal with complex concepts, such as biological construct of animals and humans, or the structure and laws of the universe that expand beyond our humanistic ability to perceive. Although we do not quite grasp most of these scientific concepts, we still create our perceptions and opinions about them, anyhow. For example, we do not know exactly how vitamins improve our health, but based on experts' suggestions (which are often conflicting, too), we develop our shallow perceptions and opinions and decide whether to take some vitamins daily in hopes of benefiting from their alleged properties. We realize our ignorance about these phenomena, but still maintain some kind of image and significance for them at any point. We find some personal rationale to make a decision about their meanings and importance for us per se.

At the highest level of complexity, we face such concepts as Creation, God, human spirit, afterlife, etc. For these odd concepts, we do not even have any scientific proof. We do not even have consistent methods or uniform means of explaining them. These concepts are not about tangible objects or ideas, but rather consist mainly of some form of speculation and myths. We have the hardest time understanding these concepts, but actually deal with them so intimately daily through our crude beliefs and religions. Our perceptions are vague and confusing, yet we create detailed images in our minds, since we are both intrinsically and socially programmed to have beliefs in some supernatural phenomenon. We can see ourselves walking right into the heaven, for example! Plenty of questions and clues exist out there to make us wonder and create our unique personal perceptions about the nature of these mysterious phenomena, yet we do not have the mindset and interest to do so!

In all, there is a wide range of perceptions that we build our thoughts and lives around. We refer to simpler perceptions as 'facts' and call most complex ones 'myths.' Of course, we do not stop to distinguish and analyse the level of complexity, nature, and factuality of our perceptions consciously anytime we think about something. Rather, we have combined all these perceptions into a vastly convoluted wisdom about the world, life routines, personal needs, and plausible realities. Even more bizarre is the fact that many people take some mythical notions, such as God, as ultimate truths to make their daily decisions and run their lives. They put their whole existence on line for their absolute faith in certain notions, such as heaven, that they have adopted as solid facts when another large group consider them as flimsy myths, if not horrendous lies altogether. Certainly, both groups, but mostly the first, have extreme difficulty to examine their identities and build plausible senses about the nature of facts and reality.

Nevertheless, we should somehow reconcile our facts, myths, and challenges, despite the confusing effects of our perceptions. By doing so, we can both get a better sense of who we are and improve our communications. We should somehow differentiate and handle our positive doubts, remain objective, and boost our decision-making power to make a living and survive, anyway. Our clearer sense of reality, away from our shoddy perceptions might reduce our burdens of living and cynicism about modern societies. After all, a simple fact to assert with confidence is that the looming natural and social hardships, including climate crisis and political instabilities due to humans' misperceptions of reality are threatening humans' sanity and existence more every year.

CHAPTER FIVE
Main Mental Reconciliations

Each set of facts, myths, and challenges listed in Table 4.1 (page 127) seem to be mysteriously interconnected when we try to align them somehow based on our intelligence and unique personalities. We do these *perplexing analyses* subconsciously or consciously for curbing our life dilemmas that burden our psyches and spirits. These ten sets of facts, myths, and challenges are analysed in this long *(tricky!?)* chapter in a philosophical format.

1. Physical Self, Spiritual 'Self', Humanness

Birth gives us a physical (outer) self—a very special privilege that we often feel, but also abuse. It provides a great opportunity for existence and contacting Nature, humans, animals, etc. This physical form (self) is the only proof or *fact* to substantiate our being, at least based on the norms of the perceived world. Thus, *being* per se becomes the most crucial and relevant 'fact' for us, too—the simplest fact that cannot be denied, especially as our sufferings constantly remind us of our pathetic lives. At the same time, what lies beyond our physical existence—a basic curiosity—is only speculation and a myth as far as we can honestly say. Yet, we are all quite anxious intuitively to know the answer.

Naturally, we cause our own sufferings when we undermine our physical health (the body), for example by drugs and alcohol. Our crooked lifestyles and values stir high stress and confusion, too, which we would then try to conceal or overcome by more pleasure, sexuality, and egotism, all leading to the demise of our psyches and further suffering. In effect, we allow our misguided brains kill the rest of the body with our weak personalities trying to cope with social pressures. Thus, we are the biggest threat to ourselves—both as individuals and human beings—and maybe even our divine spirits. This is a sound *speculation* that we can adopt as another major fact and remember seriously! Our brain is by itself just an abused organ of our physical self, too, after all.

On the other hand, our brains (senses) let us reach within and outside ourselves, think, and *feel* emotional impulses. These raw emotions and psychological reactions, along with other mental functions, e.g., analytical ability, bring us to the verge of dreams, imaginations, and divine creations. At this stage, we enter the domain of the spiritual 'self,' which is a myth. Within this realm, we become capable of expanding our being beyond its apparent limits, outside the body, where our sufferings may subside, too.

We have learned, or possibly experienced personally, that we have an extra-sensory ability to achieve a much higher level of consciousness beyond the boundaries we apply to our normal life situations. This sacred consciousness brings us in contact with beauties, energies, feelings, and inner happiness inaccessible in normal life; they are experiences of the supernatural and spiritual nature. This higher consciousness is considered a myth as we have no concrete evidence regarding its existence, and not even a uniform and tangible definition of its nature. Many people who have claimed achieving such levels of high consciousness have expressed their experiences and their sources differently, vaguely, and incompletely. We are not talking about religious beliefs or practices, although some may find religions a source of reaching high consciousness. Rather, high consciousness is more a matter of individual's mental readiness for transcendence that leads to a search for, and an experience of, selfdom and spirituality. It is also plausible that some form of spirituality is achieved through self-actualization experiences, which has been a dominant field of study in psychology. Still, in spite of scientific findings, most of us do not understand or know how the process and objectives of self-actualization (and the ensuing spirituality) can be pursued and achieved. Thus, while such experiences of spiritual 'self' or 'self'-fulfilment are beyond our normal consciousness, they rely on our state of readiness and inner search to evoke the spirituality power within us. The only hurdle is that our conditioned mindsets make us see reality from a rigid frame of mind—thru perceptions. Thus, it gets difficult for us to penetrate our inner dimensions and reach higher consciousness to release our divine potentiality and spirituality. We do not find this human dimension realistic and feasible within the context of our perceived world.

As much as our physical self is taken as an irrefutable 'fact,' we have been conditioned to accept the norms and values of the perceived world as facts, too, for defining and nurturing our physical self. We have become defenceless against the ingrained forces of our perceptions—as we have learned to accept them as facts of life and necessary for sustaining our physical self. In this context, fact-driven realities in this world refer to our perceptions of physical needs, actions, emotions, priorities, and relationships. For example, we need food to satisfy our physical self, thus we do everything to fulfil this need, including education, working, cooking, etc., as routine facts within a fixed reality. We do all these things since they are fact-driven realities we seem unable to avoid or deny. We do these activities without questioning their ultimate purposes, as if they were inherently programmed in our DNA. Thus, at the end, we have no chance of avoiding the conditioning forces that our **urgent** perceptions of facts impose upon us.

Another deficiency of our fact-driven reality is that most of us rely solely on the sensitivity level of our five senses to judge the reality of things, thus limit our grasp of the world to the level of perceptions developed by our physical senses. This is, of course, a natural and *humanly* logical way of seeing the facts of life, yet has big flaws. This means, for example, that the concept of music feels absurd to a deaf-born person, let alone his/her ability to judge the notion of enjoyment from some particular music and headache from some others. Similarly, we are all conditioned to accept certain notions as facts due to the effects of rearing, social teachings, and low personal incentives to explore the nature and purpose of existence personally thru conscious learning. We are bound by our five senses' strengths to grasp the universe and life based on their sensible properties and our preconceptions of facts. Yet, surely many other realities must exist out there beyond our five senses and expectations for tangibility and rationality.

Our physiological existence is a tangible fact and easy to see, while our psychological reality is not so clear and measurable. In spite of our superficial impressions of, and low abilities to grasp, our psyches, we have learned a lot in recent decades about our psychological dimension to a point where psyche has now been recognized as a factual reality. We are learning from our personal experiences, as well as scientific findings, that our psychological health should be given as much and perhaps a higher priority than our physical health and needs. This urgent need is becoming a serious matter of 'fact,' too!

Most of our problems, including physical illnesses and short life, have been attributed to the weaknesses and sicknesses of our psyches. Yet, in spite of this knowledge, we appear unable to do anything about this matter. We are facing so much suffering and stress, because we are becoming helpless at the presence of our growing psychological needs. The sad 'fact' is that our perturbed psyches have besieged our welfare in modern societies, whereas ideally we should be in control of them for the sake of keeping our sanities. We could connect to our neglected souls merely by controlling and strengthening our psyches that in itself depends on our ability to curb our shallow needs and desires. Accordingly, it is vital to learn actively and consciously about our psyches and strengthen them also for leading us towards *a likely divine 'self.'*

The Eastern philosophy of karma advocates that human souls are given repeated physical lives in order to heal the burdens of their actions and experiences in past physical forms. And that we are reincarnated repeatedly until we master the healing process. This regimen is allegedly for reassessing our worldly failures and sufferings until we learn to manage our psyches and redefine our physical desires and needs in line with the piety and clarity that a free soul needs. We must get our *facts* straight, apparently! While reincarnation is a myth of the highest level, the notion of aligning our physical existence and soul sounds quite rational. It is also a worthy objective we can achieve intelligently during our present (first?) chance for existence without counting on reincarnations and repeated pains of existence to get it right!

We could go beyond our physiological needs to seek solace and psychological growth, which are required for attaining a higher level of *possibly purer, hidden* humanness. Our salvation begins when the spiritual 'self,' who is inherently within us, is grasped and revived. Attaining a high degree of piety is our main 'challenge' for reconciling the 'fact' of our painful physical self and the 'myth' of redemption thru our spiritual 'self.' However, we do not know how to get there (the challenge), and we do not even believe that such a thing (which we call 'self') exists.

An inner 'self' that is strong and full of energy and wisdom seems too obscure and unbelievable; it is a myth! On this ground, someone might present a strong argument—which, by the way, reveals his inner struggle with his conscience: He may argue that, "We know the 'fact' that our body has a limited life and every second of it is precious, thus why not use it only on factual things, including the pleasures of the perceived world? And let us forget about the 'myth' that happiness comes from inward awareness and actualizing the spiritual 'self'; it feels like a waste of time and energy to search for something that may bring us some sensations we do not understand or can even anticipate its nature?" Using a counter-argument against this personal position is useless. Only personal motivation and inner conflicts might lead to awakening, a higher conscience and consciousness, and then clarity about the purpose and possibility of inward reflection and self-awareness.

Nowadays, more people are becoming anxious and stressed by their works, family lives, loneliness, social injustice, etc. The psychological impacts of this social chaos are grave. Everywhere, people are in search of salvation and remedies for their confusion and depressions. The outcome of various methods of positive thinking and psychotherapy has proven futile and many of us are in doubt if a search for the spiritual 'self' and inward reflection can be our final recourse for liberation and alleviating life's pains. Somehow, we should deal with this doubt and make a decision. This is, in fact, a serious *life decision* about the role and impact of myths in our lives and thoughts.

Overall, although myths remain mysteries for the foreseeable future, their impacts on our lives are substantial. For one thing, myths induce our positive 'doubts' productively. Even those who pretend to disbelieve myths always carry a major **doubt** in their subconscious about the existence of a spiritual 'self.' This subtle 'positive doubt' turns into a dilemma for most of us, while we feel that some efforts and sacrifice might bring us a higher level of consciousness through 'self'-realization, which could lower or eliminate our stress and hardships of living.

Whether it is due to our doubts or because of an insight, we might decide to do something about the weakness of our physical self, most likely by discovering our spiritual 'self.' At this stage, our sacred 'challenges' begin. We recognize the ambiguity of our 'facts,' encounter our 'doubts' about the possibilities of 'myths,' and decide intelligently to accept the necessary 'challenges' for reconciling our facts and myths by accepting their connectivity; or conversely, their absolute irrelevance. For example, we might conclude that physical pleasures have no relevance to (or effect on) *inner happiness* that materializes only by seeking and feeding our spiritual 'self.' Or maybe we could demonstrate a possible connection between a healthy body and a healthy mind, which would boost our sense of the spiritual 'self' leading a humble self.

Our challenges at this level, through ongoing reflections and exercises of deeper consciousness, reveal our higher qualities for becoming a compassionate human, grasping the implications and meaning of piety, and walking right into the domain of 'self.' The first challenge is to admit that life is a place for disappointments and suffering (especially since our lifestyles and economies will get more complex and unreliable every day). Therefore, we must prepare our mentalities to face these challenges the best we can. Also, our challenge is to find that elusive happiness in the depth of the mythical 'self.' We are all familiar with temporary cycles of happiness that are mostly superficial and impotent for relieving our permanent, deep suffering. Still, we also have a vague notion of, and a desire for, a sense of contentment that is complete and permanent; a real happiness that subsides all our thoughts and feelings of suffering. It radiates a deep sensation and satisfaction of *being alive*, and *being* per se.

Anyway, the ultimate objective of this particular challenge is to explore the real purposes of our physical existence in hopes of grasping the value and power of our spiritual self, which would attest to the possibility of a higher level of piety for humans. This passionate, soothing perspective of humanness would also induce our higher hope for humanity and advocating means of lowering the prevalent sources of human sufferings.

Since physical self is a basic 'fact' of existence, living has always been a cause of suffering and confusion for humans. It is quite possible that our sufferings are partly due to our misperceptions about the nature of facts—for example, the purpose of life. Of course, our sufferings are also due to our misperceptions about many ideas we take too seriously as 'facts' of life, when indeed those alleged 'facts' have no inherent legitimacy and we are only being fooled by them. We are just drowning in the ocean of our perceptions (alleged facts). We just keep swallowing more water in hopes of satiating our thirst for happiness and survival, since we have assumed and accepted our perceptions as facts of living.

It is interesting to return to Table 4.1, the list of facts, myths, and challenges, and see how every single 'fact' in that list is a direct cause of our sufferings. Similarly, we can easily detect the soothing effects of myths and challenges on our lives. Therefore, it seems plausible to make the following observations merely as another set of mysteries challenging humans forever—or at least until we develop a better sense about the purposes of our lives in such intimidating social settings:

1. Every essential 'fact' is always surrounded by one or more related 'myths,' and certain 'challenges' that we intuitively take on in order to align all these facts and myths.
2. All facts (both real and perceived ones) are causes of human sufferings, starting with the basic fact of existence.
3. Myths depict human insights that may annul or question our perceptions of 'facts,' raise our positive doubts, and mitigate our sufferings through mental adjustment.
4. Challenges are the healing processes that can help us relieve our pains and free our souls. They show our resilience and creativity to align our facts and myths, while exploring our unconscious 'self' in hopes relieving our pains of living in our diseased, convoluted societies.
5. Accordingly, another big life 'challenge' for us is to explore the nature of our positive doubts that feel like sacred insights trying to make us question the validity of the facts crippling us and their possible relationships with myths.

These five general conclusions apply equally to the other nine sets of facts, myths, and challenges discussed in the following pages, as the readers reflect upon each set diligently.

2. Life, Freedom, Doubts

Life itself—the mandate to live—is the second 'fact,' as defined and measured in terms of both its length and quality. The 'quality of life' is, however, getting a higher emphasis in recent decades, while life expectancy is increasing, too. Remarks such as, 'He did not have a good life,' or, 'She lived a great life,' reflect our stress on *how* a person lives more than *how long*. As a matter of *fact*, nowadays, we expect a special quality or outcome from life. Yet, even defining the meaning of life is hard, as discussed in Chapter Two, let alone agreeing on what makes it great or even bearable. Actually, we are learning that life's quality is only an abstract idea —another whimsical perception. We spoiled humans will soon be convinced, like our ancestors, that life is just a cycle of erratic experiences and reflections regardless of our health and wealth. Our impressions of life's quality depend also on our background, age, and state of mind. The simple activities that make life feel wonderful to a child in a developing country have no meaning for a spoiled teenager in North America and so on and so forth.

Realistically, 'life' mostly denotes a hopeful journey through hardships, occasional joys, uncertainties, loneliness, and lingering doubts about the purpose of it all, while we also wonder if God has had any role in any of this. In spite of our eagerness to grasp life's quality, nowadays, it is easier to explain a bad or miserable life—due to its prevalence. As a matter of 'fact,' our incessant doubts about many facets of our lives, along with our erratic choices and decisions, make it impossible to sustain even our sanity, let alone any sense of quality in our lives. All along, the only remedy is to keep ourselves amused with our duties and creativity as a likely healing process, which sometimes brings us some joy, too. We can only learn to embrace various challenges in hopes of making a bit sense of our lives eventually, maybe thru self-actualization and spirituality for some luckier people.

Ironically, our efforts to define the quality of 'life' bring us to the domain of myths. The most common symbol and criterion for 'life's quality' is individual's 'freedom,' which implies a relative sense of independence and salvation, despite the inevitable hassles of living, human ignorance, and growing social chaos. The word 'freedom' here is much broader than its common use, of course. This kind of freedom protects us from the evils of propagandas and social conditioning. The real freedom of mind enables us to function independently regardless of people's views and social demands. It safeguards our spirits from the vast hypocrisies and corruptions engulfing us, even within families and friends. And it is obvious again that we are talking about a myth, the myth of freedom, because living in society drastically restricts our chance for real freedom—or even basic freedom so often!

Then again, social living **must** actually contain people's level of freedom to sustain the overall freedom of the majority. This is a realistic view for freedom if we choose to live in any society. Therefore, while absolute freedom is unrealistic for any society, we can seek only mental freedom through self-realization.

No *relative* freedom manifests in our present lifestyles, either, when our options are so limited and imposed through alluring propagandas, dispiriting economic systems, and superficial social values. The freedom mottos in our so-called democratic societies are just other ways of obstructing our chances for at least mental freedom, as many methods of conditioning and advertising push our needs for materialism and phony lifestyles. The naive slogans of freedom are merely the means of abusing our intelligence and spirits. No real freedom comes from greed, materialism, spoiling our kids with more things, and pushing pomposity and sexuality. The freedom one needs for a good life is exactly the opposite, i.e., the courage to resist all those temptations for recklessness that we like to parade as our aspirations for freedom.

For real freedom, we must focus on our souls, which is still an even more obscure mythical phenomenon. It is an abstract ideal, a myth, for the practical purposes of our social and family lives, which we cannot easily give up. For freeing our souls, we must give up all the hypocrisies and dependencies of the physical world, its values, and its institutions. This is simply an impossible task when we must think and act practically, although finding our souls is an instinctual drive we cannot easily ignore, either.

In the absence of mental freedom, our challenge is to create at least a semblance of freedom in a rather stoic lifestyle, which still needs our efforts to strengthen our minds, learn who we are, and adopt a simple life philosophy. That is the only way to fight the debilitating forces in society that always undermine our mental freedom. We often doubt the authenticity of our lifestyles when our struggles to find peace do not lead to any tangible outcome. Yet, we do not stop to appreciate the clues hidden in some subtle voices in our heads that are trying to make us reassess our life choices. If we learn to manage our positive doubts, as explained throughout this trilogy, especially in Volume II, we may set out to find a more enriching path of life along with sacred beliefs and commitment. We could make better decisions by recognizing our authentic needs, rather than dampening our spirits by pursuing so many shallow needs that society pushes into our heads. We could define and prioritize our life objectives and avoid social traps that damage our integrity and independence. That is the only means of attaining a relative freedom and boosting our life's quality.

The 'fact of living' is most tangible by its nature—in the way it contains disappointments, natural disasters, and frustration. The main premise about the fact of existence is that it would be full of hardships contrary to our naive imaginations for happiness and a blissful journey. The sooner we accept this basic fact of life, the sooner we might get the right perspective and motivation to deal with it actively, instead of hoping to elude this depressing reality by more pleasures or other superficial means, and thus hurting ourselves personally, too. The main fact of life lies in its inherent demand for endless struggles and setbacks. Our sacred challenge is to make it all somehow bearable by understanding the hidden clues in our positive doubts about life and our purposes of living, and to gain that mythical mental freedom eventually somewhat, away from the seemingly factual social rules and values.

Again, it is obvious that the fact of 'life' (the mere necessity of living) is associated with pain and tough choices. The myth of mental 'freedom' is an ideal target to relieve our stress somewhat. And our challenge—the healing process—in this case is mainly the task of 'valuing our doubts' about the validity of imposed social values. Our 'challenge' is to capture at least a relative sense of freedom and peace by grasping our real purposes of living.

3. *Nature, Love, Relationships*

Nature and the universe are the most prominent and tangible facts surrounding us, although they impose the greatest mysteries for us to tackle. Studying Nature's intricacies and the complexity of its laws are always intriguing, but mostly overwhelming. The matter of Creation, why and how, is never going to be solved, yet we accept its symbols, symptoms, and mysteries as undeniable facts. We simply take our visions of Nature and Creation as facts. More importantly, we feel our deep connection to them when we step outside our routine dull lives occasionally to explore our identities. We consider human evolution a miracle of Nature and see ourselves as an integral part of the universe—just another set of facts we have adopted haphazardly! We take our connection to the universe as a crucial, urgent 'fact,' too, although no scientific proof is available, nor can we say anything sensible about the nature or implications of this connection. Still, anybody coming in closer contact with Nature understands more about his/her own vast *inner nature*. During those contacts, our deeper feelings and passion make us cognizant of our needs for mental freedom and humanness. Nature appears to brew and permeate love amidst wilderness. And despite our big doubts about the piety of human nature, we often feel an urge to find a finer sense of humanness in ourselves when we explore Nature and our urge for spirituality is aroused. In all, Nature and our connection to it manifest as 'facts' in our conscious awareness, even though we seldom get a chance to appreciate their implications consciously, too.

For one thing, we notice and believe that people's experiences with Nature often stir love and compassion, along with a sense of selflessness and resignation. Even the love between two humans is just a symptom of internal reflections and outward expression of feelings between two members of Nature. Every person is an element of Nature with basic interrelationships. Love, when not confused with desire, is then a heavenly and spiritual connection between a person and Nature. This feeling pervades the whole universe and humanity as well as one's own inner nature, which itself is Nature. The common expression, 'They found their love in heaven' is a hint that love runs through Nature (heaven) as a media of exchange between two or more entities within Nature. The love of Nature itself is the purest of all loves, as it transpires unilaterally with no expectation for reflection or response.

The unconditional love of Nature, and sometimes another human being, is selfless and soothing. It creates compassion and transcends one beyond the realm of facts to soar into a fantasy world, which is filled with beauties and myths. The insidious and pompous love and mechanical engagement in sexual activities, nowadays, suffer from the lack of Natural connection. They lack Nature's (natural) tenderness that connects a person with his/her inner and outer natures. The real love, then, remains a myth, in particular in the materialistic surroundings that one lives in these days. Love remains a myth as one constantly feels the enormous inner need for it and anticipates the possibility of reaching that state of super being. However, the harder s/he tries to find love, the less it takes the right form and meaning. Our love of Nature, although mythical, remains plausible and educational, anyway—if we understand it and learn how to benefit from it. Once we experience Nature's beauty amidst its grandeur and absorb the reflection of our love extended to, and through, it, the myth of love becomes more sensible and soothing.

In order to maintain and build constructive connections with Nature and humans, surely our challenge is to better define the purpose of our relationships and accept some practical guidelines for relating to one another, while also respecting people's need for independence and individualism. However, it is getting harder every day for people to relate to one another and to Nature. We have lost our natural ways of building even simple relationships, let alone understanding the complex implication of love that we all hope to find in our relationships so obsessively. The level of social stress and personal pain keeps rising because our challenge to define the purpose of our marriages has failed. Our challenge to connect to Nature has failed, too. We are destroying Nature in general and have lost sight of our inner nature, the 'self', as well, while we submerge deeper in our phony lifestyles. For example, we try to find love amidst our insatiable drive for sexuality, while we remain so full of ourselves.

Since we are from Nature, which is the only source of shared, collective love, we need to keep it as natural and unharmed as possible. Distracting Nature's order through pollution and misuse of natural resources threaten all facets of human life, including love and harmony for humanness along with pure reflections. We are stubbornly obstructing the survival of the only source of love and sensation, which we all so deeply and psychologically need. For being a human, and for satisfying our own unselfish needs, we should respond to our thirst for authentic love, the love that is only in the reflections of Nature.

Our challenges are obvious. With the world's socioeconomic order in such shambles, creating a balance for industrial growth and job creation, without ruining Nature, looks impossible. It is hard to believe that humans would ever overcome their rising neediness and greed for more things even at the cost of killing Nature. Yet, no price is justified for depriving humans from this unique source of love. Thus, our challenge remains to protect Nature, our nature, and our environment, if there is still a chance to reverse the effects of the harms we have been inflicting all around ourselves. We must stop ozone holes from expanding and stop the destruction of forests and all other aspects of Nature. We need to establish a higher personal awareness of ecology as the vehicle to save our source of love. This is a big challenge. Yet, even a harder challenge is to define a practical purpose for human connections and learn how to relate to one another effectively and perhaps even spread love a little more naturally with humility. The challenge is to feed our natural urge for love somehow, in spite of the abuse of this fine concept to fulfil our love deficiency and other psychological defects. Our challenge is to stop tainting our impressions of passion and compassion forever due to the symptoms of love affairs in our supposedly cultured societies and our depressing marriages.

Although Nature is the main source of true love and humans' access to their essence, it causes a great deal of pain and distress, too, like all other facts of life. The beauty and love that we can potentially derive from Nature remain concealed from most of us and this deprivation makes us suffer deeply. The fact remains that Nature is also the cause of horrendous disasters, which brings grave sufferings for humans. Nature causes floods, earthquakes, tornadoes, storms, fires and many other kinds of disasters. We cannot control them and when they occur, they result in massive devastations, deaths, and injuries. Therefore, the reality of Nature, as a powerful force with severe reactionary propensity remains an indisputable 'fact,' in spite of our love for it.

Still, love, as a myth that we can never truly conquer, remains a reflection of Nature and manifests merely through our sincere integration with it. Thus, our challenge, the healing process, is to understand our relationships with both Nature and humans. The objective is to relate more efficiently, personally, politically, and universally, in order to reduce human sufferings. We must resort to the loving aspect of Nature to understand its destructive force. Taking drastic ecological steps to save Nature would reduce our pains as well. It may seem too late for all these wishful measures to save God's Nature and our broken inner nature, yet we cannot elude the challenges ahead. In fact, we are being forced into more dramatic challenges with Nature as a result of our dire negligence in recent centuries at least. More devastations and hardships are awaiting us until we can possibly restore a peaceful relationship with Nature. Surely, we all can make at least a little more effort to prevent our selfish and careless participation in the destruction of Nature, and by expressing love and compassion to, and through, it more honestly—even to one another.

4. Physical Growth, Truth, Psychological Growth

The embryonic and genetic aspects of physical growth are 'facts' affecting one's body, health, and potentialities. It continues on a fixed path, though we may influence some aspect of this growth, e.g., by more exercise and nutrition. Particularly, brain's growth is crucial in so many terms other than directing our thoughts and activities. It stores our psychological experiences and needs and it manages our behaviour and emotions. Its capacity may even grow vastly to test and align all the 'facts', 'myths' and 'challenges' we impose on our brains. The brain's growth is measured in terms of its aptitude to make choices and decisions, and for establishing a value system and philosophy that could lead us through life via a healthy psyche. To do its job effectively, our brain sets standards and criteria to make sound judgments in search of the absolute 'truth' and a perception of an ideal world. This search remains a lifetime struggle for our minds, since we never give up the idea of perfecting our grasp of the real world—an ideal world that really makes sense contrary to all the chaos we see and must face daily in the perceived world.

However, we humans still do not agree on any behavioural standards and criteria collectively that fit the laws of Nature as well. This drastic shortfall ruins our brains' efforts, our lives, and humanity. After many centuries of thinking, experimenting, and suffering, we have not yet been able to agree even on a remotely universal truth to guide us. Therefore, 'truth' remains a myth, while we cannot stop thinking that there should be an absolute truth somewhere outside the humanistic logic and dimension. The fact that we have not found it does not mean that it does not exist. This simple fact—that there must be an absolute truth, a *Real World*—keeps our search and curiosity eternal. Our zeal to find the truth at least about simple stuff, such as the purposes of living or secret of happiness, is an innate human need. We simply cannot stop chasing this myth and our personal interpretations of it. We are delighted by our findings on some occasions, grossly disappointed in other times, and search continues. We need to live both the life of facts and the life of myths in order to facilitate our maturity and psychological growth, although we realize that we can neither grasp the ultimate truth, nor reconcile fully the vast amount of facts and myths muddling our brains.

The challenge we chase from our birth to the minute of death is to facilitate our psychological growth. The curious eyes and hands of an infant inspecting a new toy show the mechanism and means of this growth; and we can witness this thirst for the truth in all of our relationships, researches, meditations, intuitions, and contemplations. Accordingly, the general psychological growth of the public *seems* to be happening, albeit very slowly. Then again, we witness too much arrogance and naiveté also growing and tainting humans' judgments and personalities, thus hindering their psychological growth! Meanwhile, our search for the truth, as a point of reference for any likely finer humanistic standards, is derailed by our superficial needs and lifestyles. Thus, not much mental progress is possible, despite our urge and zeal to pursue our personal search for the truth. We are now just too absorbed in a fake 'truth' that society wants us to believe in, rather than the 'truth' that is inside us and must be found through our intuitions and spirituality.

Physical growth (and endurance) is a 'fact' that stirs pain and stress at both physiological and psychological levels. During the process of biological aging, we witness our body's deterioration and endure our continual disappointments about our ignorance and inability to find the 'truth.' Worries about fatal and painful diseases, and the notion of death itself, are big sources of agony. The only escape from these stressful thoughts and sufferings is to build a stronger psychological platform through meditation and 'self'-analysis. Only this psychological growth might alleviate the sad fact of physical growth along with a better sense about the 'truth' of humanity, the ultimate truth regarding the universe, and maybe even God, too. As a myth, 'truth' is hard to grasp and hold on to, but even our imagination of such ideal is soothing. Overall, our challenge is to turn the soothing myths about this eluding 'truth' into a healing process to mitigate many sad facts related to humans' painful survival (physical endurance) with little chance to attend to their psychological and spiritual growth.

5. Social Living, Everlasting Happiness, *Adaptation*

It is a 'fact' that humans are social creatures and cannot survive in isolation on a long-term basis. We need love and belongingness, and our basic needs for food, shelter, health facilities, etc. can be satisfied best in social settings. A large variety of social systems, including education, marriage, and even the simplest concepts of economy, somehow connect us to the social structure that we are defencelessly accepting as a 'fact' of living. Yet, social living is causing most of our agonies and struggles judging by humans' endless confusion and miseries all over the world. Social values and conditions, cruelties and injustice, crimes and drugs, etc. are all chewing away our mental connection to our 'self' and our fine humanness. We have lost our instincts, since they cannot help us within such a broken social structure anymore. Now, only some ineffective systems and influential entities determine what we can or cannot do, what is good for us and what is bad. Thus, we resort to artificial means, e.g., more pleasure and power, to adapt and defend ourselves in this crazy environment. Contrary to all other animals that rely solely on their instincts to make fast and correct decisions, we have lost our natural abilities and become incapable of making decisions, while struggling with a variety of niggling doubts. We cannot judge or trust the validity of social values and our options for living.

On the one hand, we cannot run away from the facts of social living and values. We are attached to them and have become an integral element of their totality. On the other hand, as helpless as we are, we also find the courage occasionally to seek a refuge or an alternative existence. We search for the elusive happiness that we believe we *deserve*. We have not found it within the realities of social living and we might have even looked beyond the world of perceived realities for a miracle that would give us this alleged inner happiness. We hope to find the source of lasting happiness, which supposedly elevates us to a rather stable state of mind with some reliable emotions and connections, including a fulfilling job and a trustworthy companion. But our emotions and connections can never remain stable and reliable. The law of Nature demands that all things and thoughts be dynamic and transient. Therefore, any source of happiness outside a person is bound to change and necessarily impact his/her emotions that induce the erratic cycles of happiness and depression.

Eventually, we realize that the ideas of a lasting happiness and a path for reaching it are simply myths. We accept that happiness is a relative term, too, as it merely reflects our reaction to a new refreshing experience in relation to a sad state of mind or after it relieves our boredom. Once the comparison with the past mood, and the freshness of the new happy experience, fades away, we lose our happiness state. Recurring boredom is a main reason we cannot maintain happiness on a long-term basis.

The big obstacle for achieving a lasting happiness is the mere fact that we hope to reach this mythical level of 'self' fulfillment outside ourselves through self-gratification. We seek happiness by relying on our chaotic social structure and values that demand compliance and hypocrisy. We rely on people's ability to satiate our needs for love and trust. However, all the clues and teachings of spiritual leaders indicate that the myth of everlasting happiness might be partially resolved only on a personal path of wisdom thru inward search for contentment. As long as we look outside ourselves to find the truth and happiness, we would only raise our addictions and dependencies on people, social order, and shallow pleasures.

However, looking inwardly feels like an abstract concept, too, which requires a great deal of meditation, sacrifice, and time for self-awareness. Besides, it is hard to imagine how and what one would achieve from all these unorthodox efforts, anyway. Thus, the idea of inward search becomes another myth, since both the likely objective and means of a *lasting happiness* are obscure.

Yet, it is within our nature, and a requirement for our survival, to continue our search of myths, including happiness, diligently, perhaps on a trial and error basis, without necessarily committing our whole focus and energy to it until we see the changes that must come from within us like flickers of wisdom. Afterward, we may devote ourselves to the task, and simultaneous enjoyment, of 'self' realization and spiritual growth. Meanwhile, we admit that the concept of an everlasting happiness is a myth, not as a cynical standpoint, but rather as a platform for adjusting our life outlook and expectations. While tolerating hardships and disappointments more patiently, we concentrate on more realistic objectives, such as peace of mind, possibly through 'self'-realization.

Nevertheless, searching for that elusive happiness would feel futile as long as we should struggle with the rising crookedness of social living, which actually misguides us about the sources of true happiness. Accordingly, our enormous challenge is to adapt ourselves to social norms, anyway, without losing our faith about finding that illusive inner sources of happiness within ourselves. This adaptation demands sacrifice and wisdom to mitigate our dependency on people and social routines without turning against everything and everybody. Is this possible and easy? Not unless we generate inner happiness and peace within ourselves through creative thoughts and initiatives, instead of focusing on pleasures and egotistical ambitions outside ourselves, fighting with people and irreparable social systems, or losing our patience for seeking the right path of living. Ironically, social living and happiness do not coincide easily, if at all! Then again, if this sad fact is actually due to humans' irreparable evil nature, do social living privileges justify so much suffering and indignity we must bear for them? Can we possibly reform our societies to be of less pain to us by revamping our own mentalities and expectations regarding the purposes of both social co-existence and existence per se?

6. Economic Constraints, Fortune/Fairness, Contentment

Another main feature (fact) of social living is the economic means and opportunities that it offers to citizens. This is an ideal concept of social living driven by an effective socioeconomic and political structure, while people are expected to make concerted efforts for everybody's benefits. In reality, though, this has never happened. Social classes and frictions have always caused deficiencies in the economic orders and governments. In our modern societies, the situation is deteriorating faster than ever, and we face more economic constraints than opportunities. People have become less secure mentally and financially in the way socioeconomic systems are controlling their lives; and naively we often even blame ourselves for missing those limited opportunities—e.g., for getting rich. We have reached a point where we can hardly rely on the existing economic systems' capacities to provide a means of honourable work and survival. Unemployment and financial insecurity often torture even the luckier employed groups living in affluent nations, as they worry about their future. Even the haughty upper class would not be safe in the upcoming economic failures. They might actually suffer the most, even though they believe they are immune against all the tyranny prevalent in the present socioeconomic environments.

In fact, our economic systems could be viewed as barriers for humanity in the way those economic opportunities are becoming less generalizable and tangible, and instead subdue individuals' pride and independence. They cause more stress and insecurity in the long run than provide a reliable source of economic welfare. Thus, our presumed economic opportunities can be viewed more as social constraints that frustrate people their whole lives. They are 'facts' that prevail in many fronts around the globe, including job opportunities, access to education, competition, technology, markets, tax systems, organization and labour discriminations, and all other social facets. These economic systems will remain painful facts of social living, while we rely on them helplessly for subsistence, and while so many greedy, incompetent executives run corporations for their own financial and egotistical benefits. As discussed in Volume III, work and organization have become main issues and sources of suffering for us all. This is despite the ideal notion about work being the source of personal security at least, and hopefully a means of self-fulfillment and happiness if it happens to be the right kind of work. In all, economic conditions in our societies not only limit individuals in satisfying their basic economic needs, but also deprive them from achieving their full potentials and self-respect, plus a lifetime of pains and worries.

In capitalistic economies, especially, people are led to believe they have equal opportunities to make lots of money and build a fortune. However, this is untrue due to economic and personal barriers, including uncontrollable factors such as opportunity and luck. 'Fortune and luck' are myths, yet many of us believe fate plays an essential role in everybody's life. If a person is born into a rich family or nation, his/her chances are much higher to get the right education, have his/her business laid out and ready for him/her at graduation, and s/he usually ends up marrying a wealthy person, too. Compare this scenario with the situation of a person born in a less fortunate family, or a poor country, with all kinds of social issues, or gets mixed up with street gangs, etc. Certainly, wealth is not a means or measure of happiness or success, but the point is to highlight the shallowness of propagandas about social equality and our beliefs about equal opportunities.

Many people who end up making something of themselves admit that good luck and opportunities have helped them; or maybe even a divine force driven their fortune somehow. This may be luck, the universe, or God. Nobody knows the nature of this external intervention, though many people have experienced it—intellectuals, rich, poor, aristocrats and commoners. We might have felt the impact of luck or a sacred entity watching over us somehow. These odd experiences occur frequently enough in such profound ways we cannot deny the existence of some external source of power out there that supports us, at least occasionally. Despite its irrationality and our passive mentality for exploring it, the myth of fortune resides in our subconscious as a possibility, and we resort to it from time to time thru prayer or meditation. That is what hope is based on and all about.

Then again, we still expect fairness from this world, despite our beliefs about destiny. We expect to be treated fairly and to receive the recognition that we think we deserve from the society, from the organization we work for, from our family and friends, etc. In reality, however, fairness is also only a myth—*maybe even related to our fate*. We can touch or exercise it from time to time, but, generally, no such thing as fairness exists. Like freedom, fairness is a relative term and subject to luck and fortune. It also depends on the state of mind of people expecting it or inflicting unfairness with dire cruelty or stupidity. Ironically, unfairness is a common, torturous fact, but fairness remains a myth!

Despite all the unwarranted unfairness, while struggling within unmanageable economic constraints, social living still demands ongoing decision-making, intelligence, originality, perseverance and other sorts of personal traits. We strive for the betterment of our economic and materialistic lives with all our might, and hope subconsciously that luck and opportunity aid us in achieving our fantasies as well, and we hope that the sources of unfairness, prejudices, and discriminations are eliminated somehow someday.

Pressed by the inevitable economic constraints as a sad 'fact' of life, while pondering the myths of fortune and fairness as likely sources of relief, our challenge is to stay content (without losing our patience, identity, and individuality). Our goal is to avoid getting completely caught up in the machinery of pervasive materialistic life and depriving ourselves from the opportunity of evolving as humble humans out of this mess. We should adapt to socioeconomics' unpleasant features somehow. We need all the opportunities and lucks to cope with the socioeconomic problems of our world. However, more importantly, we need contentment and humility to bypass the temptations of social rewards that are always against the values of divine humanness. We could at least perceive this ideal to soothe our spirits, even though we can never elude our doubts about humans' ability to reach this sacred level of sophistication. We need inner strengths and wisdom to bear unfairness and resist narrow-minded people who love to make life difficult for other humans just for feeding their Egos—to hide their deep insecurities and prove their meagre existence.

The mere 'fact' of existence forces most of us to stress on our economic and family needs at the cost of depriving ourselves of a chance to even detect our basic need for spirituality. Our realistic preoccupation with the pressing facts of living makes us miss the opportunity of exploring the finer aspects of our being.

Accordingly, our challenge remains to explore our limited opportunities and bring luck on our side by boosting our 'self' and trusting its divine potentialities, while facing socioeconomic realities (constraints) wisely as well. Despite our positive doubts, keeping some level of faith about a divine force or fortune inside us is necessary. This is not a religious remark or raw belief, but rather a useful psychological relief according to medical findings; that contentment enhances our inner strengths and health in line with more objective thinking.

Both our urge for success and our failures to find happiness due to rising socioeconomic constraints in the new era heighten our pains. Still, the only way out of this humiliating existence is to build a simple lifestyle by curbing our fantasies and economic dependencies in hopes of gaining at least contentment. We could try to adopt a life philosophy for aligning socioeconomic facts with the myths of fortune and fairness somewhat.

7. *Personal Limitations,* Enlightenment, Life Decisions

A destructive feature of the perceived world is its knack to turn humans into selfish dreamers by ignoring the 'fact' about their severe limitations. Actually, we often think we deserve the best of everything, since we see ourselves as very special individuals.

We merely develop unrealistic views about our potentialities and limitations due to shoddy ideologies and social fads. For instance, positive thinking jargons and similar schemes are becoming so popular in new societies at the cost of confusing the public vastly. Many ideas like freedom and democracy have damaged humans' sense of reality and identity as well. Accordingly, their egotistical ambitions are often driven by their raw perceptions of life, phony individualism, mushy emotions, and deep insecurities.

Naturally, positive thinking can help us improve our attitudes and outlooks, thus explore our untapped inner strengths actively. However, mere ambition does not eliminate our limitations, nor does it increase our potentialities. It only causes more frustration and limitations, since our talents and energies cannot be tapped properly before we fix our mindsets and insecurities a lot. Sadly, instead of facing reality in terms of personal and social limitations, we force ourselves to dream about many farfetched and often vain symbols of success that misguide and lure us at the cost of losing our 'self' and potentialities.

Personal limitations and potentialities are discussed in Vol. II of this trilogy, since they vastly affect our life outlooks and plans. Naturally, genetics, rearing, and educational opportunities play big roles in an individual's psychological strength and aptitude. Still, our unique talents and needs often remain hidden due to personal limitations or missed opportunities. We do not recognize and align our potentialities and limitations for setting realistic life objectives and plans. We imagine that our potentialities would flourish without first grasping and revamping our limitations to a large extent. All along, our deep insecurities generate our crooked personalities that also hinder the use of our potentialities. Overall, with no interest to study and curb our limitations and eccentricities, we merely adopt the crooked common mentalities and routines in search of success robotically.

An average human's potentialities are both limited and buried deep in his/her psyche, and thus too hard to access beyond many layers of personal insecurities and priorities in line with social pressures. Thus, for getting even a notion of our potentialities, especially divinity, we should defeat many psychological barriers thru self-cleansing and development of a rather radical mindset to observe life and ourselves in an unconventional perspective.

The natures of our potentialities and limitations also make us quite different, even if we like to believe that humans have the same basic essence. Not many people would develop Einstein's vision about the universe, no matter how seriously they tried. No education can make many of us think and perceive things like him, either. Still, we all could pinpoint and use our potentialities wisely after curbing our limitations.

We know these basic 'facts' deep down, yet get carried away by our raw ambitions, greed, social demands, or positive-thinking propagandas that claim we can achieve anything by envisioning or wishing it. Thus, many people lose their patience, minds, and lives due to their naïve impressions about their potentialities that raise their unrealistic expectations from life and society.

Naturally, it is wise to challenge ourselves with superb goals. How else can we ensure that our measures of our potentialities and limitations are valid? But the trick is to stay realistic as well. This is a big dilemma that makes the 'fact' about our limitations and potentialities both confusing and pressing. Yet, resolving all these doubts and grasping our inherent limitations, including the humans' ultimate limitation—the scary fact of death—demands major efforts for choosing a practical life path. As an important first step, we could at least avoid the obvious traps, such as faking weird personalities or pursuing imaginary goals during our strides for popularity and success. Instead, we can adopt a basic lifestyle and remain humble in gauging our potentialities, needs, identities, and limitations, including our self-development ability. Otherwise, we would only raise our limitations, push our potentialities deeper into abyss, and get lost in a world of illusions as a dreamer with a phony personality.

Understanding our limitations and potentialities is also crucial for making right decisions, especially for preventing big setbacks, depression, and possibly even losing our sanity, e.g., by choosing wrong careers or spouses. We can learn to do and say things more thoughtfully and kindly through self-awareness and by controlling our idiosyncrasies, as we gain the insight to live simpler.

It is an amazing 'fact' that the more we understand and admit our limitations, the more confident and free we feel in line with a sense of enlightenment, selflessness, and humility. These divine privileges are the results of our higher level of consciousness and self-awareness. Accordingly, as we finally stand with awe at this intersection of the wisdom path, we can make effective, radical decisions about our life path and lifestyle.

This sacred realization sounds mystical and a myth to many of us without any divine experiences. We have probably heard about mysticism, miracles, and enlightenment. However, without personal experiences in these areas, we remain sceptical about the reality of such power and its possible effect on our lives. We just keep viewing them passively with deep cynicism. We doubt our ability to grasp or experience these kinds of mythical phenomena. Yet, during some moments of weakness and need, we resort to the same kind of mystical power naturally and plea for salvation.

As noted in the previous section, many of us have an inherent, elusive belief in a power that inspires us in some moments of despair. Despite our doubts regarding this mythical phenomenon, some truth might exist about those energy sources we consider mystical. And enough clues exist about the possibility of reaching personal enlightenment if we allow our hearts, minds, and beliefs grow in the right direction. Enlightenment sounds like a myth, too, but it is a natural and conceivable reality, though it has various levels. While our basic views of luck and destiny might build our belief system, enlightenment offers a natural, active venue to find our link to a mysterious force in the universe.

Nevertheless, for most of us who are not pursuing a wisdom path towards 'enlightenment,' or are just beginning to search for it, our logic dictates that we handle it as a 'myth.' We just seek a kind of wisdom that could make our life choices and decisions easier with less stress. Together, our potentialities, belief system, and rising enlightenment give us enough energy to face the real issues of our lives and avoid irreversible situations and mistakes.

Our physical and psychological limitations and our neglected potentialities are all 'facts' of life that stir hardships and suffering for us. As our psychological strengths surpass our physical lives' boundaries, we learn to resort to mystical powers and search for enlightenment. Despite our doubts, we find even our raw beliefs a soothing alternative to our usual state of helplessness and pains. This healing process boosts our ability to make better decisions and survive. More importantly, our sound decisions empower our healing process. When our fine decisions make someone happy, relieve other humans' hardships and sufferings, or help ecology, they turn into a natural process for healing our souls as well. Yet, while everybody realizes the value of making good decisions in a timely manner selflessly and objectively, we usually miss our chances. In particular, we do not perceive or pursue our lifetime 'challenge' to manage our limitations and psyches thru a diligent, self-cleansing process. Instead, we follow the mainstream with shallow jargons, become just more selfish and naive, and damage humanity in a world rushing out of control towards annihilation.

8. Personal Needs, Inner Strengths, Needs Alignment

Essential for our survival, adaptation, and growth are a bunch of instinctual needs that we must satisfy as a matter of *fact*. Yet, we have also invented too many artificial personal needs in the new era, which we now take as basic facts of life, too. Accordingly, our growing obsession for so many artificial needs to pamper our Egos has lowered our chances vastly to attend to our authentic needs, while causing us enormous distress and suffering as well. In all, we have become slaves to our rising artificial needs.

Our personalities also evolve around our superficial needs, as we perceive them as real necessities and facts for our existence. Meanwhile, the burden of those needs manifests in our social attitudes and stress. On the one hand, people's presumed needs are deforming humans, societies, and humanity's characteristics. They are ruining our value systems and cultures. Conversely, our corrupt socioeconomic systems influence the nature and scope of our personal needs. Sadly, social values and superficial personal needs have become parallel dire forces infesting each other in a vicious cycle and tainting humanity in the process. This ominous energy is accelerating along a painful, ruinous path and only few people seem to even grasp the scope of the problem or care about the doomed destiny of humanity.

Our culture is stressing on physical needs and pleasures, while our spiritual needs are either misguided or buried further in our psyches. Thus, our psychological needs are not addressed, either. For example, only a small group actively pursues and achieves 'self-realization' as a basic psychological need. Instead, most of us focus on self-gratification, try to fake individualism, build a phony self-image, and turn into conceited characters in order to compensate for our rising insecurities. Our inflated egos manifest readily in our relentless urges for greed, sexuality, domination, power, and possession—as personal needs and rights!

Creating a right balance among our physical, psychological, and spiritual needs is surely necessary for maintaining our health and stamina. Otherwise, psychological regression relative to the degree of mental imbalance would cripple us. Other side-effects are: chronic depression, limited self-awareness, high gullibility, and minimal mental growth—all the right ingredients for many social organs to rely on to fulfil their own agendas, e.g., getting elected as heads of governments or selling more useless products to the hypnotized public.

Surely, our personal needs, regardless of their nature, type, and intensity, feel like life's necessities and 'facts' to us. Yet, so many superficial needs have burdened our psyches in recent decades, as we learn and imitate so many misleading, doomed social mottos. These shallow needs, driven by capitalism to satiate our egos and physical desires, hinder our chance for building a pure self-image and identity. Even some of our natural needs, such as sex and love, are now abused and exaggerated artificially. They have now been placed at the highest level of our consciousness as popular, urgent means of satiating our illusions regarding happiness and individualism. We embrace these superficial needs out of habit, insecurity, or obligation rather than for natural need fulfilment.

Our addiction to superficial needs has also led to our lesser stamina and motivation to attend to our real needs. Moreover, we have some deeper (subconscious) needs that are genuine, but not as clear as our basic needs mostly due to our cultures' influences. These needs stir our self-realization efforts and cleanse our souls. Sometimes, we feel the conflicts among our physical, spiritual, and psychological needs, and then we face a decision to satisfy one type of personal need (e.g., pleasure) at the expense of other types of needs (such as integrity). However, our inner strengths and souls' piety depend on our ability to identify *all levels* of our needs and favour the ones that lead to wisdom, growth, and self-realization. They are healing beliefs equally vital for our welfare like the other myths addressed in this trilogy.

Like all other 'facts' of life, our erratic personal needs mostly cause suffering as well, since they compete amongst themselves for our attention during our routine choices and actions, or keep raising our insecurities unconsciously. Even satisfying our lower level needs are causing us lots of hardships. Our basic needs for food, shelter, and security demand lots of sacrifice and mental strengths. Then, many of our medium-range needs, such as love and belonging, are often hardly attainable, nowadays, thus we suffer psychologically a lifetime, too. Sometimes, we realize that our presumed achievements are not gratifying enough in the way we had imagined. Therefore, we feel disappointed and dismayed, while we feel helpless with no chance to build inner strengths or even get a sense of them, including a semblance of piety.

When we set out to fulfil our higher (subconscious) needs, we might experience divinity, too, which reflects our inner strengths and elusive piety—our souls. This inner strength is a myth of highest order, as it is hard to feel and maintain. It has suffocated in our unconscious after millenniums of humans' struggles for survival and domination. It has been buried deep underneath all our superficial needs in our showy societies. Now, grasping and aligning our authentic needs, including spirituality, and finding a path to attain them, would be an enigmatic, tough journey that requires plenty of patience and stamina.

Nevertheless, exploring our inner strengths, by fostering our psychological and spiritual needs, is the way to reduce our life sufferings. Accordingly, our 'challenge' is to grasp, and attend to, our higher needs at some conscious level. The challenge is to align our urges for inner strength (piety) and material needs (physical and sexual) realistically to facilitate our healing process.

9. Perceived Reality, Real Reality, Health

The perceived and real worlds offer two rather opposing means of connecting to society and the universe, and thus generate most of humans' presumed facts and myths. In the perceived world, people try to satisfy their external (physical) needs by adapting to societies' rules and conditions. They have established some forms of relationships with so many organs of this world and they are rather familiar with its weird features and variables that demand our attention in our daily routines. They have internalized alluring and confusing images of this perceived world, which also gives them a subtle sense of psychological security by providing direct feedback and rewards for their efforts. Thus, it is hard for people not to see this perceived world and everything happening in it as 'real,' 'fact,' 'truth,' 'logical,' 'tangible,' 'rewarding,' and many similar criteria that reinforce both their immediate and superficial needs according to the crude realities of the perceived world.

In contrast, the real world is the means of connecting to the universe and our inner 'self.' It places an idealistic expectation on moral and mentality for some seemingly intangible rewards that are mostly one's imagination of transcendence based on one's limited (if any) inner experience. All these idealism and rewards feel abstract and fantastic—merely a myth—for our conditioned minds. Thus, the real world and the universe outside our crooked perceptions appear imaginary (a myth) to us, while all our crude imaginations (in the perceived world) appear realistic, practical, and 'facts' of life.

Turning to a real world where supposedly our souls guide our physiques is against the logic, values, and conditions that we are used to in our perceived world; it sounds like a myth. However, the only possibility for personal peace and relief is to connect to the mythical world of real realities that challenges our growing perceptions of humans' place in our so-called civilized societies. This transcendence can be accomplished by initially reconciling the facts and myths that separate these two worlds, but without resorting to religions and superstitions. We could learn about the existence and supremacy of the real world through methodical self-awareness, and then detect some aspects of this myth with the aid of our powerful, divine potentialities. We can awaken and exploit our potentialities practically in society, too, while seeking inner peace without rationalizing the wickedness and weaknesses of the perceived world that we have readily embraced and believe to be the *truth* of our existence.

The realities and facts that we accept as truths in the perceived world are only dire diseases crippling our psyches. The disease of wealth gathering and greed—the main symbols of the perceived world—has inflicted our bodies and brains. They have abolished our opportunities for natural growth and functioning,. Therefore, our challenge is to reform our crude mentalities and lifestyles by, a) bypassing the conditions and values of the perceived world, and b) excavating our divine potentialities and self-awareness for getting at least a glimpse of the real world.

We know that the most important asset for a person is his health, not wealth. Yet, we somehow ignore the immorality and the harms caused by our professions, sexuality, greed, anxieties and the stress of accumulating wealth. These symptoms of social living with no spiritual insights have paved the path to a definite self-destruction. Certainly, we hardly notice or gauge our ailment and the effect of psychological diseases until it is too late. We may realize the futility of our crude ambitions and the harm we have done to ourselves usually too late, only when we collapse from stress, depression, loneliness, or a heart attack.

Our ultimate objective (challenge) in life is to develop and maintain our psychological and physical health. Thus, measuring and reconciling our senses of the perceived and real worlds are crucial for appreciating their factuality and importance for our welfare. We can ask ourselves why we ruin our psyches, bodies, and spirits by so much nonsensical activities and thoughts spread in the perceived world in line with infantile social obsessions for materialism and self-indulgence. **In fact, dealing with these questions and reality checks should ideally be the duty of our governments and leaders!**

The answer to the question, 'Why we inflict so much harm on our health?' brings us back to the same sad conclusion: that our perceptions of 'facts' are incomplete and distorted. We do not perceive the essential messages about our ultimate life objectives, such as the matters of our physical and psychological health, in a timely manner, but we perceive many crooked features of the perceived world so readily as appealing, urgent, and necessary! We are thoroughly absorbed in, and have submitted to, the rules and conditions of the perceived world and we need a superhuman strength to pull ourselves out of this state of hypnosis.

The prevalence and power of the perceived world is a 'fact' and a major source of our hardships. This debilitating mindset ('fact') would keep us overwhelmed as long as we are not willing to challenge it. The only relief from this phony life of materialism is to transcend to the world of real realities, which we continue to accept only as a 'myth.' Accordingly, the process of healing our suffering souls imposes the challenge of maximizing our physical and psychological health. Remembering this primary human need is a big 'challenge' by itself. It is an arduous divine mission.

10. Death, Creation/Creator, Spirituality

Death is the saddest 'fact' of life. Our perception of mortality and our doubts about afterlife cause us a deep, sad feeling. Death of a close family member or a friend brings us immense sorrow and pain, and the thought of our own dismal ending is *usually* even more excruciating. The former case saddens us for losing our connection with someone we love. Our own death means losing the pleasures of this physical world as well. Most of all, however, the thought of *non-existence* per se is far more painful than all other deprivations that death causes. We *usually* get too attached to this confusing, miserable *perceived world*. These losses, pains, and thoughts are inevitable and devastating facts for all humans. Luckily, we can undermine or hide the finality of death in our subconscious most of our lives as long as a serious illness does not bring us to our senses!

On the one hand, our ability to elude the thoughts of death is a blessing for curbing the burdens of this seemingly unfair fact on our psyche. On the other hand, this low consciousness about this finality distorts our view of reality as we forget our vulnerability. In fact, a regular ritual to internalize and remember the reality of death would keep our minds focused inwardly in search of who we are and what our living purposes are—in both the worlds of perceived and real realities.

Whether there is an afterlife, and in what form, is something that we can only speculate on and wish for, in order to alleviate our fears and sadness of death. The religious beliefs and personal convictions of some sort, with respect to the permanency of soul, are the means of relieving ourselves from the anxiety of death. And, of course, our philosophical and theological ideas keep us amused about the possibility and greatness of afterlife. All these imaginations and hopes help us overcome our fears and sadness of the fact of death as well, but more crucially, they put us in touch with our inner 'self.' The questions regarding 'existence' and the purpose of life are derivatives of our thoughts about death. Accordingly, from this platform we initiate our thinking and speculations about the creation and the creator. We become curious regarding the purpose of Creation and the likelihood of a creator. Then, we find out that the notion of needing a creator for everything is only a figment of human logic and most likely way outside the reality of the universe. In spite of all the philosophies and scientific clues, we are unable to make a plausible judgment about creation and creator, existence, death, soul, and afterlife. This whole issue remains forever a myth for us to doubt, ponder, speculate, subdue our fears and sadness with, and keep our spirits high. We must face and keep doubting this myth forever, but also apply as a vehicle to know more about ourselves and awaken our unconscious needs and potentials. We might even reach a sense of enlightenment that makes up for our limitations and satisfies our need for spirituality, although our doubts about the creator and Creation continue as another myth in our lives.

Many spiritual insights, philosophical notions, and scientific evidences suggest that we are an integral part of the universe and creation. Physiologically, we are built of the same basic matter and energy that makes up the universe and which can be traced in subatomic particles and molecules. Some people go even one step further and believe that our minds, thoughts, and intelligence are an extension of a super-intelligence phenomenon, like a universal consciousness, which is the core of the universe and responsible for its creation. Keeping it at a mythical level, it might not hurt to have these kinds of corny beliefs. We can even believe that our creativity and insight flow from this universal intelligence that we access through our awareness and souls.

Maslow's findings regarding self-actualizers' emotions reflect the type of transformation that these scholars have been able to achieve. Self-actualization experiences are significant, since they provide some tangible and sensible set of evidences based on real experiments. These findings support the possibility of finding our spiritual 'self' under certain conditions. Especially, the following two quotes about Maslow's findings reflect how the subjects of his studies surpass the fears of mortality:

"One aspect of the peak-experience is a complete, though momentary, loss of fear, anxiety, inhibition, defence and control, a giving up of renunciation, delay and restraint. The fear of disintegration and dissolution, the fear of being overwhelmed by the "instincts," the fear of death and of insanity, the fear of giving in to unbridled pleasure and emotion, all tend to disappear or go into abeyance for the time being. This too implies a greater openness of perception since fear distorts." Towards a Psychology of Being, Abraham Maslow, Van Nostrand Reinhold, 1968, page 94.

"The emotional reaction in the peak experience has a special flavour of wonder, of awe, of reverence, of humility and surrender before the experience as before something great. This sometimes has a touch of fear (although pleasant fear) of being overwhelmed. My subjects report this in such phrases as "This is too much for me." "It is more than I can bear." "It is too wonderful." The experience may have a certain poignancy and piercing quality which may either bring either tears or laughter or both, and which may be paradoxically akin to pain, although this is a desirable pain which is often described as "sweet." This may go so far as to involve thoughts of death in a peculiar way. Not only my subjects but many writers on the various peak experiences have made the parallel with the experience of dying, that is, an eager dying. A typical phrase might be: "This is too wonderful. I don't know how I can bear it. I could die now and it would be all right." Perhaps this is in part a hanging on to the experience and a reluctance to go down from this peak into the valley of ordinary existence. Perhaps it is in part, also, an aspect of the profound sense of humility, smallness, unworthiness before the enormity of experience." Ibid., pages 87-88.

At the same time, humans' main challenge is to find the beauties of life that make our living so wonderful and pleasant. Maslow reports similar experiences of self-actualizers, which may initially appear contrary to the previous quote about self-actualizers' loss of fear to die during peak experience:

"The person is more apt to feel that life in general is worth while, even if it is usually drab, pedestrian, painful or ungratifying, since beauty, excitement, honesty, play, goodness, truth and meaningfulness have been demonstrated to him to exist. That is, life is validated, and suicide and death wishing must become less likely." Ibid., pages 101-102.

The perception of death is most painful amongst the other 'facts' of life. The only relief we may find for this pain and grief is to think of the possibility of our souls' immortality. This is a 'myth' that we may cling to as a defence mechanism. The 'challenge' for reconciling the fact of mortality and the myths of afterlife is to explore our inherent ability to actualize and fulfil our real 'self,' as a soulful creator of ideas and art, as a self-actualizer, and as a builder of our spirits. We have a chance and potential to achieve all these ecstatic moments in our short lives.

Therefore, we become the creator and the creation at the same time when we attain a high level of consciousness!! We become a minuscule manifestation of energy and matter transformation in the time-space dimension eternally. We are necessarily a part of the whole energy and matter in both non-physical and physical forms, then!? 'What we are' gives us the clue and ability to create a 'self' free from our Egos and in touch with our souls. We can see our real 'self,' which is immortal with a link to the creation and creator. And our 'challenge' is to discover the 'self'-fulfilling and actualizing creations that evolve within us. This is the process of reconciling between the 'fact' (and fear) of mortality and the 'myth' (and joy) of creation. The challenge is to discover how the potential ecstasy of personal creations beats the fear of mortality. The challenge is to go about opening our minds and hearts to use these fundamental thoughts within a practical path of existence.

The Role of Facts, Myths, and Challenges

The ten sets of 'facts,' 'myths,' and 'challenges' suggested in Table 4.1 (page 127) and discussed in this chapter comprise the most general thoughts boggling humans' minds, but definitely do not make an exhaustive list. Everybody can add and ponder other facts with their corresponding myths and challenges. Still, a few interesting issues have come to light: **First,** some parallel myths and challenges seem to raise our curiosity and doubts about every fact. (We have not scientifically proven this, but it seems quite plausible that, i) the facts, myths, and challenges that humans entertain are highly interrelated in many dimensions and realms, and ii) studying each set together reveals a deep insight about our thought and decision processes.)

Second, it appears that all the objects, principles, and events that we perceive as 'facts' lead to hardship and suffering, whereas the corresponding 'myths' provide soothing options for thinking and behaving, and that 'challenges' are the means of reconciling our facts and myths with the aim of cleansing our mindsets and healing our souls. Our challenges also provide the opportunity of transcending our 'self' towards the summit of enlightenment thru inner search and awareness.

Third, it seems that all our alleged 'facts' are related to the physical aspect of our lifestyles in the perceived reality world. They reflect our perceptions and contacts with the external world. That is, we look outside ourselves to establish the facts. As soon as we turn inward and look inside ourselves, we face all sorts of myths and doubts. Thus, the contents of our hearts, minds, and souls—our inner 'self' (inner world)—have been grasped and treated as myths and unreal. We have become conditioned to take things that are in the external world as real and 'facts' of life. And we dismiss or consider fantasy everything that comes from our inner world—spirits, hearts, minds, insights, and instincts.

Most of us doubt the reality of 'inner self,' yet we might get a sense of it by pondering the inconsistencies and contradictions of 'facts' and 'myths' and attempting to align them somehow in our heads. These efforts might at least reduce our dogmatism about the validity of those 'facts' if we become a bit open-minded and humbler to explore the role of myths and our inner self as well.

Finding a logical balance between facts and mythical realities —something like what we have tried to achieve in this chapter— might broaden our senses about supernatural, the absurdity of religions, and the shallowness of humans' alleged facts. It might help us sensitize the foundation of our thoughts and learn about our inner self, as we explore spirituality and gain divine wisdom deserving humans' dignity matching our higher inner strengths!

Sadly, by insisting on the accuracy of our perceptions of the external (physical) world as undeniable 'facts,' we merely cause ourselves more hardships and ignore our inner self. Therefore, we might ask, 'If our perceptions of the world are *real* facts, why do they have to be so painful? Why would God create a sad world around all these painful facts? Are these so-called 'facts' only inventions of our crude imaginations and logic? Is it in our nature to find means of paining ourselves and others, instead of looking for salvation and peace?'

So weirdly, we do not seem to get these elementary messages, despite our constant tortures within the realities of the presumed factual world. Obviously, we are conditioned to perceive facts and myths in distorted ways, but we could at least gauge our living options a bit more radically for a chance to free ourselves from the big load of dire 'facts' imposed upon us as modern ways of thinking and living. We, mainly scholars, could study seriously some fundamental thoughts that boggle most people's minds and perhaps come up with some novel ideas to reshape humanity. For example, we can see that our obsessions with too many juvenile ideologies, such as capitalism, freedom, and democracy, are not working for such flawed humans, yet we propagate these foolish ways of thinking and talking arrogantly so shamelessly with such energy. It is merely too sad how most scholars prefer to remain nonchalant about these basic existential issues!

So embarrassingly, we all dismiss the *fact* that the presumed facts nurtured in the perceived world are mostly the outcomes of humans' juvenile opinions and idealism piling up over centuries. We have developed and cherished lots of idealistic perceptions, e.g., freedom, due to the effect of our vile genes and insecurities that goad our conditioned brains. And we all let our egos make us believe we know all the facts of this world better than anybody else already! Accordingly, it should be clear how useless most of the so-called facts in societies and people's minds are.

Naturally, myths cannot help us build social guidelines and structures to serve the public, either, the same way our facts have been impotent. Yet, we have also ignored the reality (authenticity) of our inner strengths in relation to an outer source of power—besides our juvenile addictions to outmoded religions, of course. Self-awareness and 'self', feel abstract and myths, when they are actually the sources of relief from so much sufferings in a world built around a huge mishmash of irreconcilable facts and myths that have caused so much confusions, conflicts, and wars around the globe even over a bunch of absurd religious mumbo-jumbos.

The ultimate challenge for a person is to recognize and act on a simple *fact*: That since we are stuck in this formidable position about the nature of the universe and our modern societies, we might at least take on some special 'challenges' to somehow align these 'facts' and 'myths' at personal level for our own salvation. The goal is to create at least a balanced position in our thoughts and actions personally—without confusing ourselves further, of course, or letting another form of gullibility (such as religions) hamper the foundation of our thoughts. Ironically, we all often ponder and doubt the meanings or purposes of alleged 'facts,' e.g., human rights, although we have classified them as realities of life. Our cynicism about these seeming 'facts' make us question our lifestyles and choices pensively so frequently. Yet, we never consider challenging their factuality even slightly. Granted, it is hard to do so, anyway. How can we deny certain facts, such as modern humans' naïve idealism about freedom and democracy?

All other facts feel equally solid and irrefutable. However, our subtle positive doubts about 'facts' within *a perceived world* are warranted and useful, as demonstrated in this chapter.

Ironically, our positive doubts about 'facts,' e.g., the purpose of living, is quite perplexing, since 'facts' should be inherently clear and indisputable by definition. Animals lack the capacity or instincts to doubt their existence or seek a validation for it. So, why are we humans so obsessed about the purposes of our lives and the meanings of all other facts? Why do we struggle so hard to defy even the 'fact' of death by imagining afterlife, when all facts are theoretically presumed to be unchallengeable? Why would our curious brains make us doubt all our facts and myths, at least subconsciously, when it then leads to more stress and confusion? Of course, we doubt general facts erratically as well, mostly when they threaten our interests or emotions!

Are all these (positive) doubts only for awakening our sixth, possibly divine, sense to reassess our facts more realistically and intelligently, e.g., about death, by accepting our mortality without trying so idiotically to fool ourselves about an imaginary life in heaven! Since we cannot understand or change the essence of the so-called 'facts', perhaps we could at least try to, i) correct our views of them, and ii) learn to cope with them in some harmony (with great reservation and without exaggerating their meanings or validity merely because we have come to call them 'facts'.) Yet, even for this basic awareness about 'facts,' we must learn to assess them objectively. Only then we might learn to stop taking all our facts, especially our existence, so seriously and literally as undeniable phenomena. Instead, we could grasp and honour our nothingness. We might then focus on our endless 'challenges' for reconciling so many facts and myths that are besieging our lives and clouding our senses of reality and being. This cleansing ritual can soothe our pains of existence, while we also learn to value our doubts. We can do this by making smart, effective decisions, to create synergies between mind and body, spirit and ego, intuition and logic, wisdom and knowledge, etc. These alignment efforts would instigate our humility and reduce both our dogmatism and doubtfulness. A big objective of life 'challenges' is to relieve our tensions caused by our pesky positive doubts through the process of adjusting our views of 'facts.'

At the same time, understanding the sources and meanings of myths might also alleviate our stress mainly due to our growing misperceptions about those myths in the first place. For example, one of the greatest myths occupying our minds a lifetime is the myth of 'happiness,' especially when we expect an absolute and everlasting one. We have crude personal imagination of what happiness means or should be. (This fantastical perception is a product of our efforts and mentalities in modern society to seek happiness like another ideal commodity.) Our perceptions and definitions of happiness result from our erroneous impressions of, and reactions towards, 'facts' and 'myths,' as explained in this chapter. Both our perceptions and the reality of happiness depend on how we see, interpret, and deal with the facts, myths, and challenges of our lives. This basic background would be helpful in Chapter Six, where the myth of happiness is elaborated further.

Now, as a conclusion of Part II, the Nine Phases of Exploring Inner Self Chart offers a glimpse of the excruciating steps for any scholar of truth to curb his/her limitations and stir his/her hidden potentialities thru a gradual self-awareness process listed below.

Nine Phases of Exploring Inner Self
1. Build personal conviction and incentive to study our 'inner self'
2. Begin self-cleansing to acknowledge personal limitations (flaws)
3. Attain basic self-awareness (high consciousness)
4. Overhaul personal mindset
5. Align facts and myths
6. Make better life decisions, especially for redesigning our lifestyle
7. Access personal potentialities
8. Boost personal spirit
9. Reach enlightenment

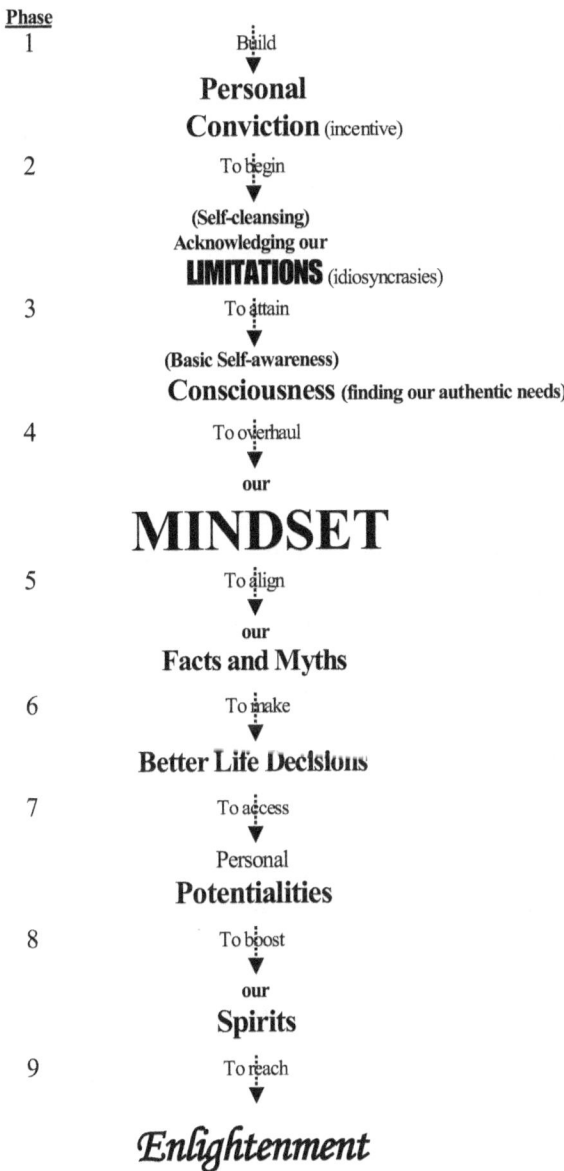

Chart 5.1: Nine Phases of Exploring Inner Self

The mission of going through the nine phases listed on Chart 5.1 is surely gruelling, but necessary to defeat somewhat the devil within all humans by overhauling our mindsets and overcoming our idiosyncrasies. Only the best among us might finish many or all the above phases—all in hopes of learning about their 'inner self,' boosting their spirits and psyches, and maybe even reaching that mythical enlightenment.

Building a fine personal conviction (incentive) is the first step to study our limitations as misguided humans, do self-cleansing, and grow our level of consciousness and self-awareness (to find our authentic needs). Then, we proceed to overhaul our mindsets —phases 4 and 5—, which makes our task of following other steps easier and more natural. Surely, all the above nine phases have their own serious, lengthy challenges. Self-cleansing and mental restoration, in particular, impose arduous demands, which in fact reveal the absurdity of positive thinking or similar jargons that insist people can change quickly merely by adopting some rudimentary beliefs or performing some raw rituals—including the ones most people do even these days to follow their religions.

Our inner strengths can help us embrace this mythical path of enlightenment. Then, our flourishing divine potentialities would promise the wisdom of enlightenment and guide us through the endless challenge of making many major life decisions in timely manners. Decision-making parameters are also discussed in some detail in Volume II, yet these decisions must be made according to criteria developed thru 'self'-awareness and enlightenment that are stressed in this volume. Some decisions have lasting effects on our lives and often the lives of others. Therefore, the challenge is to be *mentally* prepared to make proper choices, while we still have the opportunity to plan a productive life for a likely peaceful existence and salvation. Making bad choices, or postponing life's major decisions, is a reckless loss of life privileges that erupt in particular timeframes and orders without any chance of recourse.

PART III

Personality and Mood

About Part III

Part III delves into humans' gloomy search for happiness, while the rising personal stress and depression in modern societies has brought humanity to a desperate state. The difficulty of defining a general formula of happiness and how only some wise people might resolve this myth partly are also explored.

Our insecurities and other mental disorders cause self-induced stress and depressions and lesser chances of experiencing lasting happiness. Besides, finding real happiness needs lot of efforts and ingenuity than merely fighting the sources of our depressions. In all, while happiness and depression are cause and effect of each largely, we must understand and treat them separately for getting the best outcome, i.e., less depression and a stoic mindset that might avail lasting happiness.

The Addendum on page 227 regarding 'Happiness Formula' offers a brief conclusion of detailed discussions in the next three chapters that hopefully most people get a chance to read slowly and patiently regularly.

CHAPTER SIX
Happiness

The ultimate goal of knowing 'self' is twofold: To recognize its essence and keep it content—in search of that elusive happiness. Without discovering the essence of 'self,' we would never find real happiness, and without a keen desire for lasting happiness (a divine sense of contentment mostly), we would never undertake the horrendous task of knowing our 'self.'

We often believe a 'formula of happiness' is out there for us to discover eventually and live happily ever after. In spite of our rational doubts about such a formula, after a lifelong of trying and failing to find it, we still keep looking for it, because deep down in our hearts we believe that we *deserve* it. We believe that life is inherently meant to be happy; and if we do not grasp happiness, it is merely due to our weakness or misfortune. However, our only fault might be our procrastination or laziness to know our 'self,' and realizing that a relative sense of happiness may emerge only if our lifestyle satisfy 'self' fully and permanently. Otherwise, no evidence exists about life being a happy journey. Besides, not everybody deserves happiness, in particular when our lifestyle is doomed to begin with. In our crooked social setting, reaching the state of selfhood becomes impossible, due to people's rampant materialistic mentalities, shallow needs, and low self-awareness.

Nonetheless, despite these severe limitations, we still hope that some general ideas about happiness may be drawn from people's life experiences and philosophies. Although no standard formula for happiness exists, the discussions in this chapter are an attempt to establish some general guidelines for finding at least a sense of contentment.

What is referred to as the formula for happiness in this trilogy is merely a crude rendition of personal opportunities that might render peace of mind and freedom. Naturally, everybody has a unique set of needs and aspirations, which makes a common life outlook or a universal formula for happiness rather whimsical. Genetics, family background, and rearing result in personalities that value things differently and make judgments accordingly. Nevertheless, the idea is to examine the possibility of inventing a process or framework that might guide us develop a relaxed mindset regardless of our genetics and perceptions of life. After all, humans' inherent urge to find happiness may not be totally baseless or useless.

Description of Happiness

It feels strange that not even a common definition of 'happiness' has yet been developed and agreed upon in the long history of humanity. All we have after all this time is only raw speculations by some philosophers and gurus. Instead, we consider pleasures the best means of happiness! A general collection of happiness definitions can be found in, *On Happiness*, Perennial Books, 2014. In all, finding the right formula, to contain the complex feeling that our wild imaginations of happiness suggest, has proven futile so far. At best, we can perhaps describe some of its characteristics and sensations, as presented in the next section. However, even such general descriptions would be incomplete for different types and intensity of brief happiness that we experience on different occasions and situations. Moreover, even if we choose a personal interpretation of happiness, building the path to it would be hard.

We have learned that happiness is not a steady state, but rather exotic stances across the dynamic (transient) flow of feelings. We are happy for a short time, before losing even our raw tranquility, and thus seeking peace and happiness all over again. An absolute and permanent happiness is a myth and fantasy, especially within the rough modes of social living these days. A lasting happiness is psychologically unfeasible, anyway, due to so many kinds of conflicting thought processes and chemical reactions in our busy brains. Human nature also restricts our capacity for happiness, as explained in detail in the *Nature of Love and Relationships*. (See this author's list of books.) Overall, 'happiness' merely represents the highs of an emotional roller coaster our lives ride on.

Then again, we hopeful humans cannot admit our helplessness to seize happiness as a permanent state and purpose for living. We hate suffering and boredom, so we strive to capture happiness for good, once and for all. In fact, it does not hurt to imagine that an *absolute* and ultimate happiness is possible under some special conditions outside the normal boundaries of human thoughts and wisdom. If this hopefulness is combined with a self-awareness regimen, one might find at least some degree of contentment. At some level of wisdom, a moderate happiness, without ongoing emotional highs and lows, might become plausible. Thus, similar to our impression of the 'afterlife' myth, we can keep ourselves *playfully* amused with the myth of happiness, too.

'Happiness' Attributes

To describe happiness, we must explore, i) What happiness is—the 'feeling,' ii) What generates it—the 'cause,' iii) What it does to us—the 'impact,' and iv) What we do with it—the 'effect.'

The Feeling: Authentic happiness stirs a deep mix of joy, self-satisfaction, self-fulfilment, self-sufficiency, lightness, relief, love, freedom, tranquillity, transcendence, completeness, mental pleasure, inner strength, independence, and a sense of mind-body interaction. Our happiness experiences may not be as complete as described by all these feelings, but rather entail a good bunch of them in good proportions. Still, complete happiness potentially contains all the above ingredients and more, in large proportions. Overall, happiness is the sign and sentiment of a freed spirit.

The Cause: Happiness manifests in different ways as a result of an achievement or discovery, a new joyful experience, after some physical pleasure, at the end of a depression cycle, upon removal of a burden, through passion, sudden hopefulness about something, recognition and psychological fulfilment, compassion and support, spirituality, etc.

The Impact: Happiness brings us rejuvenation and immense energy, courage, humanness, and we become more forgiving and tolerant of others. We feel our spirits lifted and our outlook on life improved drastically.

The Effect: In general, when we are happy, we enjoy life much more and maintain our physical and psychological health better and longer. We are compassionate and affect people's lives more positively by bouncing off rays of hope, joy, and humour. A happy person transmits his compassion, energy, creativity, and joy to others thru positive attitude and taking on more activities and responsibilities.

A true happiness experience must entail all these four attributes in full. That is, happiness is not only a 'feeling,' and a feeling of happiness is not an end in itself. The 'cause' of happiness affects the depth and longevity of the feeling. Moreover, the feeling itself initiates a chain of internal and external reactions that impact the person's health and attitude and consequently affect other events, things, and people that surround him. Our happiness experiences often seem incomplete and short-lived, because one or more of its four attributes are missing or weak. Possibly the 'cause' has not been strong or legitimate. Or the 'feeling' has not been deep and deserved. Or the experience has had no lasting 'impact' on us. Or maybe our happiness has not made adequate effect on our actions and relationships. These types of tentative happiness experiences, or passing pleasures, are nice to have, but they are not deep and effective enough to consider a lasting happiness experience. For example, when we hear a joke, have casual sex, or find out that someone we hate is hurt, we feel happy for only a short period. On the other hand, real happiness evolves only after a successful completion of a full cycle of cause, feeling, impact, and effect. The stronger, more authentic, and fuller the cycle, the longer and more effective the experience would be.

Beside the completeness of the four attributes of happiness, the frequency of happiness experiences is obviously important, too. Generally, the feeling of happiness fades away when the 'impact' and the 'effect' are no longer present. When we forget the impact of our happiness, maybe since its 'cause' has not been strong enough, and when we lose our energy to 'affect' others or things, the whole cycle collapses and happiness ends. Therefore, we need the continuity of the cycle—the cause, the feeling, the impact, and the effect. A 'formula' of happiness is just an attempt to stress on the necessity of keeping this cycle active and vibrant. Only the cycle's high frequency and speed might guarantee a longer-lasting happiness. Thus, self-awareness is also required to feed the cycle properly and permanently in order to prevent it from leakage and exhaustion.

The causes of happiness by themselves consist of experiences and events that happen to a person accidentally, and those that he specially plans for. For instance, winning a lottery is a much less effective 'cause' for lasting happiness compared to a personal achievement resulting from diligent planning and efforts. The first kind of 'cause,' which is merely a fluke, leads only to a short-term happiness, because in essence, the cause is often not strong and genuine enough and usually not driven by authentic personal urges. Although a lottery windfall makes the winner ecstatic for a short while, it is not a legitimate cause of happiness, because the person has played no effective role in achieving the rewards. The impact of happiness would wear off quickly, too, since the same winning experience hardly happens again. Even if it kept happening regularly, its impact vanishes after a couple of weeks. Thus, the person must find other causes to rejuvenate his happiness. He might be able to use his fortune wisely to build opportunities that cause full cycles of happiness, but merely the new causes would be the real sources of feeding the cycle, not the initial cause, i.e., winning a lottery.

In all, the initial efforts and intentions of the person are crucial for creating a fulfilling and meaningful 'cause' of happiness. In addition, since the 'cause' of happiness is under his control, he can extend his efforts more consciously to recreate the outcomes that would repeat the same experiences of happiness, such as a stroll in Nature. In effect, by doing the right kinds of stuff often, the individual contributes directly and constantly to the recreation of happiness experiences. Thus, the old saying, 'We create our own happiness,' with our active involvement and awareness of the process, in particular controlling the 'cause' of happiness. The potency of the 'cause' also determines the depth of the other three elements of happiness, i.e., feeling, impact, and effect.

With this basic description of happiness attributes in place, the next step is to explore how happiness materializes for people, and whether and how the depth of their happiness may indeed relate to a person's personality. Correlating people's personality aspects (Model, Ego, Self—discussed in Chapter One) with happiness attributes (i.e., feeling, cause, impact, and effect) helps us grasp the myth of happiness a little better. We find that most happiness experiences are not genuine, deep, and effective because the four happiness elements react differently according to the personality aspects of individuals experiencing them.

The Happiness of 'Model'

The 'model' aspect of personality is the practical face of a person attempting to conceal his gullibility, neediness, fears, selfishness, Ego, and his psychological defects. Model satisfies most of our *social and belongingness needs* by trying to adapt to the rules of society and becoming part of it. It is the aspect that justifies our *actions and decisions* within fixed social norms, which Model is expected to know and conform to. It speaks and acts to impress others and obtain the psychological support we crave desperately. Thus, the more Model stresses on satisfying our crude, cursory needs for approval, belongingness, and social status, the more our higher needs, including self-esteem, self-realization, actualization, and spiritualism, remain neglected.

Ordinarily, moving up the 'personal needs tree' enhances the cycles of happiness, as long as the individual is aiming for the opportunity of satisfying his self-actualization and spirituality needs. So, finding real happiness becomes impossible when an individual stops at a low level and keeps striving for the same lower need satisfaction repeatedly. Remaining stagnant at a low level is against Maslow's theory that presumes people realize, plan, and strive for their higher-level needs intuitively. Stagnation is against humans' basic instincts. In reality, however, it happens quite often as people do not know or care about their higher-level needs—mostly because their Model and medium-range needs keep them occupied on a substandard path of life. Even if Model was not so dominant and we appreciated the ultimate needs of our being, we do not find time, or know how, to aim for fulfilling our higher needs, e.g., spirituality.

Persisting at lower personal (psychological) needs, e.g., for love or social status, actually results in frustration, because no amount of love and social status seems sufficient; and a small breakdown in their supply feels disastrous. Like some addiction, our tentative happiness comes from satisfying our mental or physical dependency. Attachment to this urgent and fleeting need satisfaction stirs anxiety and self-pity, as this habit creates only more craving for attention and dependency on others.

The 'cause' of happiness for Model is generated by other people's recognition of his work or attitude. Therefore, even his tentative sense of happiness breaks repeatedly while he remains at the mercy of others. It is impossible for people to understand an individual and give him enough credit regularly for who he really is, let alone who he is pretending to be as a Model. In fact, people detect the superficiality of the Model eventually and the approval pipeline starts leaking again. Therefore, he now must strive to find a new group of people to confirm his existence. This mental conundrum is never fixed until the person stops feeding his addiction and begins moving up the ladder of the needs tree to gain some sense of independence and fulfilment.

We could be rude and consider a Model driven personality a phony character with no originality and authenticity. We could even take him as a charlatan or hypocrite trying to manipulate others by pretending to be compassionate. Yet, he is a simpleton at best eluding his real identity just in hopes of impressing others or hiding his idiosyncrasies. He struggles to manage a secondary (phony) personality, which reflects his apprehension about his primary personality or inability to build one. These inner conflicts for Model prevent the development of a legitimate 'cause' for happiness.

Sometimes, Model adopts a stronger and healthier personality for improving himself. This is an honourable exercise and a great achievement if he succeeds internalizing some of the Self's traits thru the Model he has adopted. This high achievement provides a legitimate 'cause' for happiness. In such exceptional instances, the Model might help the person proceed towards independence and a 'self' dominated personality through self-awareness.

While some moderate Model is useful for social adaptation, etiquette, and recognition, Model domination reflects either a person's deep neediness or his immaturity and insecurities. A Model driven by immaturity imitates a personality with needs that are neither in line with his own nor authentic per se. He merely pursues some inferior needs just for playing the role of a particular model, e.g., as a powerful gang member.

The 'impact' of Model's performance and achievements would be at best a tenuous happiness, thus not heartfelt. Often, his conscience turns against the Model and perhaps induces an internal resentment and competition with this fake personality. We might recall those instances where we did not feel so proud deep down when in fact our Model was quite satisfied with the performance and outcome. For example, as part of the initiation in a fraternity or sorority, we might engage in activities that are normally not quite a part of our real character. We do things to get the acceptance of others or satiate our sexual urges perhaps. Afterward, we often feel down and confused as our conscience asks why? Why have we behaved so contrary even to the basic perceivable principles of decency? Role-playing a Model, we advise our kids not to lie or cheat, but then do exactly the same things ourselves, sometimes even in front of them.

A Model feels excited and happy when he makes up stories about his wisdom or courage to get the respect of his family and others. However, the Self, observing the masquerade from inside, knows how cowardly he has twisted the facts to serve his Ego. Happiness of Model is thus shaky, because the person knows in his deepest subconscious or unconscious that he is merely serving his Ego with no Self-respect or satisfaction.

The success in selling 'who one pretends to be' presumably constitute a Model's cause of happiness. If the result is effective enough and repeatable, it would only encourage the person to pursue the needs of Model and depress his own (the natural ones) even further. The 'cause' of happiness is weak, anyway, yet those repeated tentative happy instances goad the person to reinforce the 'model' personality, thus accelerate the destruction of his real personality or jeopardize the option of growing a more authentic and independent character.

The tentative rewards that Model receives for adaptation and approval do not serve him in the long run, anyway. A Model is always running the risk of being exposed to others eventually, often when he becomes most popular and highly attached to the incentives and causes of his happiness, which he is now counting on like an addiction. In this process, he keeps quarrelling within himself—with his deprived real nature, which he is personally trying so hard to suppress. Like any actor that often loses his own identity by playing the role of a special character continuously, a Model gets confused about who he really is. The more a person is successful as a 'model' personality, the faster he is detached and alienated from his inner needs and instincts. He often learns to like his phony personality and actions, as a Model, while losing his identity and feeling more anxious without knowing why.

A Model often transforms into a happy-go-lucky person, due to the effect of positive thinking propagandas and social appeal to always portray a positive attitude. Yet, deep down, he often feels unhappy, frustrated, unfulfilled, and tired of playing games all the time. Constant doubting of our identities subconsciously damages our psyches. However, it is even worse for a Model, because his disguise becomes superficial and ineffective faster if he cannot portray the positive reflection of a truly happy person constantly regardless of how he really feels. Sometimes, we are bound to keep a happy face to pretend we like our jobs, are happy with our marriages, to appear tactful and respectful, etc. Keeping a happy face, as a gesture of mannerism and social behaviour, is probably justified, as long as we do not get absorbed into this superficiality deeply. As mentioned before, using Model to reinforce our inner needs and reach selfhood (and maybe a natural air of optimism) is honourable and a productive process.

Sometimes, a person keeps switching from one Model to a different Model, hoping to find his real niche. He usually does it when he does not get the expected result from a certain Model, or because he becomes frustrated after playing that role for a while. When a person fails to play a special role properly, or as people detect his shallow personality, he should find a new mask. His mental health suffers from switching from Model to Model even more than the case of a person who has a more stable role to play, even as a Model. There would be no deep 'cause' of happiness in a cycle like this, as the person becomes highly confused about his identity and mission in life, since every switch leads to deeper self-pity and disappointments. A simple version of this situation is when a person cannot decide on a career and switches between jobs and every time finds a reason to quit. He cannot figure out his real vocational needs (and potentialities).

The Model's 'cause' of happiness, e.g., getting approval and acceptance, not only undermines his authentic needs leading to self-fulfilment, but also encourages him to become shallower and phonier every day. His time and energy are wasted on projects ineffective for his psychological growth or improving his flaws. Of course, the underlying reason for being a Model is insecurity and immaturity in the first place. Thus, he is unaware or careless about his other personal needs beyond the needs of the Model, anyway. In fact, his urge to repeat the same experience to stay happy only reinforces his conscious or subconscious efforts to suppress his instincts even deeper and run away from his real needs faster. Accordingly, Model is less likely to ask, 'Who am I?', because he keeps justifying to himself why he likes to be somebody else.

In all, for a Model, the 'cause' of happiness is something or somebody, which he generally has no, or very little, control over. When the 'cause' of happiness remains so shaky and irrelevant for Model, the other elements of happiness, i.e., the 'feeling', 'impact', or 'effect,' always remain too tentative as well.

The 'feeling' of happiness is shallow and usually offset by the constant, subconscious fear of losing the momentum when the impact of his pretensions wears off. His happiness cannot make a major 'impact' on him, since the presumed rewards are irrelevant for realizing his higher psychological needs. And obviously, a Model cannot 'affect' others (especially people with low Model orientation) positively, as he cannot connect to anybody truthfully. Even when he does something for someone, it would be insincere and merely out of fear of losing that person's approval, or for satisfying a selfish purpose, e.g., manipulating someone, or he is simply trying to conform to some rules just to maintain his status, e.g., his job. And, of course, the cycle of happiness itself is often impaired quickly in the case of a Model, when the approval and acceptance channels dry up even temporarily.

It is interesting, and sad, how our social environments and values encourage Model attitude (compliance and hypocrisy) in particular. And it is even more interesting how, in fact, Model personalities help satisfy the dependency needs of one another by promoting phony social values and norms, even as they realize their low sincerity and the vanity of the words they exchange. By giving and receiving compliments, Models support one another's psychological needs for social status and approval as ultimate goals. Like an addiction, a Model craves attention, although he knows it is phony and perhaps even a way of being exploited. Salespeople recognize this weakness of Models (in the general public) and use it to the extreme. Models usually act and say things differently in the presence and absence of a person, which often is a sign of both their hypocrisy and desperation. Sadly, 'model' oriented personalities are increasing in society and they are pushing phonier social values and behaviour, too. Therefore, we find more depression in society than real happiness. Model orientation and depression are highly correlated.

The Happiness of 'Ego'

The 'ego' aspect of personality handles our value systems, senses of rivalry and superiority, judgments and punishments, desires and expectations. It reflects the *real intentions* of our words and actions, and our *reactions* to other people's words and actions. An egoist is self-centred with extreme expectations and narrow perceptions of others, and he is harsh and hasty in his judgments and punishments with a dramatically biased value system. Ego is an exact opposite to Model in many ways, in particular frankness, impatience, and pomposity. Therefore, a person's Model and Ego often clash and cause extra headaches for him. Yet, they also help each other, e.g., when Ego is so strong it can even besiege and abuse Model as a strategy to manipulate another person.

Unlike Model, an egoist's needs often extend across all levels of the personal needs tree. In particular, he is too ambitious with a high need for achievement and recognition. He has an extreme need for control and doing things his way. Yet, his achievements remain non-actualizing, because his self-serving goals supersede the senses of purpose, piety, and selflessness required for self-actualization. Thus, while an egoist may have many achievement experiences and casual thrills, they are seldom actualizing and they hardly stir lasting happiness.

An egoist attempts to use a scheme or his charm (through Model) for attracting and exploiting others. However, an egoist does not have the patience and motivation of a Model to indulge people merely for the sake of friendship. If his hidden intentions are not satisfied fast thru Model's pretensions, he gets frustrated and resorts to a different strategy, e.g., aggression, to fulfil his important and urgent need for self-gratification.

The Ego's 'cause' of happiness relates to the outcome of his selfish actions and intentions. He works hard to serve his Ego for the highest level of thrill and satisfaction. He must keep boosting his Ego to feel happy, while getting things done in the *manner* he desires is often more important for him than the outcome itself. He can forget his failures and forgive himself quickly as long as he succeeds in making everybody follow his lead. He is fully convinced that his judgments are always appropriate, logical, and fair. When he seems to compromise, he is simply using Model for manipulation and exploitations.

Tenacity and dogmatism are merely the products of all idiots' rampant egotism. They simply believe they know everything and have the answers for all the problems, while others are ignorant and inferior to them in logic and vision. Their high needs and expectations from others and themselves often remain unfulfilled, since their goals are unrealistic, their expectations from others are more selfish than rational, and their directions are too rigid, but also because people's Egos clash all the time. With a demanding personality, seldom an egoist feels happy with the outcomes or the means of achieving them.

Egoists' inflated Ego and obsession for success push them to take risk and set tough (and often unrealistic) objectives. Their needs for control and self-importance, however, stop them from putting their guards down to find contentment and their Self. They have wrong perceptions about the means of satisfying their needs, especially the higher ones for which a self-actualizer must depend only on himself, instead of exploiting others to succeed.

An egoist's 'cause' of happiness also relates to other people's reactions to his expectations. His happiness is at the expense of people he exploits. It depends on someone else's submission, defeat, and willingness to play along with his manipulation and exploitation games. Surely, in most cases this expectation cannot be fulfilled, and thus causes many frictions.

An egoist's 'feeling' of happiness comes from short-lived, shallow gratifications, because his objectives are self-serving and usually achieved by pushing others. Therefore, he should keep manipulating others and struggle for more signs and symbols of achievements to boost his Ego and maintain his shaky cycles of happiness. The more he relies on people to achieve his goals, the more he must feed this cycle (by pushing others) to maintain the momentum. Even tentative satisfactions from his achievements merely boost his Ego rather than soothe his soul. He is *ruled* by his Ego and lives to satisfy it—an endless struggle to preserve his pompous identity.

His shallow feelings of happiness cannot 'impact' him, as he has no time or patience to stop and internalize his fulfilments and their true meanings. He often does not even know, or care about, the real purposes of his struggles, while he follows some routines aggressively. Artificial goals, such as maximizing his wealth and power, justify all his struggles. His triumphs have no relationship to his essential and inherent needs. And of course, when he is unaware of the relationship between his needs and triumphs, his rewards and achievements cannot impact him deeply. The only 'impact' of his fulfilments is his growing eagerness to repeat his mischievous and exploitative activities that boost his Ego and give him some wicked feelings of satisfaction.

Accordingly, he has no ability to affect others, either, except for the burden of his manipulative attitude that intimidates others. Thus, for an egoist whose fulfilments come at the expense of hurting others, the 'effect' of his accomplishments is negative. Egoists' plans and actions are always calculating and self-serving for specific personal interests, either for an immediate benefit or future exploitation. Doing things for the sake of 'affecting' others positively does not mean anything to an egoist unless it has some advantage for him personally, and this scenario seldom happens.

The happiness cycle for an 'egoist' is too short, therefore he requires extreme momentum to maintain even a tentative sense of happiness. Otherwise, frustration and stress take over quickly. A tremendous level of effort is required to feed the cycle and still real happiness is hard to maintain.

Establishing a working relationship with others is extremely difficult for an egoist even when he tries to use his/her Model to manipulate and exploit as many people as possible. Especially, establishing a mutually agreeable marital relationship based on teamwork would be very difficult for egoists. Volume III of this trilogy discusses some of the implications of egotistical family quarrels and competitions between partners to keep the upper hand in their relationships. These kinds of games and attitudes are, unfortunately, prevalent and somehow even encouraged in our societies as a means of establishing partners' individuality and presumed independence. They often lead to psychological struggles that hinder partners' communication and happiness. Work environments are becoming quite difficult to tolerate, too, due to the rising number of egoists and psychopaths running our organizations, nowadays. The negative effects of these people's managerial style have now brought the level of social stress to a record high.

The Happiness of 'Self'

'Self' is that aspect of personality that holds our basic instincts, feelings, and needs, including spirituality. It holds our creativity, potentialities, genius, and psychic energy. This pure aspect of our personality also contains our innocence, conscience, and regrets. Self is our *real being* outside the conditioning rules of society, aside from the value systems that we have adopted and adapted ourselves to. Perhaps a symbolic representation of Self can be found in Tarzan whose instincts and feelings are intact and pure. Yet, Tarzan is only a raw picture of Self, since his potentialities and spirituality power remain untapped.

We all meditate in some form, consciously or subconsciously, to get close to our Self, although we often know very little about the meaning of Self or the means of reaching that pure state of being. When we go to a church, mosque, or shrine to speak to our gods, we are doing some form of meditation to contact our Self —our soul. We need to do this meditation, at least in private, in order to heal our physical and psychological hurts from living. We need to go somewhere in Nature alone and think, quiet our minds, and grasp the messages of our inner voices. These are the basic experiences of Self that most of us have enjoyed at least a few times. However, on most occasions, we do not recognize and appreciate them as a device for entering our most intimate, yet neglected, state of natural being and for finding some relative freedom at least. We bypass the opportunity to delve into our Selfhood after a short pause at the entrance every time we happen to meditate.

Unlike the situations for Model and Ego that require external stimuli for approaching some form of happiness, the happiness of Self is automatic. The only requirement is to acknowledge the Self that is within us ready to be explored and nurtured. It is surely not a straightforward, easy task, but it is possible to get at least a little acquainted with Self. The first step is to believe in the possibility of being a better human being for our own sake at least and then learn how. Afterward, we can use the power of Self to overcome the negative influences of Model and Ego at any opportunity. Every time we let Self overcome the Ego's or Model's attempt to taint our deeds and decisions, we get one step closer to realizing Self. It cannot happen overnight, but practice and active meditation would give our Self the power to overrule Model and Ego more often with deeper sincerity when they rush to dominate our existence and behaviour.

How is the happiness of Self automatic? And how happiness attributes, i.e., cause, feeling, impact, and effect apply to Self?

The 'causes' of happiness for Self are several. The main cause, which is perhaps less tangible to people with no or little experience of Self, comes from the achievement of being a Self dominated personality per se. We can rather imagine how a caged animal feels once it escapes. We know how much risk and trouble prisoners are willing to endure to find a way to escape. Reaching Self-dominance resembles those freedom experiences, except that finding Self would be even a more meaningful and permanent experience. Once a person learns to recognize and free his Self from the captivity of Model and Ego, he enters the world of eternal peace and tranquillity in which happiness is automatic. There is no need to feed a cycle of happiness in order to maintain it, as long as one stays in the kingdom of Selfdom. The happiness of Self is inherent. Merely our superficial needs and the influence of Ego and Model suffocate this natural source of happiness.

Although the main cause of happiness of Self is so prominent and potent, some other causes are also interesting to discuss.

A Self-dominated person finds the opportunity and strength to recognize humans' inherent (but hidden) potentialities. By saving the energies normally wasted by Model and Ego, Self focuses on the means of actualizing himself. He concentrates on thoughts and activities that nurture the real nature of a person rather than the ones that hurt and destroy his physical and mental abilities. Generating valuable ideas, exploring the creative domains of mind, and developing the vision of a universal existence, provide happiness experiences that replace, or at least mitigate, the crude, mundane mission of living and surviving. The purpose of one's existence becomes vivid and meaningful. Simple thoughts and activities derived from the energies of the inner 'self' turn into self-actualizing and spiritual experiences. Oneness with the vast universe that rules our beings manifests as unique moments of ecstasy and experiences beyond the meanings of the worldly pleasures. These are some other 'causes' of happiness of Self.

A 'self' dominated person does not rely on the outside world to induce a 'cause' of happiness. He finds authentic sources of fulfilment without exploiting others or expecting approvals from people. He is not threatened or dissuaded by the punishments of the power-thirsty authorities of our world, nor does he care about the luring rewards of compliance. He is neither attached to social systems that control him, nor detached of the harmonic worldly relationships that complement his being along with an urge for co-existence. The challenge for maintaining this delicate balance constitutes some other 'causes' of happiness for Self.

All these 'causes' of happiness are Self-directed and free from outsiders' control. Thus, the happiness generated through these experiences is manageable much better by the individual and remains more consistent and repeatable by him. He is in charge of the 'causes.'

The Self's 'feelings' of happiness, induced by self-controlled 'causes,' prolong rather continuously, and they are authentic and deep, with a lasting impact. There are hardly any interruptions in the 'causes and feelings.' In fact, for a Self-driven personality, the 'feelings' and 'causes' are usually the same thing, since the cause of happiness is inherent for Self, as noted earlier. This natural property gives the whole cycle of happiness more momentum, intensity, and continuity. Maslow's account of self-actualizers' feelings provide great evidence of how deep those sensations are, and how they directly relate to, and connect with, the causes. (See quotes from Maslow on pages 172-3.)

The 'impacts' of Self-controlled happiness are fundamental and also coincide with the 'cause-feeling' interconnectivity. The impacts are psychological, spiritual, and a lasting source of deep tranquillity.

The 'effects' are also paramount and continuous. A 'self' dominated person has a different view of people, events, and things. In particular, he has a great deal of compassion towards everybody, despite his profound knowledge of people's inherent impurity and frequent malice. He feels connected to the whole universe and knows that he is an inseparable part of it, including all the badness within and outside him. Thus, everything he does affects other things and people automatically and directly in a positive way, simply because they reinforce his own 'cause' of happiness. To him, giving and taking are the same things with an equal meaning and effect—like the kind of selfless feelings we have towards our children. Altogether, the Self's four elements of happiness have an integrated and integral interconnectivity that drive a potent cycle of permanent and self-nurturing happiness experiences. This cycle accelerates even faster once one's ability of utilizing the potentials of Self are largely developed.

Personality Aspects' Role for Happiness

The above discussions of the three aspects of personality suggest that happiness can happen only to Self. The happiness of the other personality aspects is at best shallow and temporary. In the real world, however, often one or two of a person's three aspects of personality overwhelm the other(s). We may remember many evidences supporting the dominance of a particular personality aspect over others during our interactions and relationships. Overall, however, we usually do not detect enough of our own Model or Ego the same way we notice them so quickly in other people. This low awareness about ourselves is in line with our tendency to ignore our psychological needs and defects unless we make a point of exploring them. We simply deny our Model and

Ego, despite the comments and clues we receive from others as well as our own conscience.

We do not believe or admit that we are anything but a pure Self. We do not like to admit that our prominent Model prevents us from grasping who we are and what our purpose of living is. We would never accept the idea that our strong Ego is depriving us from sensing compassion and having a tranquil and happy life. Obviously, until we acknowledge these sad facts, we would not find the courage and incentive to study our Self. Unless we admit that we have become slaves to Model and Ego, we would never believe in this book's ideas about Self and happiness.

We hate to admit that our weaknesses and unhappiness in life are the result of letting Model and Ego run our lives. Even if we get the courage to admit it to ourselves, we have difficulty taming these crooked aspects within us. How would a Model or Ego consider adopting a more 'self' controlled personality? Initially, he would not even have an idea what being a Self means, how it works, what it requires, etc. However, realistically, if he were going to give up, or at least tame, his Model and Ego, he would first require a tangible understanding of Self and the way he may act and behave from within this aspect of his personality. He is estranged to Self, and actually, his Self has never had a chance to grow. Without a relatively comprehensive grasp of Self, the switch would be impossible regardless of our efforts. Playing Self (e.g., as a Good Samaritan) without understanding its meaning is just another attempt for building a different Model personality. To remain realistic, the switch to selfhood must be gradual and in line with one's appreciation and practice of a Self-controlled life. Even our religious rituals and pretensions cannot show us our Self until we realize the nature of, and means of capturing, Self through self-awareness and sincere self-cleansing.

This book talks about 'self' in different dimensions and from different angles. In essence, 'self' is one of the main themes of this trilogy, as it emerges frequently in all the topics and chapters. In particular, the seven basic elements of 'self' are discussed in

Chapter Thirteen of Volume II. We try in many ways to explain what 'self' really means, how we can find it in ourselves, and how we need to use its potentialities to make our lives tolerable and perhaps happy. Still, at the end, what this trilogy can offer is merely a general idea of what 'self' really is. Everybody should explore it individually and usually find a personal interpretation of 'self' in terms of definition and application, though this innate source of energy manifests and directs us through life. Therefore, an ultimate definition of 'self,' or how it leads to happiness is rather personal. Merely by trying to become a better human being —by learning humility and sensing our nothingness—would get us there. Detecting and defusing our Ego and Model bring out the Self automatically.

The degree and depth of our happiness depend on the varying prominence of Model, Ego, and Self at any time, and thus our happiness experiences find different qualities and properties. We all have *a kind of* multiple personalities due to one aspect of our personality becoming more dominant in various instants. This also indicates that expecting a constant happiness mood is almost impossible even for a Self-dominated individual. Although a Self-controlled personality has the highest chance of carrying a tranquil and happy life, the other two aspects of his personality emerge occasionally in small doses and disrupt his mood. When Model or Ego takes over temporarily, even a 'self' dominated person thinks and behaves erratically. The firmer his Self-control, the less frequently Model or Ego finds a chance to interfere. Yet, the random dominance of Model or Ego is normal. We should expect erratic moments of distress even when we have a genuine Self-dominated personality. There are several reasons for these moments of weakness erupting.

First, our temporary switch to Model or Ego, as a requirement of coping and living, might cause experiences that ruin all our past 'Self'-hood triumphs, and thus lead to a sense of discomfort and delusion. For example, we might submit to adultery or some other mischief in a moment of weakness. This experience brings us a cycle of depression that overrides even an enduring cycle of happiness. Our conscience might bother us for a long time.

Second, it is possible that occasionally we neglect to attend to our semi-developed Self. Although the happiness cycle for Self is automatic and self-nurturing, staying a 'self' dominated person demands constant *awareness*. If we forget our need for ongoing meditation and development of Self, the 'self'-control process stops, Model and Ego take over, and the happiness cycle breaks.

Third, even for a 'self' dominated person, moments of doubts and questioning erupt frequently, especially when it becomes necessary to adapt himself to social demands and get along with people. During those moments of self-doubt, we question our choices and paths, we think about our sanity and philosophy of life, we think about our responsibilities and financial obligations, we suffer from our solitude and loneliness, we think about our relationships that we are hoping to 'self'-control, etc. Under these circumstances, we are psychologically vulnerable and undergo a state of mild depression, if not something more serious.

Naturally, recognizing and strengthening all seven elements of Self, as explained in Volume II of this trilogy, would also be essential for maintaining the cycles of happiness by developing higher 'self'-control.

Nevertheless, some variations and inconsistencies in the level of our happiness should be expected, even for a 'self' dominated person. Accordingly, developing 'self'-control, perseverance, patience, and stamina becomes important for managing these irregularities in our lives as well. The more we grasp and practise a 'self' dominated life, the better we can deal with, and defeat, the periods of temporary distress or doubts.

CHAPTER SEVEN
Depression

Recognizing the role of personality aspects in creating happiness experiences is only half of our challenge. The other half relates to our ability to detect and defeat the ongoing cycles of depression. Happiness and depression are contending forces that clash in our psyches all the time. Therefore, our search for happiness is futile when sneaky waves of depression bombard us regularly. They are either generated from within us, often unconsciously, or induced by outside sources. Yet, our three personality aspects play their roles regarding the nature and length of our depressions as well as happiness. Ego causes mostly depression and Self stirs happiness more often, although Model and Self also create depressions.

Like happiness, the sources of depression must also be gauged in reference to the three aspects of personality even more closely due to their unique roles in both causing and fighting depression, especially those from outside sources, such as financial or marital issues. Moreover, the same elements of happiness, i.e., cause, feeling, impact, and effect, also apply to depression. Thus, we can assess the forces of depression from within the same framework, i.e., by gauging the influence of each personality aspect on the four elements of depression.

We should actually study our depressions on two grounds in line with the three aspects of the personality: First, we must find out how each of these personality aspects generates self-induced depression. Second, we must study how a person dominated with any one of these personality aspects deals with depressions caused by inner (personal) or outer sources.

One danger of depression is that people do not grasp its nature and source, and thus have difficulty analysing it. They prolong it simply because they accept depression only as a reality of social living—due to inevitable hardship caused by others. However, depression is often a sign of mental disorder and inner struggles. It should actually be viewed as a warning signal to pause and find its source realistically by relating it to a specific personality aspect and the underlying message coming from it. Finding its source, internal or external, is also vital. That is a potent way of learning about ourselves and reaching a higher sense of being. On the other hand, chronic depression is harder to grasp and heal.

The Depression of 'Model'

The self-induced depression of Model accumulates furtively due to his inability to move up the 'personal needs tree' and fulfil his higher needs, including spirituality. He is not quite aware of those needs and that his neglect to fulfil them hinders his psychological growth and self-image. Yet, the lack of fulfilment stirs boredom, which is obviously a hidden source of depression for everybody. Furthermore, his needs for approval, love, and sense of belonging cause him stress and self-pity when they do not happen enough in reality or he doubts their authenticity. He gets disappointed with himself and others, so he keeps developing new tactics to get the love and approval he needs desperately. He tries to play his role as a Model more precisely and effectively, thus becomes phonier. He exhausts himself by wasting all his energy seeking attention and recognition, instead of satisfying his authentic inner needs. All these strenuous efforts and reactions are the hidden causes of chronic self-induced depression. Overall, ignorance about one's higher needs, how to attend to them, and the real sources of one's boredom are the inherent 'causes' of Model's depression.

The depression of Model is quite deep, as he feels too helpless without a large dose of external attention on a regular basis. His only sense of psychological security in life is given to him by outsiders and he must try hard to maintain this socializing flow as a safety net. This incessant struggle (strategies and activities) for acceptance and love by itself reinforces the cycles of depression vigorously and frequently and makes the task of self-redemption too difficult. In all, his focus on his low-level needs comes at the cost of ignoring his other psychological urges.

With respect to 'externally induced' depressions, Model is quite vulnerable, because he is always too anxious to cope with external forces and fit within society somewhat like an obsession. The 'causes' of his depression relate to any of social, financial, political, or relationship problem that he is too eager, but unable, to solve. When there is a problem in one or more of these areas, it means a conflict exists between a Model's *urgent* expectations and reality. This conflict feels too harsh to Model, since it usually means rejection or his inability to adapt. He takes the matter too personally due to his low self-image and high oversensitivity. He feels defeated, misunderstood, exhausted, and ignored, especially considering all his efforts to be loved and understood. Somebody or some entity is not taking his efforts or needs seriously. It does not matter how in practice he deals with these external sources of his depression. He may take a legal action, retaliate against his companion or spouse, try to become accommodating, leave the company he is working for, etc. The vital point is that internally he has to deal with the pressures of coping and rejections, which he has a hard time accepting as a reality of life.

Model's obsession for being always understood and accepted hardly matches reality, while he also naively over-trusts human nature. Therefore, he faces a major dilemma often when people's reactions seem odd and unfair to him. A rejection, in any form, is quite personal and unbearable for him emotionally, even more than it may hurt his Ego, and thus results in a deep depression. As expected, Model is mentally prepared to hide the setbacks and his emotions, instead of confronting his opponents assertively. In fact, Model develops a strong defence mechanism to take rejections nonchalantly on the surface and jump to find other opportunities to satisfy his need for acceptance and approval. However, every rejection brings him deep disappointment, plus the added stress of hiding his frustration. Thus, he suffers for it internally longer than if he somehow dealt with his stress and people's aggression more assertively or just ignored them rather stoically.

The cause, feeling, impact, and effect of depression for both types of self-induced and imposed depressions follow the same pattern. The 'causes' of his depression are numerous as noted throughout this section. The 'feelings' of depression are quite deep and devastating for Model, although he attempts to appear calm and collected for playing his role (as part of Model), which is still another source of pressure and stress. The 'impact' and 'effect' of such depression are obviously harsh and harmful to him and people around him. Most likely his oversensitivity and repeated rejections (two other causes of his depression per se) lead to low self-image, self-loathing, and passive aggression, which he would try to hide and control as much as possible, too. Signs of his neediness for attention and affection also show in his swift, occasional outburst or even showy parades of compassion. The irony is that, with spreading negative 'effects' on others, due to his neediness and suppressed depression, he annoys the same people he relies on for attention. He turns into an oversensitive person who expects unconditional attention and love, but is often unable to offer true compassion to others despite his pretensions. People often have difficulty handling such ultra sensitive persons and bizarre (uneasy) situations that erupt during their interactions. In all, everybody has difficulty building the right level of Model to adapt professionally and socially and get adequate approval without becoming, or looking, too needy and rejected.

The Depression of 'Ego'

The self-induced depression of Ego is caused by his inability to achieve enough of his goals and high expectations, in terms of not only results, but also the *means* of attaining them. He becomes extremely agitated and depressed anytime his plans fall through or people resist, or forget, to do what he demands. Moreover, Ego regularly attracts conflict and contradiction. S/he likes to control everybody and every situation and gets depressed often because controlling others and events are both difficult and unreasonable expectations. Arguments and clashes of Egos always erupt among individuals, leading to frustrating situations and the loss of a great deal of energy and productivity. Ego does not forgive and forget. He does not accept even an occasional submission, i.e., blaming himself instead of others. Every discussion, competition, battle, transaction, and simple matter he is involved with has to end in a 'win' situation for him, but more importantly a 'loss' or 'defeat' for somebody else. When this is not the case, he gets upset and depressed. In addition, since he is too preoccupied with 'winning and success,' instead of 'learning and contribution,' he has a hard time exploring his self-actualization potentialities and needs. He may continue to win and feel successful, but builds up lots of stress and anxiety in the process, since he cannot internalize the meaning of a real achievement. He feels depressed and empty, in spite of all the symbols of winning and success around him, such as wealth and fame. His successes are not heartfelt and satisfying his 'self,' since they are not selfless and authentic. He may hide or dismiss his inner conflicts and lack of deep satisfaction, but the burden of depression in his psyche keeps building up stealthily. These are some of the big 'causes' of the self-induced depression for an Ego-driven personality.

The externally generated depression of Ego is similarly due to his high expectations remaining unfulfilled and his Ego's clashes with the demands, shortfalls, and Egos of other members of the society or organizations. He has a hard time having a peaceful conversation without the interference of Ego and an inevitable contradiction or clash.

Thus, for Ego, the causes of both self-induced and externally induced depressions are very much the same as well. They both result from expectations not met and competitions not won. His depression experiences are caused either when he tries to exploit others and they resist (self-induced), or when others are imposing their own rules and expectations that do not appeal to him, thus become Ego-threatening (externally induced).

The 'feelings' of depression are severe and recur frequently due to the pressures on him to fulfil a wide range of his needs in peculiar ways through selfish schemes. Ego must make constant efforts to push others for some (often unreasonable) goals, excel in everything, and win all the competitions, even when rewards are not significant or the issues are not important. Since these egotistical schemes and processes go on constantly, their rewards and disappointments also recur continuously. These 'feelings' of fulfilment and depression hit him based on the outcome of each experience. They are exhausting and depressing. It would be like a gambler feeling happy with every hand he wins and depressed for every loss. At the end, the fast cycles of happiness-depression feelings become a nerve-racking loop and a stressful mechanism even when the cycle is at its peek during a happiness experience. The psyche anticipates the depressions that may come tomorrow or any second, and also recalls the depressions of yesterday(s).

The 'impact' of depression experiences and cycles is obvious. The nervous breakdowns, neurosis, stress and heart attacks, which are sweeping us our feet in large numbers every day, are mostly the impacts of endless depression cycles and experiences caused by Ego. The 'effect' is also clear. The level of pressures we are putting on one another with our Egos constantly is simply killing our spirits, not to mention the stress and exhaustion they cause. In families, in work places, in our simplest transactions, and every time we get into action or interact, our Egos interfere. What could we expect the 'effect' of a neurotic or overanxious individual be on others, other than causing more damage to this vicious cycle of impacting self and affecting others adversely every day, to what disastrous end—only God may know.

The Depression of 'Self'

The self-induced depressions of Self are caused by his regrets about personal impurities that he is incapable of controlling while living in a chaotic environment. Self feels sad about the impurity of human nature, especially when friends and family members keep disappointing him more often than not. Self gets sad when he feels helpless in expressing himself and when his Model and Ego take charge temporarily, while Self feels obliged to keep them in check. We suffer, consciously or subconsciously, when Self, which is our conscience in this sense, fails to restrain Ego and Model. When our innocence is threatened, Self gets sad. When our potentialities are not used effectively, Self feels empty, unfulfilled and depressed. And when our spirituality needs are neglected, Self feels lonely, unprotected, helpless, and dejected.

The externally induced depressions come from the chaotic environments that Self is expected to adapt to. The realities of social living initially restrict the growth of Self. However, more importantly, these socioeconomic and political settings impose value systems and conditions unacceptable to Self's integrity. A major contradiction always exists between what these settings expect from a person and what his Self can submit to.

For both self-induced and externally induced depressions, the 'causes' are merely the symptoms of social living that are mostly out of one's control. Yet, despite one's limited power to induce change, Self has a much better capability to absorb the waves of depression without getting affected. While there are experiences of depression, the 'feelings' of depression are mild, infrequent, and manageable. This is because Self (that is perhaps partially aware due to a person's conscience) recognizes the 'causes' of depression as his personality defects (the Self in the process of development). Self realizes that these weaknesses are impossible to bypass and ignore completely because of the realities of social living. Self knows that these mild depressions are natural during the process of growth. During the transition from the *perceived* world to the *real* world—the process of cleansing our illusions—depressions are the results of our regrets for past mistakes and memories. We may never get the chance to become fully purified as a refined Self, which means some waves of depressions attack us due to our unique vulnerabilities and humans' innate impurity. Yet, the depression intensities are low and Self is aware of their nature, causes, and likely healing powers. When Self knows the causes of depressions, it uses this clue to heal itself rather than store it as a psychological hurt.

Thus, for Self, even the impact of a depression experience has a learning and healing nature, rather than being an obstacle along the cycle of happiness experiences. In fact, these experiences help the growth of Self, as they reinforce the process of self-control, meditation, creation, and self-cleansing. During these periods, we also learn a lot about our true potentialities and creativity along with finer impressions of the universe, Nature, and our existence. Thus, we might say the 'impacts' of a depression experience for Self are more positive than negative.

The 'effects' of depression experiences are at the very least neutral for a Self personality. Often a depression experience leads to a temporary withdrawal and meditation. During this period, Self does not deal with others and issues. Instead, he concentrates on the 'cause' and 'feeling' of the experience, strives to learn a lesson, and builds more stamina and creativity. After a period of solitude, Self emerges with much more energy, compassion, and wisdom that can only have positive effects on others.

*****

Depression experiences are too pervasive and powerful because they occur regularly to every aspect of personality separately or concurrently. We feel depressed too often because one or more of our personality aspects may be hurt at any time when its unique needs and urges are jeopardized. Depression experiences have different implications for each of the three aspects of personality in the long run as well. Model and Ego depressions have extreme repercussions on both the person himself and people around him. For Self, however, a depression cycle is mostly a learning and healing opportunity to achieve his objective of Self-control faster. It provides an opportunity for reflection and self-cleansing. Thus, as Self goes thru these normal depression moods, he learns more about humans' vulnerability and weak nature as a general rule. Thus, he learns compassion and patience and uses these attributes to impact others positively all the time.

Luckily, by studying our personality aspects, we can pinpoint the causes, natures, and sources of our depressions, which in turn offers an opportunity to learn better about ourselves and a higher chance of defeating our depressions.

CHAPTER EIGHT
The Formula of Happiness

The cycles of happiness and depression clashing regularly lead to additional personal frustration and stress. Even small events, e.g., someone's simple whining, spoils our mood and often even ends a thriving happiness cycle prematurely. We feel our mood swings often, yet do not stop to grasp the crucial life lessons they offer. For one thing, we forget that controlling the sources of ongoing, self-induced depressions is more urgent and useful than looking for that elusive happiness. We ignore that our own idiosyncrasies, obsessions, oversensitivity, relationships, phobia, uptightness, and raw ambitions prevent us from feeling peace and happiness. All along, we only blame people and life for our depression while we rush to forget ourselves by shallow pleasures. We try to suffocate our depression as quickly as possible, instead of learning to pause and fathom the real source and message of any depression.

The Happiness/Depression Cycles

The four elements of 'cause,' 'feeling,' 'impact,' and 'effect' of a happiness or depression experience determine its longevity and nature. Happiness experiences last when Self is dominant and we are free from our wicked thoughts and urges driven by Ego and

Model. Conversely, depression comes more often when we focus on serving the needs of Model and Ego.

In Chapter Six, we set out to explore the possibility of finding a meaningful and lasting formula of happiness. Overall, though, we can say that, "Unless we build a 'self'-control mechanism to at least monitor our ongoing cycles of depressions and assess their causes, the idea of capturing happiness is futile and unattainable."

Nonetheless, we face a major dilemma all our lives: On the one hand, we are limiting our chances for real, lasting happiness by empowering Model and Ego beyond the modest roles they should play in a healthy lifestyle. We just do not see or care how they are keeping us from achieving happiness, while we struggle with our greed-laden ambitions and fantasies. On the other hand, overcoming the urges of Model and Ego, especially in a crooked environment like ours, is definitely not easy. We cannot grasp and revive the obscure, weakened Self quickly to fight off the powerful, wicked Ego and Model. We need high self-awareness and lots of self-cleansing first, then patience, practice, evaluation, and growth. Only when we view Model and Ego as big obstacles and learn humility, we have a better chance of defeating them and revamping their roles in our lives and decisions.

Finding happiness is an idealistic objective, anyway, although we may get at least a glimpse of it occasionally if we can curb the incessant cycles of depression. Lasting happiness is an immense ambition for common people who are driven mainly by their Models and Egos. A 'self'-driven life and personality can help us somewhat to escape the perils of the socioeconomic and political settings, and even so, it would be an impractical and imprudent practice these days. We simply cannot ignore the inefficiencies, ineffectiveness, corruptions, and abuses rooted in socioeconomic systems and authorities we elect to run our communities and countries. The entire democratic process is screwed up even in developed countries, while the rich rules the means of controlling people's minds and votes. We have to get involved and we are eventually forced to play their games somehow to defeat them when necessary. Certainly, we cannot confront Model and Ego driven people merely by our Self. Our bureaucratic systems and organizations are also the replicas and tools for 'model' and 'ego' personalities (executives) that are running and controlling those organizations. We would be crushed fast within the Ego-driven mechanisms and destroyed under the influence of Model oriented societies instantly. At best, we would be isolated and rejected. It is too late and naive to behave like Mahatma Gandhi or Martin Luther King these days.

Choosing and keeping the right balance of personality aspects is a daunting personal issue and choice. We could try to develop enough Self to attain some happiness, and at the same time, we need some Model and Ego to help us survive in current chaotic societies. What is the right mix? How much pain and insecurity can we bear due to our survival needs, financial pressures, work demands, economic instability, etc.? And how much happiness can we really bring to ourselves by leaning more toward our Self? These are major life decisions to make, especially at the younger age, for building the foundation of our thoughts and a practical life philosophy. We face these dilemmas throughout our lives, anyway. All along, we change our minds, priorities, and decision criteria regularly to adapt. Accordingly, we get more confused as we age and weigh the challenges of survival and pleasure versus the amount of time and efforts we can (or are willing) to extend in search of true happiness. Volume III of this trilogy tackles this dilemma in some detail.

Happiness (peace of mind) is an integral part of our thoughts about life and subsistence. And our happiness discussions show how fragile the whole issue of life philosophy can be, considering the huge conflict that exists between the path to happiness and the path of survival. It appears as if 'happiness' and the 'practicality of living' are opposing ideas that cannot be easily reconciled into a meaningful philosophy!

It is interesting to study our *mood* when we are neither happy nor depressed, thus appreciate the value of this quiet mood for our welfare. What kind of a state is that? Contentment? A normal state? This analysis is beyond the scope of this book, although it seems that we live in that *resignation* state more often than we are either happy or depressed. However, if somebody asks us how we feel at any moment, we suddenly lean towards a sense of satisfaction (happiness) or boredom (depression). This shows the burdened state of our psyches, despite our show of resilience to conceal our deeper, painful sentiments. In all, sustaining a sense of contentment and mental stability over a long period would be blissful, but rather abnormal for human nature. Therefore, as we navigate between the moods of happiness and depression rather frequently, we cause so much turmoil for our tired psyches. We overuse our nerves and drain our spirits. We cause our sufferings.

Still, the possibility of happiness through 'self' exploration is a reality that we can rely on for developing our life philosophy. We should stop doubting that happiness is an intrinsic virtue of 'self' and that Self is the only place we should look for happiness. We might then focus only on our doubts and decisions about life practicalities, because our confusion about a viable path of life is hindering our chance for happiness through a state of 'self'-hood. With this kind of life philosophy, we can even entertain our deep belief (expectation) about deserving happiness as our legitimate right of being *an intelligent being*. Deserving happiness is a viable claim if we can deal effectively with both our idiosyncrasies and the practicalities of living that create too many depression cycles. A basic formula of happiness is offered in the Addendum at the end of this chapter.

The Ideal Personality for Salvation

Seeking an ideal personality resembles the conventional attempts to define, or develop a philosophy about, 'pure humans.' But the *ideal personality* noted here merely refers to human traits useful for coping with social mandates *practically* and possibly attaining some personal enlightenment and contentment, too. We already agree that human nature is impure and humans are quite incapable of gaining high qualities within the crooked standards of modern societies. Still, we might envision the characteristics of an *ideal personality,* at least as a guideline for gauging our behaviour and detecting our flaws that hinder our happiness. Surely, not many people can hold such a high standard of being, which requires a deep alignment of Ego, Model, and Self, as noted in Chapter Six.

An ideal personality stresses on Self, around 60%, while he utilizes Ego and Model about 20% each only for managing his relationships in society without being fully isolated or dominated. Actually, studying the three personality aspects and finding their right mix is also crucial for aligning our personalities with our philosophical ambitions. After all, the main goal of developing a 'self' driven personal life philosophy is to curb social hardships and possibly even find happiness (peace of mind).

In the desired personality, a person's needs and motivations are 'self'-directed and 'self'-controlled. When Model and Ego's needs compete with Self's needs and motivations, it is assumed they are not too conflicting and excessive, and applied only for practical purposes. In fact, this low portion of Model and Ego emerges only as a defence mechanism, and not for offensive or dependency purposes. They are merely tentative measures for adaptation and assertiveness, anyway, while we should remain a good judge of the level of Model and Ego we use, how often, for what purpose, and that their use is totally necessary. Maintaining the right balance is a big challenge, but a definite requirement for developing a life philosophy and finding tranquility or at least minimizing life's hardships. The Self, Ego, and Model attributes of an ideal personality are explained below, while an enlightened man's characteristics are discussed throughout this trilogy.

Envisioning and aspiring an 'ideal personality' helps us build a 'self'-oriented and 'self'-motivated life philosophy, and vice versa. That is, by learning about, and elaborating on, the purposes of personal life philosophy, we also learn about many traits of the ideal personality, which is guided by Self. The long discussions of fifteen fundamental human thoughts presented in Table 2.1 of Chapter Two provide a solid platform for building both an ideal personality and a typical personal life philosophy. Readers may wish to go back and review those discussions again. Meanwhile, the remainder of this chapter delves into the attributes of the ideal personality in further details.

The 'Self' Aspect of the Ideal Personality

The higher a person's level of self-awareness and transcendence, the lower would be his/her neediness and attachment to worldly values. Accordingly, an ideal personality with a right mix of Ego, Model, and Self puts little emphasis on materialistic or egoistic desires. Unlike Ego and Model, 'Self' has minimal ambitions, if any at all. Still, even such enlightened individuals need Ego and Model randomly for social coping, defending themselves against people's prejudices and malice, or for being assertive to protect their dignities and relationships.

A 'self' driven person seeks inward gratification, not external rewards. Even his/her love and belongingness needs are unselfish and global, instead of possessive and focused. While s/he enjoys the blessings and happiness cycles of social living and loving, s/he disallows such needs besiege him/her or compromise his/her plans. Especially, s/he learns how to deal with the love-deficiency syndrome that pains most people these days. Overall, the physical needs of Self are minimal and merely for running a healthy life, while facilitating his/her psychological and mental growth.

Naturally, reaching even a relative 'self' orientation is hard, let alone gaining all of its divine qualities. We all depend on other individuals, groups, and organizations to satisfy our basic needs, including love and belonging, while they impose their own needs and rules on us through this interdependency. This rising level of interdependency in society, especially for dealing with personal insecurities and psychological deprivations, jeopardizes people's chances of exploring their Self. They feel obliged to use all their strengths on coping and finding external acceptance. Thus, they find little energy and motivation to attend to their higher needs that support Self's intrinsic attribute. We prefer to stay needy than becoming self-reliant! It feels easier and more natural, after all!

A *personal life philosophy* aiming for 'self'-hood and lasting happiness starts with a commitment to develop and sustain our mental freedom by satisfying our higher needs. The goal also is to free ourselves from the temptations of, and dependencies on, the lower needs that society stress on. By developing a personal life philosophy and a personal plan, one strives to minimize one's reliance on external sources beyond minimal limits essential for our survival in society. This means self-reliance and self-control, while fulfilling specific needs that support a 'self' oriented life philosophy, which largely says, "My limited needs are *mainly* 'self' generated, 'self' controlled, and 'self' satisfied."

However, the self-reliance and self-control traits do not mean or lead to selfishness. On the contrary, self-reliance is based on a belief that everybody has modest abilities to think and behave without too much dependence on society or others to define his/her choice of lifestyle. With this basic belief, Self is incapable of assuming self-superiority. A 'self'ish person cannot be selfish. Instead, a desired personality is self-reliant, since he appreciates his 'self' objectively. He does not need to exaggerate his being and beliefs to attract others' approval, though he knows the innate value of 'self.' In fact, self-reliance is for living more practically, since Self knows that reliance on others is doomed, especially in our highly egotistical societies. Of course, Self's experience and knowledge are personal with no urge or interest to advertise them. The 'ideal personality' enjoys a humble sense of 'self'-approval and 'self'-value to replace the need for external approvals. It is both interesting and depressing to witness how we sometimes even pretend to be humble and submissive as a Model in order to manipulate people or receive their approval to feed our egoistic needs. A self-reliant individual does not need to go through these humiliating hassles and playing games regularly to feed his Ego.

In fact, the concept of 'self'-value is crucial for developing a modest, realistic self-image within an ideal personality, because societies suffer largely these days from the imbalance of personal 'self'-value. Only a small portion of us really understand our 'self'-worth, while the majority either overvalue or undervalue themselves. This odd confusion is not only our fault, but rather an epidemic transmitted to people from their parents, culture, and society. Mostly, they are creating this false image of us in our minds, whereas people's true self-image must be based on their 'self'-worth after a careful self-analysis and self-development. When we let our habits and idiosyncrasies stifle our potentialities, we undervalue ourselves. Conversely, when we believe in and exaggerate our importance in this universe, we let Ego dominate our personalities and we overrate ourselves. Both conditions hurt mostly the person, but also people close to him. False self-images created by erroneous self-valuation have destroyed our societies' structure. They have hindered personal communications, mutual respects, and people's sensitivities to each other's needs. Even our efforts to help people, such as positive thinking propagandas and self-image development seminars, only raise the burdens of living by advocating erroneous self-image and 'self'-worth, thus causing recurring cycles of self-absorption and self-alienation.

To encourage positive thinking, our social norms appear to dictate that 'we are what we think (and who we think we are).' This implies that if we think of ourselves as a rather invincible, know-it-all person, we would in fact turn into such a personality. Thus, we imagine and parade a superficial superiority, which is created by our twisted minds when no other viable criteria exist for measuring the real value of Self and not even knowing what Self is like. As a result, we have just become the most arrogant humans in the history of mankind. Ironically and sadly, in fact, we humans have become least trustworthy and pure than ever. Therefore, our arrogance only reflects how far off the chart our personal self-images and self-values are. Actually, the absurdity of positive thinking and playing phony personalities based on erroneous self-images must be clear if we review the discussions in Chapter Five about the intricacy of going thru the nine phases of self-realization (Chart 5.1).

An *ideal personality* and valid personal philosophy, therefore, requires aptitude for objective 'self'-valuation to build a positive self-image without getting arrogant or conversely losing our faith and confidence in our abilities. Comprehending and correcting our impression of 'self'-value is another important (but difficult) exercise included in our personal life philosophy. This delicate valuation process starts with a conscious belief and decision to explore our authentic needs through self-cleansing as part of the nine phases of Chart 5.1. In the process, we learn more about Self and humility to develop self-acceptance and self-approval. This would be a part of the process, or state, of awakening, as we let our Self become in charge of our lives. Thus, we set the stage for deeper 'self'-awareness and 'self'-control.

Relying on 'self'-value and 'self'-approval (in line with our life philosophy and lifestyle) is much harder than just discussing it, of course. When we do things—let us say write a novel—we normally assess our success by external results, e.g., the number of copies sold and the amount of money made. Without such seemingly tangible feedback, we have difficulty accepting our contributions' value. We become doubtful of our achievements. The trick with 'self'-approval for personal achievements is that we must not care much about receiving social recognition. Yet, it is ordinarily hard for us to ignore the feedback, even if we learned not to care about a reward to highlight our accomplishments.

Ironically, the words 'value' and 'approval' *customarily* refer to general comparison, judgment, and agreement by more than one person. The 'value' of every thing is established usually by the price that several people are willing to pay for it after judging it relative to established norms. 'Self'-value, however, is mostly a subjective and sentimental judgment with no general value or perception. As practical people, we underestimate our personal and mental assets, and instead emphasize on materialistic values based on universal judgments—which we assume are objective, yet also negotiable! The reason is clear. We like to use our times and thoughts for achieving or creating things that have value beyond our views per se in order to get a tangible reward for our efforts. We often doubt our own judgment or might even sense our general bias and dogmatism, especially with respect to our efforts' values. In real life (perceived world), we are expected to create only products that help us sustain our costly habits and lifestyles. Therefore, cashable creations appear more useful and precious to us than any personal integrity, 'self'-acceptance, and 'self'-approval.

Conversely, 'self'-value is an inner assessment that requires humility and a different point of reference for doing things in line with our philosophical (and/or divine) objectives, thus it is hard to compare and gauge its worth. It is not expressible, nor can it be measured in terms of equivalent cash, assets, or people's respect. It takes a lot of courage to depend merely on 'self'-value to judge our accomplishments. Making this drastic change in our mindsets is hard. A similar argument applies to 'self'-approval compared to external approval. While the latter gives us confirmed love and acceptance, 'self'-approval requires self-reliance and solid criteria to make objective judgments and assign tangible values for our efforts. Still, we often doubt the validity, value, and relevance of our 'self'-imposed criteria (e.g., integrity, principles, or humility) in a society with such a highly superficial orientation and deep influence in all aspects of our daily lives.

It would be interesting to study the concepts of 'self'-value and 'self'-approval within the contexts of the needs hierarchy model and self-actualization sensations. History is full of high-achievers like Van Gogh and Mozart who have had difficulty satisfying their basic needs for food and shelter, while creating masterpieces that others did not value sufficiently at the time. Yet, they had seemingly had the highest degree of 'self'-value for their creations. Nonetheless, we wonder how their achievements could have felt actualizing to them without external values, love, and approval to satisfy even their basic mental and physical needs. It is interesting to know if and how Van Gogh and Mozart might have avoided self-doubt and appreciated their real 'self'-value while constantly haggling with, and worrying about, basic life demands and their lower level needs. Judging by the sheer size of their achievements, though, one would *expect* them, and many similar artists and high-achievers, to have climbed up to the highest levels of the needs hierarchy and felt fully actualized Yet, most likely they had not truly, despite their vast potentialities and knacks for self-actualization. They might have had a huge level of 'self'-control and 'self'-value to bear the absence of external valuation and approval, while needing love and financial support so badly, too. Overall, it would be difficult for most of us to feel actualized when our self-actualizing efforts cannot help us sustain a basic life for our dependent family.

Maslow's 'needs hierarchy theory' seems to break down in instances when a person's achievements bring him to the verge of self-actualization without his lower needs being satisfied. He may feel actualized or not, depending only upon his approach towards 'self'-value and self-doubt, and his ability to face normal social pressures rather nonchalantly. Or conversely, his ability to set his ambitions aside, become practical, and move down the personal needs hierarchy. After all, living in society pushes our Egos and Models to act in many weird ways, and in return, our Egos and Models often push us in odd directions on Needs Hierarchy tree.

The 'Model' and 'Ego' Roles for Ideal Personality

A small amount of Model and Ego is in fact desirable for helping us handle the rules and expectations in societies, especially with Model and Ego-driven majority of people we should associate with for exchanging services and emotions. Without Model, we may appear rude and uncaring to those who are used to judging others based on appearances and etiquettes. Self may appear cold and uncaring in the showy and allegedly tactful socializing these days. In all, our presentations of the 'self'-induced ideas and facts are better received and understood in a 'model' format, if at all. This Model aptitude helps us merge, communicate, and get along with others more effectively, while keeping our private identity. Sadly, even Ego aptitude becomes necessary on some special occasions just to survive.

A small dose of Ego can help us assert and defend ourselves rather than remain passive all the time when we face people's offences and pressures. Self advocates patience, forgiveness, and tolerance as the main traits of the ideal personality. However, often, even the ideal personality has to protest and maybe even rebel against excessive cruelty and unfairness, which are normal symptoms of our modern societies. We should judge and oppose people with our managed Ego and tactful Model occasionally when it becomes absolutely necessary.

Volume III of this trilogy deals mainly with the realities of our lives, critical decisions, and relationships that we must maintain with others and society. From those discussions, it becomes clear that, for practical purposes, we should engage in some activities by using Model and Ego for role-playing. Many examples are given in Volume III where the three personality aspects converge to create a best possible decision, action, or reaction. In a crude sense, our ideal personality emerges and takes control of our lives effectively even in those chaotic situations with the aid of Model and Ego. The important point, however, is that we ('self') should not allow Model and Ego exceed their shares of contribution in the ideal personality. As we struggle with many hardships and dilemmas a lifetime, it would become a big temptation and easy for us to forget the essence of the ideal personality and allow Ego and Model take charge of our minds and lives gradually. The ideal personality has to remain 'self'-controlled at all cost and prevent a takeover by Model or Ego. This constant awareness and resistance constitutes Self's most challenging task.

Addendum: The Formula

The discussions in Part III show why prescribing a particular 'formula of happiness' would be imprudent at best. It is hard to establish a standard or criterion for real, lasting happiness due to many factors. For one thing, individuals' unique perceptions and combinations of personality aspects (i.e., Model, Ego, Self) make their expectations and approaches in life different. Their personal needs and deprivations also make their definitions and feelings of happiness different. Moreover, happiness moods and experiences are unique in depth and length. These and many other obstacles make the chances of finding and applying a fixed 'happiness formula' questionable. Yet, we all hope to unravel this mystery, too, along with many other life puzzles.

In the final analysis, happiness is an abstract perception that eludes a comprehensive definition. Perhaps the best definition we can invent for common purpose is that 'happiness' is the outcome of profound experiences that impact a person's soul deeply, boost his outlook on life, which then affect others positively, too.

Nonetheless, the following general guidelines can be derived from the discussions in the last two chapters regarding the basic characteristics of happiness:

1. Happiness is not a phenomenon out there that can be defined and accessed independent from the *particular* personality of the person experiencing it.
2. Happiness does not have a fixed path and it cannot be gained without making extensive changes to one's own personality, mindset, outlook, and lifestyle.
3. Contrary to common perception, we surely do not deserve happiness as long as we expect to find it within pervasive, crooked lifestyles and shallow mentalities.
4. Without a 'self'-control mechanism to monitor and manage our endless cycles of depression and determine their causes, the idea of finding happiness remains vague and unattainable.

5. Pleasures can at best replicate merely a tentative sense of happiness. They do not stir happiness or remove depression.
6. Happiness is an intrinsic property of 'self.' Therefore, it can be generated from within us automatically without so much toil for superficiality. All we need is a simple knowledge of how the principles of happiness work within 'self,' and how to nurture them in our minds. The first principle, surely, is to minimize the roles of Model and Ego in our lives.
7. The biggest challenge for finding happiness is to believe in, and boost, as much of the 'self' aspect of our personality as we can. We must monitor every one of our actions, reactions, communications, and encounters to gauge the influence of Model, Ego, and Self, as well as the motives behind them. Ultimately, we should learn to become a better human being with lots of humility.
8. A mature personality resembles a perennial flowering plant, where its innate properties stay intact, in spite of the cyclical winters of depression. Thus, happiness is automatic when one's personality is well groomed and kept in balance. Yet, explaining any happiness experience is like describing the beauty of a particular flower that has its own unique needs, properties, and fragrance.
9. Happiness requires high self-awareness. Not only Self must be strong to cultivate the plant of happiness, but also special attention to the properties of the flower itself is necessary. We should train ourselves to stay aware of the happiness of our 'self,' the same way we look at the flowers of a particular plant consciously. If flowers are not healthy and strong, we assess the situation and adjust the watering, fertilizing, or change the environment (the soil) of the plant. Similarly, the happiness of 'self' needs monitoring to adjust personality and correct a noted lethargy in one's self-cleansing regimen. The awareness of 'self' is discussed in several parts of this trilogy. It simply means knowing and remembering 'who we are,' 'what the purpose of our living is,' and the vulnerability of

our lives leading to the inevitable death. We must be familiar with the seven elements of 'self' reviewed in Chapter Thirteen of Vol. II. Being conscious of our physical health as well as psychological growth are other means of 'self'-awareness. We need 'self'-control over our physical and psychological needs (i.e., social and inner temptations) in order to avoid mental deprivation or stagnation.

10. A real happiness experience has **four main attributes**. It has a legitimate and worthwhile 'cause,' it generates authentic 'feelings' of inner joy and fullness, it 'impacts' the person in a meaningful and deep way, and as a result, the person can 'affect' other individuals, events, and things in a positive way as well. For lasting happiness, we should pursue mostly those simple experiences that can entail all these four elements fully and consistently. Thus, happiness cycles should be deep and continuous, despite the inevitable cycles of depression.

11. Happiness cannot rely on external sources and whims. The events and experiences causing happiness are only important to the extent they can create the four attributes of happiness regularly. Therefore, small experiences that can be attained quite readily are potentially more powerful in steering and generating happiness experiences. For example, gardening joys, once appreciated, can become a major source of lasting happiness and 'self' growth. When we explore the details of a good piece of music, especially *old* classical music for those who like it, we discover small notes and creations every time we listen to it. The easily repeatable joys of art, music, and gardening reinforce the cycles of happiness in our psyches quickly. We appreciate and associate with the genius behind the art and music, even though somebody else has done the creation aspect of them. We can grow a habit of producing those basic experiences that keep happiness cycles running perpetually and smoothly. When it comes to our own artistic creations, the intensity of happiness caused by our achievements and self-actualizing experiences would be

ten folds. Such personal achievements, i.e., inventions or arts, enrich our lives and propagate the intensity of our happiness experiences by affecting other humans, too.

12. Happiness runs in parallel with the realized level of personal potentialities. Following our dreams in line with our realistic sense of our potentialities and limitations has a big chance of stirring happiness experiences. Conversely, following some rampant dreams just based on hope, false pretences, positive thinking, or our misleading perceptions of our potentialities, most likely lead to stagnation and depression experiences.

13. Happiness experiences would be much more frequent and rewarding once we choose and follow a path of wisdom with a sensible life philosophy. Abolishing our gullibility sources, e.g., blind pursuit of, religions, positive thinking gimmicks, or unfounded spirituality rituals, is an important step towards wisdom and happiness. Through our search, we learn about the essential dimensions of our 'self,' including our inherent spirituality urge. Accordingly, we would not only learn about our ignored potentialities, but also access our inner strengths that free us from the limitations of a mere physical existence. This wisdom path gives us the power to resist the imposing and conditioning value systems, while staying realistic about our ambitions, relationships, and social responsibilities.

14. Happiness cycles are interrupted less frequently when we learn to recognize and avoid the traps of depression cycles, especially when they are self-induced by our Ego and Model personality aspects. When 'Self' induces depression, such as our sadness about human impurity, the experience should be used for learning, healing, compassion, and creating.

15. Happiness cycles are intensified when we learn to pause and ponder our rational doubts about objects, people, and events. Through this awareness process, we develop a personal life philosophy to deal with reality, make the right life decisions, and fulfil our responsibilities effectively.

PART IV
Philosophy and Reality

About Part IV

With our new wisdom about the workings of human personalities and thoughts as well as the prevailing facts and myths covered in the last three parts, we should now try to define the parameters of a plausible personal philosophy to help us build a simple life path and maintain some degree of contentment.

*****

CHAPTER NINE
Thoughts and Wisdom

Our thoughts are boundless and intriguing for exploring many magical facets of existence. Yet, the simpler goal of thinking is to plan and control our lives. We hope our thoughts can help us develop our life philosophy and *primary wisdom*, which we need for coping within society, making good decisions, and getting a deeper grasp of people and God. Naturally, our philosophical thoughts find much more value for directing our lives compared to our mundane thoughts, which merely waste our brain cells and energy too often. Yet, the soundness of our thoughts also depends on our level of consciousness and self-awareness, while we must know (and justify) the sources and purposes of our thoughts, too. Our thoughts are supposed to bring us wisdom, not stress and confusion. They should also help us develop our self-image and self-worth, instead of causing self-pity or a sense of loneliness.

Yet, unfortunately, humans' thoughts are seldom devoted to the right stuff of life. Therefore, most of our decisions and actions remain a matter of habit and personality, instead of reflecting a thoughtful life philosophy and primary wisdom. We allow our juvenile thoughts derail our lives and deflate our spirits, instead of helping us control our erratic emotions and see life's essentialities in a proper perspective.

The complexity of social life and our relationships forces us waste so much time and minds on shallow thoughts mostly for solving our problems and dealing with stressful facets of life. Our thoughts are often scattered and skimpy merely for responding to our urgent needs to compete and get richer. We often ponder our options, solutions, or ideas just to fight with others or manipulate them for some evil purposes. Thus, we seldom find the motive and time to reflect deeply and build a simple lifestyle that could eliminate the need for so much painful thinking regarding trivia or worrying about irresolvable life issues. If only we realized the vanity of our naïve desires, we might stop our endless, stressful thoughts and pains. Instead of dwelling on self-indulging needs that our Egos push on us incessantly as matters of life and death, we might allow our delicate imaginations and insights elate us beyond our superficial reality to the sacred spheres of tranquility and freedom.

Unfortunately, most of us do not know the best way of using our brains. Sometimes, we think too much and too long, to the point of losing our sanity or major opportunities of our lives. Sometimes, our thoughts are sporadic and meaningless like some form of daydreams. Sometimes they create scientific theories and techniques that are vastly perplexing and amazing. Sometimes they goad evil actions, or conversely lead to personal awakening along with most sacred, humble sentiments. Sometimes they are self-destructive and sometimes stir tranquility and a sacred sense of beauty. We can also learn to relax and meditate by thinking in certain ways, or by stopping our thoughts a while. Meanwhile, the miraculous, vast scope of our thoughts reflects the complexity and intricacy of human nature. These divine experiences give us a chance to reach higher levels of intelligence and humanness if only we understood our naiveté, sentiments, brilliance, arrogance, and ignorance that besiege us, all at once or in rotations. We only need to know the right thoughts to make our lives meaningful. We also need periodic moments of no-thoughts, which we can induce through some type of meditation.

Surely, the *extent, content*, and *intent* of our thoughts depend on the person's primary wisdom, personality, mood, and motives. However, we all share the same fundamental thoughts about life intuitively (as discussed in Chapter Two). They are the deepest, most primitive thoughts that we reflect upon regarding existence. They are the underlying thoughts behind the whole philosophy, processes, and actions of life. These fine thoughts are specifically posed in our psyches and become relevant in line with our life perspectives and priorities in various phases of our lives. They also raise three philosophical questions.

Three Philosophical Questions

Three related philosophical questions occupy our minds during life's three main phases, i.e., i) childhood/adolescence, ii) middle age, and iii) old age.

In the **first phase**, childhood/adolescence, we ask ourselves, *"What is my life going to look like?"* During this phase, we are anxious, doubtful, and inquisitive about our future and fate, but do not realize our deeper needs and beliefs. Despite our curiosity about the whole existence, we do not understand or question the main dilemmas and purposes of life per se. We get involved with the so-called life 'practicalities,' which seem to require our urgent attention as basic matters of survival. We are also driven entirely by social norms that hardly reveal life 'essentialities' besides the basics for survival. Thus, many of our life essentialities, such as our spiritual and psychological needs, do not get our attention.

Although all the thoughts listed in Table 2.1 of Chapter Two sometimes circle in our heads vaguely and subconsciously during the first phase of our lives, we remain unclear and passive about the purpose of life and our goals. During this 'confusion' period, we mainly strive to master social norms and means of adaptation. We grow some raw ideas about how we would like to shape our future and then make tenuous plans to get there. Still, we remain uncertain and apprehensive about our decisions, the life we must lead, the resources and results, our abilities, and the opportunities that may be offered to us, fate and luck, etc. These are the years we have the highest level of doubts about our future and success, and, at the same time, *success and future* is our whole definition of life. We have little notion or concern about the purposes of life and our deeds, as long as we fulfil the expectations and teachings of our parents and society. We imagine that life and society are defined properly already, though we do not like many aspects of them. We just assume that by now humans have fathomed what life's purpose is and what society tells us is based on millenniums of proper thinking and experimentation. We naively trust history and social values overall. Even worse, we trust our emotions and our friends' views about the youths' needs. We assume that we should set our actions and decisions in line with those common needs and definitions. By doing so, we also believe that success and happiness follow automatically, and that this process would make us a perfect person to lead a complete life.

In the **second phase** of our lives, i.e., middle age, we start to question the purpose of the life we are leading. We ask ourselves, *"What is this life?"* During the first phase, we seemed to have many objectives that made sense and had special value to us. In spite of our many doubts, we had embraced some inherent hope and optimism about future. We had tried to achieve those logical objectives, as though they had been the main purposes of life. Now, in the second phase, however, those thoughts and feelings do not make enough sense. Now, we question the value of the outcome and content of life itself, even when those childhood objectives have been achieved. It seems we keep doing the same things over and over without getting an inner, deep satisfaction from life. It is not merely the boredom, but a sense of deficiency and failure that often besieges our thoughts and feelings. This becomes the phase of reflection. Our hardships to survive appear to surpass our appreciation of the outcomes and life's values in general. We work hard, tolerate injustice and unfairness, accept socioeconomic pressures, humour people's phony Models and annoying Egos, and fight with our bosses and families constantly with no sign of relief in sight. Thus, we question the purpose of the life we are leading. Often, we believe a drastic decision is needed to free ourselves from this suffocating trap. However, we also have many doubts about the alternatives, our options, and solutions. It seems we have no choice but to keep struggling and postponing all those risky choices or actions that might change our present life path, *most likely for worse, we fear!* And before long, we arrive at the third phase of our lives, still hesitant and doubtful about our options and decisions.

In the **third phase**, old age, we project our lives' ending and recall all the struggles, thoughts, and doubts we have endured in the earlier phases of our lives. At this point, we question the value and purpose of it all even harsher in **total disbelief**. Our thoughts centre on the question of, *"What was this life (all about)?"* We regret many things we have or have not done and the things we had spent so much energy and time on naively, not to mention all those useless worries and all those abuses we had to endure. Even at this phase, some of us might still question the purpose of life just out of curiosity or anger. Yet, most likely we have given up on finding an answer, or believe it is too late to do anything about it now, anyway, even if we could define a purpose for life. The risks of choosing a new life path or lifestyle feel even higher and more intimidating now. We can finally feel the sad 'conclusion' clearly and regret many of our past deeds and beliefs, as we had trusted life, society, culture, our families and lifestyles naively.

There it is! The story of our lives as portrayed by the wisdom of three philosophical questions boggling our minds, exhausting our bodies and psyches, and depleting our spirits a lifetime during the three intimidating life phases.

Phases of Life	**Underlying Philosophical Questions**
Youth	What will be (my life like)?
Middle Age	What is this (that is happening)?
Old Age	What was it (all about)?

The Ultimate Wisdom

Some precious lessons lie in humans' three main philosophical questions. Each question may not reveal as much wisdom as they do together. They offer the gist of the deepest thoughts, doubts, and dilemmas that engage intelligent people as they mature. They are ultimate visions, conclusions, and valuations of life for most us whether we reflect on them consciously enough or not. Together, these three simple questions can offer a great source of potential lessons and wisdom.

In fact, if we grasp the gist of these philosophical questions early, we might be able to develop the foundation of our thoughts and life path properly to live with lesser stress. We may be able to plan a more practical life for ourselves, choose a simpler lifestyle, and possibly find happiness, too, by always remembering and using these philosophical questions as our primary wisdom.

Of course, these three philosophical questions hardly occur to many people living deeply in their delusions within the perceived reality world, not even in their subconscious, or they just refuse to stop and reflect upon them for a minute. This fast-growing group of narcissists in modern societies has deprived itself from any type of thinking, anyway. However, the rest of us surely arrive at these questions in due time if we are lucky to live long.

At each life phase, we sense and live thru the corresponding philosophical question daily mostly subconsciously, but we seem unable to find a suitable answer for it at the time. Only when we arrive in the next phase, we grasp the absurdity of the question(s) in the earlier phase(s). We get a tentative and awkward answer, too. On the other hand, if we consider the questions we would be asking in the future life phases, we often get plausible answers today as well as a chance to build a proper mindset and realistic expectations when we live in that life phase. We simply realize, not emotionally or cynically, but intelligently, that all life phases would be questionable and paradoxical, no matter how we strive to make sense out of life and how diligently we plan our actions.

Our most likely answer to Phase One question, 'What my life will be like?', is rather easy to anticipate in the next life phases. That is, regardless of our level of success and deemed happiness, we would still doubt the value and meaning of our lives even when we are in the prime of our lives, i.e., the second life phase. Sadly, the third question by itself implies that we would not find solace or good results for both first and second questions, either.

Surely, we are not aware of the depth, effect, and importance of the upcoming questions when we are in a lower life phase. Our optimism and arrogance would not allow it. In phase one, we do not know and believe that more fundamental questions await us, which, by the way, negate the importance (validity) of the first question (What my life would be like?). That is, no matter how our life turns out, we question its meaning and value, nonetheless. We could try to hide behind positive thinking or similar mottos to override the nagging reality about existence in our subconscious. But our psyches and spirits cannot be fooled forever.

Similarly, we do not expect the question in phase three to be so harsh, nor expect such deep sense of helplessness, despite all our wisdom and wealth after a lifetime of efforts and suffering. No matter how much we try to make sense of life and our plans and pleasures, no intelligent person would find a plausible answer for the *enigmatic* question, 'What was it all about?' Again, some radical, carefree individuals might resist this conclusion and insist that life is full of meanings and pleasures. Well, everybody is best capable of judging his/her deep senses and existence. It is merely a matter of personal wisdom and sincerity with one's self! It is just a matter one's intimacy with his/her psyche and spirit!

Perhaps it is in our nature to believe only in what we can feel or expect *now* (in this very minute) despite all the philosophies and prophecies that circulate about existence, and despite even the ongoing clues about the faltering state of humanity that our psyches and spirits sense. Yet, for the very same reason, it seems we devote our lives to adventures and thoughts that would prove to have no substantive meaning or value whatsoever at the end.

We follow some crude ambitions a lifetime, seek more pleasures, and worry about trivia, which we often regret later when we view and review them retrospectively in the future phases of our lives. This dire conclusion also suggests that perhaps we have all been 'living in the now' too much already, more than what we like to admit. That is, we judge our future needs only based on what we feel urgent today, instead of using our imaginations and realize that our perceptions of life (according to the values of the NOW) are questionable and most likely erroneous. We need the wisdom of foresight to make our lives simpler and reassess the purposes of our needless struggles and desires.

Many of us who pass through the three phases of life would admit that these three basic questions have besieged their minds in a profound, and often shocking, manner. Some have struggled with those questions more closely in each life phase. Some might be less candid to confess or have lived without enough reflections for whatever reason. Some might have been too overwhelmed by their Egos, self-gratification, or daily social pressures to think at all or properly. And some lucky individuals would not face these three questions, especially the last two, because they have found a path of wisdom that directs them through the three life phases smoothly. Their life experiences have been rather unadventurous, but possibly more peaceful and fuller in a stoic lifestyle perhaps. These lucky people have somehow come to terms with the three questions, especially the last one, very early on in their lives.

The lessons we can learn from these questions are drawn from a projection of our state of mind and feelings in the upcoming life phases. These questions could serve us as hidden clues about the futility of submitting to the common processes and standards of life. The lesson is that, sooner or later, we would discover the emptiness of our egotistical objectives. The lesson is that if we realize what would, and would not, matter when we are in the second and third phases of our lives, then maybe we would focus our minds and actions in the right direction, in a timelier manner perhaps. The lesson is that the standard formula of happiness that our parents and society teach us is not viable for human survival. The lesson is that perhaps we should ponder and find a basic path of wisdom to prevent our future shocks about life's futility, and to prevent our minds and energies being wasted on social struggles and shallow desires. If only we knew what we would be thinking torturously in the future phases of our lives, it might get easier for us to sort out our priorities and establish a personal philosophy that feels more sensible for now and future phase(s).

We learn a lot from our experiences, except that they do not pose or answer the three main questions of life in a timely order. We do not get the opportunity, either, to reverse past situations and conditions or to relive the lost years. The old saying that, "Everybody needs two lives: One to experience, and one to live," finds its significance mostly during the last phase of our lives. We would be willing to give up everything we have, all our wealth and worldly attachment, just for a second chance to think better this time. We would do some (or many) aspects of our lives quite differently if we could replay our three life phases, just because we now suddenly think differently, more philosophically maybe, so late in our lives. Alas, we never get that chance! Alas, we do not develop, and benefit from, the wisdom of foresight and the nine phases of mental restoration (for exploring our inner 'self') noted in Chapter 5, either, to address the three fundamental life questions in time! Alas, we become so overly engaged with our social and family obligations to find the time and nerve to look beyond the norms! Alas, our insecurities and idiosyncrasies limit our sense of reality and urge for self-realization!

We need a radical mentality and courage to understand and believe in the significance of the questions we would eventually ask ourselves in the future phases of life. If so, we could start *thinking forward* indeed. By thinking deep about the ultimate and eventual question of, 'What was it (all about)?' as early in our lives as possible, we might change our vision of life. We might appreciate the wisdom of this (third phase) question when we are in the first or second phase of our lives. Putting ourselves in a future state of mind is very difficult. Yet, only through forward thinking (the wisdom of foresight), we might invent an 'escape scheme' now, because in the third phase, it would be too late to escape the painful thoughts of, 'What was it?', or the regretting thoughts of, 'What could be!' Later, we cannot do anything with these questions other than getting ourselves more depressed.

It happens that an 'escape scheme' (relief) can be found only on a path of wisdom. To become immune against the question of, "What was it?" in the third phase of our lives, we need the right mindset to help us develop a philosophy of life for assessing and professing our purposes of living honestly and practically. Then, we must apply those thoughts and philosophy to our actions and decisions consciously in the light of *forward thinking*. Finding our authentic needs and purposes in life prevents the question of, 'What is this life?' from materializing in the second phase of our lives. If we plan wisely, we might not have to ask this depressing question from ourselves as a haunting reality of our lives during the entire middle age.

At the same time, it should be reiterated that one must have an advanced mentality and willpower to appreciate the gist of these questions and the premise of 'forward thinking' life philosophy. Surely, that is a high expectation to consider for average human beings. This radical mentality about life is too depressing and contrary to social values to spread in society, especially among the youths, as people are taught to stay positive and work hard mainly for social rewards. Then again, keeping people, even the youths, in dark a lifetime is another kind of human travesty!

'Forward thinking' and possible escape schemes are reviewed further in Chapter Twelve to emphasize that the three questions of, 'What will be?', 'What is this?', and 'What was it?' should be contemplated in a package within a proper perspective to raise our self-awareness and chances for tranquility. Accordingly, we might succeed in refining our 'perceived' world's outlook with our new sense of 'real' realities that have different meanings, emphasis, and significance for us. This approach might relieve our excruciating self-induced sufferings that we have helplessly accepted as our inevitable fate.

Overall, it is useful to consider *forward thinking* as a primary philosophical principle for building our foundation of thoughts, beliefs, and actions. After all, we have the choice to think outside the box to enrich our psyches and spirits or just keep indulging our childish dreams for self-gratification, happiness, and success.

Human Thoughts' Mishmash

Whether we like or not, believe or not, the concepts discussed in this trilogy circle in our heads often, as we suffer daily, try to learn about our existence, hope to find some truth about the world and people, and remain perplexed about leading a rather purposeful life. Sometimes, we might even reflect upon some fundamental thoughts more actively when we encounter life's dilemmas and question our existence and plans. However, a large volume of trivial thoughts always distracts our minds, causes stress, and limits our chances and time to analyse our deeper thoughts. Our needs and sufferings stir lots of mundane thoughts by themselves and hinder our ability to think straight and assess the chance of finding a better life path. These are very basic, hurtful facts of life! Still, our curiosity regarding existence and finding happiness cannot be eluded, as humans' brains are becoming more active every decade in our chaotic societies, although mainly preoccupied with more trivia.

Some people might finally find the wisdom and willpower to curb their rampant desires and thoughts in order to think deeper and feel freer. They try to maintain their integrity and sanity by defining life more realistically. However, the rest of us struggle with our unrelenting, torturous whims and thoughts all our lives, unable to decide about a basic life path. We suffer from stress and depression and must consume a large amount of antidepressants to go through another day. Some resort to crimes, self-destruction and self-deceit to elude the dreadful reality running their shallow identities. Ironically, our deep urges and sufferings often trigger many spiritual questions in our heads about 'life,' too. We cannot avoid our inherent curiosity about life, which are regularly raised through some fundamental thoughts. We lose our sleep and peace when our spirits demand real justifications for our artificial needs as well as our egoistic ambitions and lifestyles.

Human brain appears to operate like an engine with many complementary (but clashing) parts that must work together for the ultimate purpose of running a volatile machine called human. Keeping this engine efficient to run an instable cranky machine (laden by erratic thoughts) is hard, but necessary. Clearly, when the engine is not balanced and strong, it would not provide good efficiency and output. A particular part might not function well from time to time, like when we have our doubts or face difficult dilemmas. Thus, our job is to identify the problem and repair the part, so the engine can return to full efficiency. The engine needs regular checkups and tune-ups, like the times we need to halt our thoughts and quiet our minds. The engine might boil sometimes like the times when anger and egoism dominate us. In those dire moments, we should just slow down and stop for a while to let the engine cool down.

Nevertheless, we know intuitively—like a kind of magical power—about our need for *fundamental* thoughts to define life, and grow our convictions for self-actualization and spiritualism through a personal life philosophy. Only then, we believe, we can begin to justify our existence as an intelligent person somewhat. At the very least, we like to feel some basic senses of peace, love, and compassion in line with valid thoughts.

Some fundamental thoughts laid out in this volume can help us with our special objectives and decisions of life that are noted in Volume III. Together, our life experiences and fundamental thoughts build our 'primary wisdom,' which entails our outlook, personality, and the means and methods of handling life matters, especially our major life decisions and plans. An efficient and sophisticated engine would drive our decisions and plans during the journey of life. This solid engine would help us endure life turbulences and get us to our destiny as smoothly and safely as we deserve. We do not want substantial breakdowns or regrets because of our naive mishandling of the engine. On top of all these difficult tasks, the toughest mission for our thoughts (this intelligent engine) is to keep our spirits intact and elude pain and depression, as discussed in Volume II.

Still, our thoughts are much more complex with graver goals than being envisioned solely as an engine to run our decisions and plans. Beyond its use for worldly affairs, our fundamental thoughts should also help us find a divine vision of life and our spiritual connection to the universe. We realize our thoughts' values for daily life, but more importantly, they should transcend us beyond all the worldly decisions and plans. It should help us grasp, believe in, and find a path of wisdom deserving the dignity of human beings in the form we have evolved, even considering our huge flaws, ignorance, and ongoing mistakes. We might find tranquility now that happiness is so illusive. We might even gain a higher morality considering our intelligence and the long history of 'thinking humans' seeking salvation. An advanced foundation of thoughts can help us transcend to divine domains not sketched in our pitiful societies within a delusional perceived world. Such sacred findings can offer the most crucial resources for thinking and living, but sadly, we have failed miserably so far to develop this platform even for mitigating human pains worldwide. That is the reason humanity appears more doomed every decade, while even our leaders and scholars refuse to see the absurdity of social structure we are relying on to guide humans. Surely, under the current conditions, the rest of us are too lost and misguided to worry about next generations' dire prospects.

Managing Our Thoughts

Most of our thoughts are mechanical, mundane, erratic, fanciful, and often stressful. Our dreams, crude ambitions, hallucinations, paranoia, misperceptions, and personal idiosyncrasies are causing this mishmash of human thoughts. However, we intuitively also strive to manage our thoughts in order to be effective, objective, happy, compassionate, and avoid the stress of needless musing. Overall, we like to manage our thoughts for three purposes:

1. To better understand and support our inner needs, major life decisions, and plans.
2. To develop and maintain a feasible life philosophy and find a path of wisdom to reach peace of mind and maybe even enlightenment.
3. To stop all our thoughts occasionally in order to give our minds a chance to rest and our souls an opportunity to heal.

Managing our thoughts implies an ability to manoeuvre within these three states effectively, while minimizing our preoccupation with all those mundane, liquid thoughts (the 80-90% portion). Our success depends on our characters and backgrounds, but also personal efforts to control our thoughts at least 30% of the time. Even this minimal awareness of our thoughts is vital for running a healthier lifestyle. We spend lots of times on routine decisions and plans (purpose number 1 above). We waste so much time on soft thoughts, too, such as daydreaming, reminiscing on varied social encounters, and struggling with our dire paranoia and other idiosyncrasies, including jealousy, spite, and rivalry.

With these types of raw and liquid thoughts, we develop more untenable expectations and unauthentic needs every day, which lead to further psychological deprivations, insecurities, and crude thoughts. We suffer needlessly and worry uselessly. Sometimes, we stir disruptive thoughts with no foundation or significance for our physical or psychological needs, but only due to our anger, paranoia, spite, etc. These futile thoughts cause us more pain and confusion and push our nervous system to explode eventually.

In all, most of us need a plan (along with high consciousness and convictions) to re-distribute our crude thinking habits and energy to minimize the soft thoughts. Accordingly, we would use our minds, times, and energies on realizing and aligning the three purposes of thinking noted above routinely.

Managing our thoughts mainly means controlling the types of ideas that we allow into our heads. We strive to restrict troubling thoughts with little or no consequence in the end. We rely on our fundamental thoughts (primary wisdom) to set our life priorities and make our major life decisions effectively away from personal whims and social pressures in complex socioeconomic settings. The times we spend on enhancing the foundation of our thoughts through meditation and reading is never too much. Studying the opinions and prophecies of truthful thinkers and philosophers enforces and supports personal thoughts and individual creativity.

Finally, we could learn how to meditate and stir the moments of 'no-thought,' and how often. We do so by consciously freeing our minds from musing—perhaps by amusing ourselves with basic activities, such as gardening, that halt serious decisions and thinking, but provide feelings of joy, discovery, and satisfaction.

We might try to alleviate the repercussion of futile thoughts in two major ways: First, we could build a general life philosophy to direct and minimize the level of our trivial thoughts, and to limit those activities that induce such confusing thoughts. Second, we could attempt routinely to give ourselves a break from thinking by goading our minds to only feel things, or stop thinking and feeling altogether on some occasions—like the time we do a deep meditation. Balancing these two methods (i.e., thinking deeper to strengthen our life philosophy versus creating regular no-thought moments) provides the best results, of course.

A 'no-thought state' can be reached once we learn to relieve our minds from trivial thoughts, which usually revolve around our shallow needs, plans, and how to elude our stress and pains. In a no-thought state, we find peace and freedom, which is the same objective we have for developing our life philosophy with a diligent (active) mind. Thus, the question is how often we should force our minds to relax partially or totally compared with times we should spend on thinking actively and deeply for enhancing or gauging our life philosophy.

On the one hand, we expect our minds to be always sharp and alert for defending ourselves, and in constant control of our plans and decisions. We also need a sharp mind for our self-awareness exercises and keeping life trivialities out of our heads as well. On the other hand, over-thinking and planning, merely for survival, is driving most of us to the verge of insanity in a corrupt setting where hardly anything makes sense anymore. Thus, it has become vital to find the right timing and means for quieting our minds and managing our thoughts as often and prudently as we can.

This paradoxical situation (i.e., keeping our minds in full alert versus total quiet) follows the same pattern that has surfaced throughout our discussions about humans' irreconcilable doubts, dilemmas, and inner conflicts, as integral characteristics of living. The foundation of our thoughts is merely formed around similar dichotomies, such as doubts versus decisions, facts versus myths, perceived versus real world, life versus death, challenges versus suffering, stoic versus practical personality, independence versus dependence, solitude versus socializing, trusting destiny versus active planning, etc. Nevertheless, we should learn to use the right meaning, mix, and balance for these complex dichotomies, along with a philosophical framework to reconcile them collectively as well when necessary. After all, this hug paradox seems to be the underlying property of life, thus demanding a refined foundation of thoughts for navigating in the ocean of uncertainties forever. Accordingly, the task of reaching this comprehensive balance in our lives also unravels the mysteries of life and happiness.

The Significance of No-thought Experiences

Keeping our minds sharp versus maintaining enough no-thought experiences is a major dichotomy as noted above! However, it particularly requires a special mindset and ritual that we usually expect to find amongst gurus and spiritualists. Thus, grasping and practicing it would be a challenge all by itself.

At one extreme, J.K. Krishnamurti has commented that:

"Only when there is no movement of thought, life is full of significance." Truth and Actuality, Gollancz London, 1977, page 70.

A mystical truth lies behind this philosophy merely because no-thought moments are not the means of forgetting ourselves or losing our senses. On the contrary, we actually learn more about ourselves during such moments through a feeling of selflessness within a divine sphere, thus sense the majesty of both Nature and our being per se, i.e., the significance of humans being part of it. That is how some no-thought moments produce the highest level of significance for us, merely by the opportunity of becoming more in contact with our 'self.' Wandering leisurely in a beautiful garden or a field, occasionally the glory of Nature manifests and absorbs us when mundane thoughts and feelings are absent. In such moments, we become conscious of our being within eternity as we stand in awe appreciating and admiring that grandeur and order. We feel and enjoy our inherent relationship with Nature. In those moments, at the height of our conscious awareness of this heartfelt existence, our thoughts are silent, yet our subtle feelings are deeply serene and meaningful. We simply get absorbed in the depth of the real reality and feel delighted. And sometimes even get enlightened.

No-thought moments do not include the moods created under the influence of alcohol or drugs, when one loses control of one's thoughts, feelings, and self. Even movies or routine recreations might help us forget our problems and stop our thoughts, which have limited benefits. However, they do not stir true no-thought moments. These artificial settings for forgetting ourselves do not induce the energy that natural no-thought states stir. Meditation and no-thought states entail full awareness and conscious efforts for self-control. Yet, most importantly, the value of a no-thought state lies in the high energy and freshness it generates, instead of lethargy or ignorance of self. Instead of getting high with drugs or suffer our regular drinking hangovers, we could depend on more precious means of creating our no-thought moments. We feel and know how much we need these moments, but we use our corrupt, creepy ways to induce them—mostly through alcohol, drugs, and sex—again as another crude phenomenon of modern cultures.

We can induce or capture no-thought moments in many ways. Music has special power in creating such moments. Without the need for an artificial substance, such as drugs, *the right kind of* music by itself can penetrate our senses very deep and touch our souls. Gardening or strolling in Nature and artistic experiences revive our sense of 'being' and connecting to our souls. All these simple experiences, music in particular, have been proven to stir brain hormones, create serenity and vigour, raise our spirit and awareness, and enhance our health. Such experiences are vastly precious, as they relax (and also connect) our body and mind. They help us recreate and prolong our no-thought moments. Yet, natural no-thought moments through divine and philosophical reflections offer the highest level of potency for self-realization and enlightenment.

Furthermore, no-thought moments release a tremendous amount of creative energy through deeper perceptions. For the person who knows how to appreciate and generate no-thought moments, this energy turns into significant thoughts, deeds, or creations subsequent to a no-thought experience. Actually, this transition turns into a natural cycle as a person rotates between no-thought and thoughtful moments automatically. This is an odd phenomenon of the real world. And strangely enough, we are all subconsciously aware of it and apply it occasionally, like the times we withdraw from people and society to sort out our life issues in a quiet corner personally. However, we neglect using this device more consciously and frequently for personal growth and defining our spiritualism as well. We do not take advantage of this inner strength within humans, since we do not know how to delve into a state of full awareness. And also because we are afraid of loneliness even for a few hours to achieve a no-thought moment effectively. While the cycles of 'no-thought vs. focused-thoughts' sound quite useful for developing our philosophical principles, they can also help us deal with our stress as well as major life issues and decisions.

Enhancing our level of awareness regarding the process and purpose of no-thought moments enables us to benefit from these experiences more systematically and fully. Managing no-thought experiences is a complementary routine during our search for the path of wisdom and healing our chronic depressions. No wonder we get attracted to gardening, music, artistic expressions, and similar no-thought experiences to reach our inner energy. We choose and pursue these activities and hobbies subconsciously to relax our thoughts and overcome our depression. However, we have not learned to become aware and appreciate the significance of these amazing no-thought experiences and understand why we seek them so intuitively. Therefore, we do not absorb the whole energy that resides in a no-thought experience.

At the same time, moments of full significance also arise when there is a movement of a significant thought—somewhat contrary to Krishnamurti's assertion quoted on page 249. Certain thoughts are significant in themselves and also give significance to our existence when we embrace them. These are thoughts of new creations, thoughts of humanitarian actions and decisions, thoughts about our 'self' and authentic needs, thoughts about our relationships with Nature, and thoughts regarding our souls and existence. These thoughts make life full of significance. All other thoughts are symptoms of life necessities or personal deficiencies and do not particularly give any significance to our being.

Significant thoughts give special significance and meaning to our actions and enrich our lives. In parallel, no-thought moments offer certain experiences that are full of significance and glory by themselves, because they bring us the inner peace and freedom that our souls require away from our daily encounters, thoughts, and efforts to adapt in society.

In essence, life is full of significance in both cases when there is a significant thought and when there is a conscious no-thought moment. Self-actualizers' feelings of completeness, when their significant thoughts generate a new concept, meaning, or value, show how significant life is for them in those moments—and they express it excitedly to the extent that explaining such exotic experiences is possible. Equally important, no-thought moments signify our existence, too, when we closely sense life's beauties and values. These are the major two ways we contact the real world. In fact, these two ways of 'significant life experiences' are related. Our significant thoughts and consequent discoveries lead to special and intensified feelings that push us into no-thought experiences and tranquility. Conversely, we get inspired during no-thought moments, which trigger new significant thoughts. Self-actualizer are more aware of their 'self,' soul, the universe, and the spirituality aspects of life and humans. They are attracted to Nature and simple life experiences that induce no-thought moments regularly. The person with significant thoughts has a special appreciation of no-thought moments and experiences, and seeks those moments with high passion and anticipation.

Overall, significant thoughts and no-thought moments seem to both complement and induce each other—rather than posing a dichotomy, as initially suggested. They are not merely exciting and educational, but also make us wonder if similar wisdoms link the two sides of so many dichotomies humans face, including the ones noted on page 248. It is interesting to test those dichotomies somewhat deeply, too, to unravel their secret linkages, especially humans' growing urges for both dependence and independence! Maybe if we first learned how to be independent individuals with 'self'-control principle and compassion, we could also depend on one another much better!? Maybe! *Another Dichotomy resolved!*

Thoughts and Sufferings

Our psychological needs have become quite complex in the modern world, as we have become both too oversensitive and insensitive at our own perils. Our overactive Egos and Models make hasty judgments regarding events and people, while we try to adapt in society, seek attention and acceptance, etc. Our endless efforts and thoughts feel purposeless and suffocating quite often, while our rising superficial needs are hardly ever satisfied. In fact, our unsatisfied needs stir more suffering and our sufferings instigate more psychological needs (mostly the need for compassion and a loyal companion). Now, everybody demands a lot of attention to go through life and maintain his/her basic sanity at least. When we suffer, we *need* somebody to guide us or something to distract us. Thus, we often end up going out shopping! Or we engage in some kind of mischief, mostly sexual or drugs. In all, our rising needs and sufferings are now the cause and effect of one another!

On the one hand, our needs and sufferings create unsettling thoughts, which stir more illusions and pains. On the other hand, only through our thoughts (valid reasoning) we can restrain our shallow needs and vain sufferings. Only significant thoughts can revamp our niggling thoughts. Friendships and consoling also help a bit, sometimes. Yet, ultimately, we should come to terms with our sufferings on our own through rational thinking. Carl G. Jung says:

"Suffering that is not understood is hard to bear, while on the other hand it is often astounding to see how much a person can endure when he understands the why and wherefore. A philosophical or religious view of the world enables him to do this, and such views prove to be, at the very least, psychic methods of healing if not salvation." Psychology and the East, Art Paperback, 1978, pages 210-211.

Therefore, building our foundation of thoughts seems crucial also for enduring and curing our sufferings by grasping their sources.

On the other hand, J.K. Krishnamurti suggests that a no-thought state can transform suffering into passion and compassion:

"When you suffer, psychologically, remain with it completely without a single movement of thought. Then you will see out of that suffering comes that strange thing called passion. And if you have no passion of that kind you cannot be creative. Out of that suffering comes compassion. And that energy differs totally from the mechanistic energy of thought." Truth and Actuality, Gollancz London, 1977, page 85.

Both Jung's and Krishnamurti's approaches are important for mitigating our sufferings and facing life's hardships. Regardless of our success to attain the high passion Krishnamurti suggests, quieting our minds in a no-thought state periodically gives our brains a break and enriches our spirits. It mitigates the effects of insignificant thoughts and activities overwhelming our lives and causing our sufferings. However, before getting into a no-thought state or meditation, we should detect the causes of our depression and suffering through a thoughtful self-therapy, as explained in Chapters Five and Nine. In that regard, Jung's suggestion is more essential in the long run, at least until we master 'self'-control. In fact, without self-awareness and full consciousness, a no-thought state cannot heal our sufferings permanently. Only significant thoughts and insights with full consciousness provide a platform for gauging and halting insignificant thoughts and desires, which might lead to salvation and solace. We should learn to distinguish between significant and trivial life issues and how to apply the former to defeat the latter. Then, we can assess the nature of our sufferings through wisdom and self-awareness.

Our suffering intensifies when we cannot grasp its source or insist on creating foolish excuses for it. Often we create some imaginary reasons or merely nag to justify our suffering and our feeling of self-pity, perhaps hoping to attract people's sympathy, too. All along, we only increase our suffering for no reason other than the weakness of our convictions and souls, out of laziness in general, or not taking proper actions to elude our self-imposed mental slump. Often our suffering is due to our high expectations from life and people. Sometimes, we doubt or deny the causes of our sufferings and do not admit that our stress is a symptom of a fundamental problem, which can be addressed only through deep self-cleansing and self-awareness. We ignore our inner feelings (conflicts) that signal the vanity of our lifestyles, or quickly turn them into the feelings of defeat and uselessness. Sometimes, we suppress our thoughts and the symptoms of our hidden problems, e.g., neediness or greed. Sometimes, we let some elusive concepts like love and happiness ruin our grasp of reality. When we doubt our inner feelings and instincts about our suffering, we dampen our interest or motivation to adjust our life outlook. Not knowing our reasons for living, or adopting erroneous purposes, raise our sufferings, too. We are often too stubborn to accept the fact that our shallow mentalities are causing all our sufferings, and instead keep pushing the same crooked values and methods that have proven impractical and stressful. A good example is our bizarre approach in marital relationships, while continuing with the same methods and expectations. We cause our own sufferings through our idealism and whimsical thoughts.

We all have personality and psychological defects that create pain and problems for others and us. Our idiosyncrasies differ based on our unique needs, interests, and willpower, of course. Yet, the healing can begin only when we stop doubting the fact that our peculiar defects and obsessions are causing most of our sufferings. We must admit our paranoia and hang-ups, and learn how to view, curb, and cure them. We need commitment and courage to overcome the main barrier, i.e., our denial of the depth of our insecurities and flaws. We have some lingering doubts about our identity and purity, but fail to stop and analyse them.

We must realize that nobody out there in society is going to change to accommodate us and reduce our sufferings. The chance of finding our soul mate or even a reliable companion is quite low, too. The odds would not rise if we keep imagining otherwise or dreaming. We should learn to accept, and live with, all these painful facts of existence. Actually, we must expect the matters to worsen in coming years in terms of both personal eccentricities and social burdens. We must accept the hard reality that no one understands and cares about our sufferings and real needs the way our imaginations desire. Life's hardships would hit us all our lives with very limited, if any, compassion. This is a sad reality to accept easily against the pervasive social fad that pushes positive thinking so recklessly!

Enough sacred clues and warning signals are often around us about our misunderstanding of life, but we just insist on ignoring them. We could at least pause and ponder their possible relevance and significance. Soon, we might even feel their divine messages if we learn their secret meanings over time as our faiths grow. Our anxieties often reflect our inattention or misinterpretation of the sources of our sufferings. We feel helpless, as our efforts do not even bring us relief, let alone lasting happiness. Instead, we feel desolate and lonely, and we get more exhausted and sadder every day with our search for love and happiness. We desire to correct the whole world and make everybody grasp our concerns. We like to inform our friends and family about our hurt feelings, failing relationships, and deprivations. Yet, it seems, the more we try, the less we succeed to communicate with the rest of the world. Our frustrations and anxieties keep rising and we look in the wrong places for remedies. Yet, we refuse to mull over our value systems and adopt a simpler lifestyle. We simply like to believe we have already figured out the meaning and purpose of life. And we seem adamant to stay the course, despite all the pain our lifestyles and mentalities give us daily!

Another problem is that we look externally for the causes of, and the cures for, our sufferings. We look for the faults of people and systems. We ignore that mostly our own idiosyncrasies and persistence to take the perceived world too seriously produce our sufferings. Our ignorance of our inner powers inhibits our real potentialities to manifest and energize our existence. Our primary wisdom and thoughts are lacking a strong foundation. Grasping these concepts is difficult for a person who is trying hard to find a decent job and meet his financial obligations, but keeps failing due to discrimination or job shortages. Still, if he develops the wisdom for exploring the real world, realizes his inner powers, and seeks his few real needs to replace many superficial ones, then perhaps he would stop caring too much about finding a job altogether. He learns to create his own job, accept a lower paying job, or maybe even ponder the possibility (risks) of living without a job if he has the psychological strengths and resources to do so. The bottomline is that *ideally* not even joblessness must become a cause for chronic stress and suffering. It should *ideally* induce more creativity to explore other options and opportunities for living. Then again, the rise in the number of homeless people in modern societies probably indicates that already many people are either too carefree or unlucky to find a simpler lifestyle!

Still, life's inevitable struggles become a bit less painful and overwhelming if we learn to manage our thoughts by adjusting our expectations and attitude. Only we can feel and defeat these self-induced causes of our sufferings. We could learn to ignore those insignificant life events and expectations that enforce our erratic thoughts and sour our spirits. Just a mere acknowledgment of our idiosyncrasies can mitigate the feelings of frustration and helplessness that cause our sufferings. Our awareness can help us subdue these known (deep-rooted) causes of sufferings slowly. Only we can adjust our mentalities and adopt a more practical life philosophy. Revamping our lifestyles and attitudes can subdue our sufferings, and maybe even curb our personal idiosyncrasies and desires causing them.

To build a simple life philosophy and foundation of thoughts upon our personal experiences, we could study the visions and prophecies of great thinkers to make a finer judgment about the meaning of existence. We can weed out the influence of social conditioning on our thoughts and crippling our reasoning power. We can refute senseless common perceptions and norms that have made us so phony. We can resist the temptation of living and thinking for external approval, sexuality, greed, and power—as they are the sources of our sufferings. We can learn to manage our pains and paranoia by pinpointing the insignificant thoughts behind them. We can refuse to comply with superficial standards and expectations propagated in society.

In the end, only our significant thoughts, along with managed no-thought rituals, can alleviate our sufferings somewhat. Most people try to forget their thoughts and themselves for healing. But some of us do the opposite. We strive to think deeper and more philosophical in hopes of finding the meaning of life for healing our psyches. Doing both alternately is usually the best.

Our thoughts soothe or sour our psyches, as we spend hours contemplating our needs, pains, joys, and goals, yet our fantasies and disappointments kill our energies and spirits. We seek all kinds of pleasures to elude reality or subdue our senses of defeat and helplessness, yet we do not learn how to manage our lives and families with humility. Our exhausted brains wander in vain for salvation, since life's realities are getting harsher and sadder. The vicious cycles of dreams and daunting disappointments raise our doubts about the meaning of our routines and the purpose of living altogether, while our existential worries and cynicism stop us from making sensible plans. Still, we cannot give up!

Common Sources of Suffering

In spite of our unique personal reasons and remedies, most of our sufferings have common themes. Learning about the nature of epidemic sufferings in new societies can heighten our awareness and lead to novel and faster solutions. Of course, the intensity and nature of our sufferings vary according to people's sensitivity, insecurities, weaknesses, surroundings, and outlooks as well. Yet, the common sources of mental sufferings usually relate to some kind of personal needs deprivations, such as:

- Financial burdens and worries
- Social pressures, sexual deprivations, and loneliness
- Paranoia, greed, jealousy, spite, etc.
- Psychological defects and chemical reactions in brain
- Personal insecurities and the lack of social recognition
- Personality imbalance due to excessive Ego or Model
- Stress, fears, physical issues, unfulfilled dreams, etc.
- Incomplete or problematic relationships
- Lack of self-actualization and spirituality
- Boredom

Often a bunch of the above sources mix and cause niggling thoughts and sufferings. Their intensity relates to our perceptions (thoughts) about their causes, importance, and effects, however. Remembering this fact and managing our thoughts help mitigate our sufferings, mostly by redefining our long-term life purposes and plans. Saying that our thoughts raise our sufferings does not mean our pains are not real, but merely to stress that solutions are usually found easier if we unlearn the conventional methods and criteria of assessing and resolving our problems and sufferings. We could become more creative in detecting and admitting the roots of our suffering, especially those related to our flaws. We might even find ways of circumventing social inconveniences and pressures. What we see as a problem might not be a real issue at all in a new perspective. Instead, suffering is mostly an emotional reaction, which is hard to quantify or set a rigid criterion about its validity. Usually, our minds assess a recent situation in reference to previous experiences or erroneous expectations (as a criterion) to gauge its effect and intensity. Our conditioned brains do tricky and hasty assessments that instigate the feelings of self-pity and suffering. Therefore, we must discard the patterns and directions of our conditioned minds, and instead, depend on self-awareness to assess the causes and effects of a recent painful experience in a compassionate manner. It is easy to let our self-pity, pride, and spite spoil our mental state and raise our sufferings accordingly.

Instead, we can grow up and curb our sufferings by becoming forgiving and compassionate.

We can do 'self'-therapy or seek the assistance of experts to overcome the depression caused by psychological defects, or merely due to our Ego and Model dominance. All we need is an initial awareness and honest assessment of our basic weaknesses, which cause sufferings for us and others. We can help ourselves if we really believe that some mental *adjustments* are necessary. However, we almost never see our idiosyncrasies or just trust our abilities to overcome them casually. It would not be an easy task even if we ever muster the humility to admit that changing our attitude would be necessary.

Obviously, some sources of sufferings are harder to control. This usually happens when brain chemicals or external forces stir or reinforce our sufferings. For example, financial burdens are always tangible and possibly due to no fault of our own. Even when caused by our basic flaws such as laziness or extravagance, we still suffer, maybe even more, though we could at least try to do something about it. If we are rather realistic, use our potentials properly for making a living, and do not waste our energies on useless habits or ideas, then our financial hardship is probably not our fault. Or when we have difficulty with our relationships, it is often hard to adjust the situation. Often, it is also hard or unwise to get out of them without causing a different kind of suffering for ourselves and others. Still, some alternatives might exist to alleviate these sufferings. Maybe these difficult relationships can be tolerated with some mental and attitude *adjustments* when the situation itself cannot be rectified. Maybe smart, sincere couples can find a more practical relationship model to help them interact easier and more productively, even if it would have to be a rather passive relationship along with partners' higher independence.[*]

---

[*] Relationship models are explained in this author's book, *Relationship Needs, Framework, and Models*. Relationship models should be designed more precisely in the near future, though, in line with finer research.

We can choose a more self-controlled personal life path and develop a sensible mentality away from our lifelong prejudices. A sound foundation of thoughts shows us the need for passion and compassion, flexibility, mental stability, finer beliefs, grasp of 'self,' a sense about the true means of happiness, and a personal philosophy goading a simple lifestyle. During this long process, as our wisdom grows, we might gain some insights about life's mysteries, too, which would be a sacred personal achievement, but never a definite, universal interpretation, because nobody can ever offer a comprehensive meaning for life.

Our sufferings, their causes, and our incessant search for a more peaceful means of living are merely the symptoms of our negligence to strive for self-awareness and the wisdom of a *'self' driven* life. Once we learn to live under the guidance of 'self,' based on the real world's criteria, we would not face as much pain in our lame societies. In the real world, away from our rampant fantasies, our wisdom might defuse the sources of our suffering and confusions. We learn to anticipate the situations, thoughts, and feelings of deprivation that cause suffering. We might even succeed to turn our depression to our advantage in the form of passion and compassion, which are usually the main keys for discovering a few notions about the big mysteries of life as well.

We can readily grasp and fight the common sources of our sufferings. However, some deep causes of sufferings relate to the inner needs' deprivations, including spirituality. This occurs when we neglect to ponder significant matters of life, and instead stress on many nonsensical ambitions, thoughts, desires, plans, actions, and decisions.

Our psyches are burdened by many sources of suffering since childhood, as we grow within, and adopt, many crooked social values. For example, a child may show frustration and suffer when one of his grades is not high enough or if he is not getting enough attention at school from his classmates and teachers. His conventional thinking (and sense of competition) makes him feel inadequate when he feels unappreciated or when he gets any grade lower than 'A,' since he has established it as a criterion for self-worth. These ordinary experiences feel like big failures or rejections to him and valid excuses for suffering. They lead to deep insecurities that might ruin a person's life forever, even as a grown-up well-educated person if he does not learn how to see and cure his misperceptions. Only through some kind of mental restoration and foresight, he might unlearn his addiction to giving the matter of competition so much significance. He needs a finer criterion and practical principles for success in order to avoid so much added sufferings all his life. Instead, many of us absorb and use a lifetime the crude criteria for success and self-worth spread in modern societies so naively. Especially, competition has now become a devastating habit in line with people's rising arrogance. Therefore, our seeming failures damage our psyches and turn into permanent quirks we cannot avoid or repair easily.

A fundamental cause of suffering is loneliness. It hurts many of us all by itself, even when we are only slightly ignored or lonely just a few hours. We are simply not prepared to bear even short loneliness, or maybe even the impression of it. Of course, many options exist these days for groups or individuals to work together to alleviate their loneliness pains. Still, learning about the positive side of loneliness can reduce our fears of it, too, at least partly. During our 'no-thought' experiences, we learn how those moments of solitude (loneliness) could be relaxing, educational, peaceful, and maybe even spiritual. Surely, loneliness on a long-term basis is more complex than occasional ones. Still, studying and creating no-thought experiences can help mitigate loneliness sufferings, learn some self-reliance, and perhaps induce higher consciousness along with exceptionally divine feelings.

The sacred energy and passion that a no-thought experience or loneliness creates can actually fulfil our higher personal needs, such as self-actualization and spiritualism, which automatically generate tranquility and a better sense of our being. During such divine moments and conditions, we can create beautiful thoughts and objects along with divine sentiments that override the pain of loneliness many folds. The only problem is that our fears and conventional view of loneliness do not let us test and appreciate the merits of solitude. We have now become desperately attached to things and other people, thus built this tremendous paranoia and phobia about loneliness. However, in the real world we are actually alone and stay lonely, even if we have a house full of friends and family.

The importance of socializing aside, recognizing the merits of solitude early on in our lives is also vital for preparing ourselves for the high chance of even our families disappointing us at worst conditions when we need their support. Learning the art and privileges of solitude is actually becoming essential now, since both living and family relationships are getting too cumbersome. More importantly, the fear of loneliness can be cured only by discovering the joy of 'self'-fulfilling experiences that erupt only from loneliness and are extremely beautiful and full of passion.

Sufferings due to boredom relate to a lack of vision or passion to explore one's innate potentialities and divine needs, including soul-searching and soul-evoking adventures. Boredom reflects our negligence to find our niche and developing it. We all have some hidden potentials that press us subconsciously to emerge. They demand our attention or else we feel unfulfilled and empty. Exploring and nurturing our potentialities is tough, however, as it requires plenty of varied sacrifices, hard work, and patience, plus an incentive to study the issues raised in this trilogy about Self and self-awareness. Yet, once developed, our fine potentialities provide a chance for self-growth and 'self'-actualization, which are the two best antidotes for sufferings. These divine experiences are just for inner fulfillment with no other ulterior motives. They fill our lives with joy and creative energy, which would subdue our stress and banal sufferings due to boredom.

If our suffering relates to greed and jealousy, then it should be obvious how we might at least try to get rid of it. Why do we continue to look for more of the same things, which we cannot consume in our lifetime anyway, is difficult to grasp. How much wealth and power is enough? We can only ask our Egos! These basic insights simply show the absence of a reliable foundation of thoughts in society to guide our lives and mitigate our sufferings.

CHAPTER TEN
Life and Self

Surely, a solid foundation of thoughts is the engine that drives our decisions and actions in the journey of life. During this confusing journey, we follow a customary path loaded with social norms and values, which we may call 'human life's structure.'

Human Life's Structure

We have different lives and destinies. Yet, within the large scale of the universe, we all travel the same journey and reach the same destination. Like other species, we have a wide range of strengths and weaknesses, special habits, life expectancies, defence mechanisms, certain habitats, and existential thoughts, etc. Our modern idealism and fairly high intelligence goads our drive for individualism and a variety of goals and lifestyles. Yet, a natural process defines the path of our existence. Both the natural laws (our instincts) and social order push us to chase a rather tedious path of life hypnotically. While driven by our odd genetics, we walk within certain social parameters uniformly rather blindly. After all, we are still just one minute part of the universe, despite our big Egos, amazing initiatives, all the skyscrapers we can build, and the amazing technologies we have mastered.

Like a tree that has roots, a trunk, branches and fruits, the structure of human life is also constructed around a *foundation, purposes, activities, and outcome* during three life phases. In the first phase, we prepare ourselves for the life that lies ahead of us. We spread our roots and build our strengths and primary wisdom to get ready for the challenging and demanding phases awaiting us. In the second phase, we develop our careers and family lives, which, similar to the trunk of a tree, comprise the main body or purpose of our lives. In the final phase, we expect to reap the fruits of a lifetime of efforts and growth. This common vision and approach to life feels natural to everybody. But are our thoughts' foundations, life purposes, activities, and outcomes sensible for a thinking human or are we still living soullessly like a tree?

During these rather distinct life phases, we do similar things to prepare ourselves to live, multiply, raise our offspring, and die. In the process, we hope to satisfy our physical and psychological needs, both the instinctual ones and those we have developed artificially throughout the history. We have created things and thoughts that we believe are useful to us, although we can never be sure about that. We have already demonstrated how some of our demented thoughts make us destroy our cultures and lives. We kill each other directly, or engage in life activities that would eventually destroy our societies and humanity.

Nonetheless, all these human attributes have evolved into a peculiar life structure based on our perceptions of our identities and needs and now *it* directs us coldly within globally predefined parameters, although some of us are richer or happier. Within this ordained structure, everybody participates in social processes and routines, instinctually or habitually, and pursues similar ambitions as a matter of social coexistence. We entertain familiar thoughts and follow similar lifestyles to survive within this structure. This framework also imposes a rather fixed mentality and a common set of goals for us to follow, which demand a handful of major decisions along with plenty of doubts and dilemmas that we must wrestle with during the three distinct life phases.

This is what we can call the structure of human life. We just try to adapt ourselves to this bizarre human creation and plough on. However, does this life structure make any real sense? How sensible following the guidelines of this shallow life structure is? Is it possible to build a sensible foundation of thoughts and life philosophy in this environment, and if yes how? We must answer these questions to our 'self' and soul.

At the same time, understanding the structure of human life is significant for identifying the purposes of the main decisions and plans needed in life. The intention is not to generalize life. Like a tree that has many branches signifying its uniqueness somehow, individuals' distinctive dimensions are interesting by themselves. They influence human progress, preferences, and mentalities in making decisions and behaving. Our decisions and actions vary, since we see the same things differently, and since we judge a situation or person according to our personalities and beliefs. However, despite our differences in judgment, values, decisions and actions, we are forced to follow the same journey—a general life structure *supposedly* fitting our social values and culture. This life structure reflects the basic commonality of human thoughts and actions in pursuit of their personal goals, for the purpose of survival, adaptation, and receiving other people's approval and cooperation. Our needs and efforts to adapt produce a uniform structure for humanity, although its mechanisms have become dysfunctional, nowadays. Sadly, this horrific structure is the best our collective visions and efforts have been capable of building. What we humans have created and call civilization, nowadays, has actually become a big source of human suffering.

We cannot challenge this inevitable truth about humans' life and their perceptions too much. However, we cannot dismiss our innocence and ignorance for following this life structure rather unconsciously according to shoddy facts and myths surrounding us. We have learned certain things about life and ourselves, but the unknown reality is getting wider in scope and damaging our personal lives and mental health significantly. We know that our physics (and existence) is only a by-product of an accident, when one *particular* sperm luckily finds its way to a *particular* ovary in a special moment. But our souls? We do not know where it comes from and where it returns to, if anywhere at all. As long as our physics is healthy and conscious, we build a personality and a set of characteristics that contain both our physics and soul. Some of us learn better how to envision and combine these two features of humanness—physique and soul—, whereas most people only mingle in the perceived world at the physical level with no time or chance to enrich their spirits despite their religious rituals.

Analysing the features of our prevalent life structure is useful for building our foundation of thoughts, while realizing the main sources of our suffering. Thus, Volume III studies humans' life structure, its characteristics, and the way we helplessly follow its guidelines rather robotically. Many questions can be raised about the validity of this structure and our hypnotic attachment to it. At the end, we may still believe that it provides the best option for living in spite of our inability to justify its values and purposes. However, by learning something about this dull life structure, we might be able to gauge and change at least a few aspects of it for ourselves in order to get a bit more sense about our being per se. Most of us are hoping to figure out the meanings of our activities and ambitions within this frivolous life structure when we say we want to 'find the meaning of life.' Chapter Two's discussions and Appendix A on Page 88 has probably explained some of these vital enquiries about humanity.

Life's Major Decisions

Most decisions relate to our reflexes, such as walking, observing, listening, etc. They consist mostly of crude, subconscious habits with no substantive thoughts. The second group of our decisions requires some thinking, yet still relate to mundane duties of living, such as cooking, eating, shopping, going on a vacation, choosing a movie, etc. They recur regularly within the same thought frame.

These two groups of decisions have no long-term effects on our lives, besides fulfilling our basic needs and keeping us alive. As long as we stay rational, their outcomes are not too consequential for us or humanity. A wrong choice would not change the course of our lives.

The third group, however, contains high risks and requires conscious, significant thoughts. These major life decisions are essential due to their severe, lasting impacts on our welfare and happiness. They involve other people and external factors that we cannot control. Thus, their outcomes are quite unpredictable, yet affect the quality of our lives seriously. They change one's life direction and they might cause lifelong agonies and depression. Indeed, they often result in rather irreversible entrapments (e.g., a bad marriage) or the loss of precious opportunities (e.g., about our career plans).

The problem is that we often fail to recognize the importance of our major decisions until it is too late and we face many deep disappointments and regrets. We do not know the right factors and do not realize the gravity of our decisions when we should make a good judgment, especially when some sort of infatuation infects us. Instead, we choose to be optimistic and adventurous. We just get sloppy or merely ignore the potential risks, especially when we do not have a proper decision criterion and a valid life philosophy to support our analyses. To measure the risks, we follow almost the same basic, shallow approach we apply to our mundane decisions, except perhaps we get more obsessed with some misleading factors (e.g., sexual attraction) that we find most urgent and valid all of a sudden. Our idealism, emotions, fears, genetic qualities, personality, and other reasons, make us lose our alertness, patience, and sensitivity to distinguish the long-term effects of some decisions. For the same reasons, in fact, we often emphasize on wrong factors (excuses) naively when making our major life decisions. Often our decision criteria are superficial and influenced by the perceived world's idealism, e.g., a chance for happiness, success, or having a companion. Most of us are emotional, driven by our sexual urges, and 'live in the now' too much already. We are lured by positive thinking propagandas. We are too absorbed in our illusions and phony personalities to grasp life essentialities or the importance of certain life-changing decisions. For example, when we marry a person for his/her money, infatuation, or other superficial reasons, we get ourselves entangled in a situation with high potential for disaster.

Sometimes, we ignore or casually undermine the risks and hope for the best, instead of the worst; or we assume that dealing with the consequences later, if necessary, would not be too hard. We cannot anticipate how differently we would feel and think in the future and what new criteria would all of a sudden make us look foolish regarding our past sloppy decisions. We are usually obsessed with our lousy justifications and false assessments, so we also ignore everybody else's advice, or our subtle inner voices that attempt to caution us. We simply ignore what might happen later, as long as we get something we crave so badly now, e.g., a companion or a taste of love. Laziness is another major factor for our indecisions or ignoring the risks of our emotional or hasty decisions today.

Another factor for our sloppiness towards major life decisions is that people interpret life's essentialities differently according to their personalities, ambitions, and outlooks. Some pursue life for pleasures only, some seek power per se, some stress on wealth accumulation, some crave constant approval and love, and some become stoics or idealists. Each group has its own standard of 'essentiality' for similar decisions, though they have a somewhat similar understanding of the overall nature of social structure and its perils in line with new societies' pervasive evils. In all, people have very peculiar life outlooks and insecurities that make them rather careless with their important life-changing decisions.

At the same time, the youths' frustration with social chaos is another (somewhat justified) reason for their reckless decisions and behaviour. TV shows like American Idol reveal the vanity of social structure and youths' struggles to fit in. Their naiveté and lack of preparation for facing the sad reality of our shoddy culture is astonishing and worrisome. It is disheartening to watch the huge wave of dreamers coming for audition and to hear so many of them insisting that singing and fame are their only goals with no plan B for their futures. That is their final decision! At least that is what they are saying now!

The main point is that unless we plan our lives extra carefully, nowadays, we must prepare ourselves for major disappointments and suffering throughout our lives, although eluding life's painful features is mostly impossible, anyway. We normally have little appreciation of major life decisions in terms of their complexity, or how deeply they can spoil our lives, usually forever. We do not know we are too vulnerable and bound to make big mistakes in today's chaotic social environment. Thus, we create all kinds of self-induced causes for a lifelong suffering.

Even when we realize the deep lifetime effects of certain life decisions, decision-making process and requirements are too complex all by themselves, nowadays, as explained in Chapter Sixteen of Volume II. Even governments and corporations have major difficulty in making proper decisions in the present social structure. They do many kinds of feasibility studies for business purposes based on economic and financial data and forecasting algorithms, yet the world economy is in such disarray. Even these sophisticated economic models and studies have proven to be full of flaws and used only for justifying governments' agendas and giving us an impression about officials' knowledge and efforts to do the right things. Some of our personal decisions have much severer consequences on our lives, but are even less analysable than economic data, while we do not have proper decision criteria or models to aid us, either. Instead, too many emotional factors always interfere with major personal decisions both before and after we take an action, as we lose the control of many factors and people involved in the implementation of our decisions.

Nevertheless, before making any major decision, we should predict and remember its risks and prepare ourselves to face even the worst possible consequence. As a basic example, someone quits his job to accept another one, without doubting the chance of not being happy in the new job. He is either naive to think that things would definitely work out as he plans, or losing the new job and looking for a third one is not of a major consequence to him. If he is confident to find another job quickly, then, of course, the consequences of quitting his present job is not substantial. In this particular case, the decision feels simple, assuming his view of the future events and circumstances hold true. However, even when we feel certain about the outcome, still things often turn out differently. Our decision criteria and social circumstances often change fast frequently without any prior indication. Therefore, being too optimistic or adventurous might not be a good strategy for many people. The gravity of some decisions, e.g., choosing our prospective spouse, is even clearer, relative to the previous example about a job. Again, trusting our naïve views of social systems or people's promises is a personal responsibility. Thus, we should only blame ourselves if we are not careful and smart at the outset before making our major life decisions. That is how we often cause our self-induced sufferings.

Despite the risks of procrastination and looking indecisive, it is rational to take our time, maybe even weeks, months, or even longer, to make some decisions that we might not even classify as a major life decision normally. Simply some decisions' nature, sensitivity, or complexity needs much more thinking and analysis before we finally feel ready to make those decisions. We should feel comfortable to do so without letting our own or someone else's pressures or impatience affect our timing unduly.

Naturally, we all usually sense these basic requirements for planning our lives and the importance of major decisions in life. However, we do not scrutinize on them seriously with enough patience or we let our emotions or insecurities make us ignore their importance. Volume III of this trilogy reviews some of the common major life decisions due to their significant risks and impacts on the quality of one's life. Nevertheless, this trilogy's discussions offer a long list of 'major decisions' we must make, as we face major dilemmas about:

- The main purpose of life in relation to our purposes for living.
- Means of capturing happiness and peace (which most likely demands the skill to master a stoic sense of contentment.)
- Our values, beliefs, and principles.
- How to manage our thoughts and stir no-thought moments.
- Our authentic personal needs and how to go about satisfying them, while curbing our superficial needs.
- Our long-term objectives and a plan to achieve them.
- The kind of life philosophy that fits our personalities, needs, and plans.
- The risk oriented opportunities and timing of them.
- Our real potentialities and limitations.
- Our inner-strengths, identities, and personalities.
- How to monitor our three personality aspects and develop our 'self'-control.
- The career we should choose.
- The means and criteria to choose a spouse.
- Having children or not, how to nurture them, and what our role should be.
- Gaining our financial senses and living within our limits.
- Etc.

The above decisions and actions also raise many fundamental questions such as the followings:

- Why do we feel, act, and choose in certain ways?
- Why do we educate ourselves or learn things?
- Why do we need friends and companionship?
- Why do we work?
- What are the sources of our fulfilments?
- What are our financial resources?

- How should we set our life priorities and expectations?
- How do we feel about, and handle, our relationships with both people and Nature?
- Etc.

We ponder the above topics regularly, but only superficially within the context of our mundane busy lives. They appear to surge from our subconscious mind, more in the form of an inner voice (or conscience) that demands practical and philosophical answers. Actually, these questions reflect the inherent urgency of 'life' and 'self' decisions in some combination, depending on how deeply we view them or act upon them. We cannot avoid them even if we are the most pragmatic 'life' oriented persons. These questions, and our corresponding decisions and actions, inherently construct the structure of life. We face them regardless of our understanding of our inner needs and the soundness of our foundation of thoughts. Still, most of us do not pause enough to contemplate these life-changing topics in some depth in relation to our purposes of living and for being a better person. Volume II of this trilogy discusses 'self' decisions and Volume III deals with 'life' questions and decisions in some detail.

'Life' and 'Self' Decisions

According to this book's discussions, two categories of decisions are essential for humans: 1) Those needed for fulfilling our socio-economic needs and raising our families. Let us call them 'life' decisions. 2) Those related to our subtle drive to understand our inner needs, identities, and spiritualism. Let us call them 'self' decisions. In this regard, we feel a subtle urge to grasp our being, build and pursue a sound life philosophy in line with a sensible foundation of thoughts, make fine long-term plans, and maintain high 'self'-awareness and 'self'-control. The goal is to satisfy our divine self-actualization needs by learning more about our 'self.'

To people who do not grasp, or care to realize, the essence of 'self' and its unique needs, no decision about such matters seem necessary, let alone considering them 'essential.' This majority in society has no patience or interest in these kinds of questions and efforts. Therefore, they concentrate solely on 'life' decisions, i.e., socioeconomic matters and relationships. Even then, they simply follow the crowd and common criteria to make their decisions, instead of thinking outside the box to consider the validities of their decisions and lifestyles personally. On the other hand, for the minority who believes in validating their 'self' and leading a 'self'-controlled life as a crucial guide and philosophy, stressing merely on socioeconomic decisions and actions seems ridiculous. They believe the other group is not only missing the real meaning of life, but also causing their own agonies and stress merely out of their arrogance and naivety—not to mention their higher share of irresponsibility for causing the chaos for humanity.

For a prudent person, nevertheless, it feels essential to at least understand the implications of, and relations between, 'life' and 'self' decisions and routines. We need this basic awareness to stir some degree of harmony between social adaptation and personal enlightenment. It is hard to imagine how we can go through life without a notion of 'self' included in our foundation of thoughts to support our decisions and actions. In fact, personal problems and social pains seem to be the outcome of our shortsightedness, and the lack of a good foundation of thoughts and 'self'-control. Yet, social passivity about 'self' is the most popular option these days even for those allegedly religious or spiritual. Thus, many of us continue our lives in vain without understanding our reasons for living and suffering.

On the other hand, only a tiny group can concentrate solely on 'self' questions and decisions just for self-awareness and divinity, e.g., the way monks and sages live. They gather the strengths and courage to break away from the mainstream and pursue seclusion and enlightenment as their sole path of life. Naturally, this weird mentality and routine feels impractical to most people, so we do not spend much time explaining it.

At best, grasping a basic sense of 'self' would suffice to most of us. We just hope to combine the benefits and wisdom of both 'life' and 'self' decisions for building our faiths and attaining a high level of personal fulfilment and peace as a modest human without relying on religions. At least, we might be able to regain a relative sense of freedom and mitigate our sufferings. At this middle ground, we can learn about ourselves and our life options without abandoning much of our regular life commitments and pleasures. Still, the wisdom we might earn from even basic 'self' decisions and routines, e.g., by learning humility, would also help our social life. 'Self' oriented and 'self' driven decisions always enrich our lives and boost the quality of our 'life' decisions. But only rounded 'life' decisions might help our neglected 'self.'

The 'Self' and 'Life' Impasse

Ironically, 'life' and 'self' appear like two conflicting forces that drive the magical realm of human existence. The more we stress on 'life,' even as a necessity for survival, the more we lose sight of our 'self,' which reflects our identity and sense of being. We can say, 'life makes us lose hold of ourselves.' Conversely, 'self' requires letting go of 'life' vastly, at least in the form we perceive and live it only based on our desires and ambitions. Our struggles to find 'self' within 'life' (or 'life' within 'self') only increase our inner conflicts and we get more impatient and frustrated with people and ourselves. All along, both 'life' and 'self' manifest as abstract mysteries that we can never decipher, let alone integrate. We try hard to find a meaning for life at least. However, it just persists to remain a mystery, like a vague notion only teasing and confusing us. We feel the same way about 'self,' too, that seems to be an even more ambiguous concept than 'life' beyond our reach. However, we know that both 'life' and 'self' are real, as inherent features of human existence, although we seem unable to define or find them. We suspect 'life' would reveal its true meaning only if we find our 'self.' And we suspect 'self' would emerge only within the context of a divine, meaningful life, which is also simple, so unlike humans' present lifestyles. These plausible hypotheses suggest that 'life' and 'self' are actually complementary (rather than conflicting) forces for signifying human existence. They are prerequisites of each other and only together reveal their own particular meanings and significance. Only together, they pervade the fine essence of an enlightened human as well as life's eluding meaning and value. It appears that understanding 'life' and 'self' together might give us the best opportunity to outline our life path and minimize our suffering.

Luckily, many of us believe that our curiosity and struggles to find life and self are quite justified and maybe even a divine urge. Many clues suggest that our seemingly vain attempts to find the essence of our existence, the 'self,' within 'life' is not a naïve adventure or ambitious, but rather an instinctual drive that might be the key to our salvation. And our seemingly futile struggle to discover the essence of 'life' within 'self,' the free being, is not a passing romanticism, but rather a natural calling.

This intricate paradox boggles our minds a lifetime, too, while we also hope to make the right decisions for living, at least for stopping our naive or egotistical choices that cause us too much suffering. It gets difficult to build a reliable life philosophy when we seem to have difficulty understanding even the meanings and contents of life and self as two main pillars and puzzles in the realm of our mysterious existence. Still, despite this paradoxical barrier, we must find a means of developing a solid personality and foundation of thoughts for making those major life decisions listed on pages 273-274. In fact, the difficulty of making such vital decisions stems from our failure to figure out, or actively seek, the meanings of life and self together at some basic level at least. After all, it seems very difficult for most of us to align 'life' (our tortuous worldly desires) with 'self' (our soothing spiritual drives).

Ultimately, the secret for finding a relative peace of mind and happiness lies in our ability to build a flexible mentality, in which both 'life' and 'self' choices are simultaneously and continuously interactive, and justifiable, too. Both 'life' and 'self' orientations are important within the structure of human life and require our parallel scrutiny and proper decisions. As noted, however, our emphasis on 'life' decisions, has just limited our ability to bring meaning and serenity to our daily routines and grasp our 'self.' Anyway, a proper mix of 'life' and 'self' decisions can enrich our lives and reduce our sufferings.

The Substance of 'Self' and 'Life' Decisions

Our occasional encounters with spirituality urges, while enduring our mundane lives, might raise our interest for 'self' awareness and 'self' growth. This simply means making our life decisions more based on non-materialistic values. For example, we might consider devoting a big part of our lives to humanitarian causes. These moments of awakening happen to many people. Some pause and cherish those experiences—mostly for soothing their souls and building the foundation of their thoughts in line with a celestial philosophy that can help them learn more about their essence and 'self.' They discover new stuff about themselves and their inner strengths every day. They might even take these signs seriously as a divine guide to explore the seven basic elements of 'self,' which are discussed in Chapter Thirteen of Volume II. This gives them a chance to explore the role of their spirits in both the real world and our soulless societies. Still, most of us bypass these callings fast impatiently, or do not follow them up seriously. Thus, we never explore the alternatives to our mundane lives. We continue to suffer a lifetime when we never get a chance to discover who we really are and free our souls.

For those devoted to 'self' and seeking a profound foundation of thoughts, the bigger challenge is to transform those thoughts into practical actions for humanitarian benefits. We might have been successful in preparing a sense of 'self' commitment and some kind of foundation of thoughts to guide us through life. Yet, when it comes to act upon our commitments or convictions, we fall short of our objectives and standards. When the time comes for us to act with integrity, we fail to adhere to our principles and 'self'-control discipline We are lured by money, love, pleasures, greed, sex, and other 'life' distractions, as seemingly precious privileges of living that overwhelm our profound commitments and character. Or we just get lazy in pursuing our objectives and beliefs sometimes. Or we lose our patience and conviction.

For many reasons, we often fail to implement the ideals and principles we had chosen for building our foundation of thoughts. This damages our self-image when we take this failure as a sign of our irreparable personal weakness. We give up our spiritual vision of 'self' and commitment to grasp the depth of our being. We adopt a phony or passive/aggressive personality just to live.

Realistically, we do not know how to handle the inner voices and questions circling in our heads about life and 'self', especially if we are busy with our daily obligations or when the messages contradict our lifestyles and values. However, with patience and practice, we can learn to absorb these messages and give a benefit of a doubt to the possibility of a more serene life outside the prevalent social structure.

Sadly, the majority of us fail, as we look for a quick solution and salvation, or at least a sign of divine wisdom, when we have not even learned how to do a basic self-analysis, be humble, or create a 'no-thought' experience for ourselves to meditate and get a better sense of our 'self.' The means of facing these obstacles to boost our spirits is addressed in Volume II of this trilogy.

Transcending to the real world sphere and realizing our 'self' occur gradually, of course, by learning the basics first to mature, and then by getting deeper into our unconscious mind and 'self.' During this slow process of transcendence to a new realm and realizations, we learn more about our true identity, including our weaknesses and potentialities. Only through sacrifice, positive doubts, humility, and wisdom, we might climb up the mountain of the truth slowly and reach the summit. Only through patience and faith, we can achieve selfhood and feel the outcomes of our meditations and beliefs. Nobody can leap beyond his/her *primary wisdom* (which also evolves slowly) for a higher vision of life—especially not by drugs, artificial stimuli, or raw positive thinking.

CHAPTER ELEVEN
Actions and Adjustments

Despite a subliminal urge to discover 'life' and 'self' all our lives, we only focus on managing our strenuous and showy lifestyles. We strive to survive and possibly be happy by being friendly and making ourselves popular around people. Of course, deep down, we dream that our actions and life would have some meaning and value eventually as well.

Still, the purpose of our endless struggles often feels doubtful. Even our sensible decisions and actions often lead to no *tangible* outcome, if not disasters and disappointments. It hurts, especially, when we cannot find peace with others and within ourselves after making so many tough, heroic adjustments in our mentalities and attitudes. Especially our family and friends' lack of sincerity feels so unsettling, if not insulting. Often, it feels like we are staggering on a wobbly path of life, hoping for some kind of miracle and enlightenment to save our souls or die in peace gracefully at least. We wonder whose fault it is that we do not get the right results from all the efforts we extend to find basic peace at least.

With such busy, agitated state of mind, our eccentricities and insecurities also grow, while our personalities form around some naïve beliefs and expectations from 'life' with little zeal for 'self' realization. We simply become more needy and greedy, pamper our Model and Ego in hopes of capturing happiness and success, and wait for some rewards. Sometimes, we stop and gauge the value of our diligent actions and plans to no avail. We doubt our competence and decision-making ability—now or when we had had a chance to make better life plans and maybe grasp our 'self' better. We might even admit our normal sloppiness and naiveté in handling life's challenges.

In all, we blame one or a mix of, 1) social disorder, 2) destiny, and 3) personal negligence for our failures. The way we see and handle these three likely bottlenecks also affect our plans lives. Accordingly, discussing them in this chapter might enhance our awareness and decision-making, which have been essential topics of this trilogy, after all.

1. Social Disorder

We face and rely on many people with odd personalities daily, especially at work and in our families. Ironically, most of life's major decisions and actions need the participation or knowledge of other people. Thus, we are highly at the mercy of society and people when everybody is so self-centred and impatient, thanks to materialism killing morality and compassion. Social gullibility and malice have accelerated as well, and the situation would only deteriorate due to the vanity of social values and structure. Thus, even when we plan our lives and take timely actions to secure our futures, a good chance exists that people, and social disorder in general, sabotage our efforts either intentionally or ignorantly.

Our roles and options for coping in society and organizations are addressed in Volume III of this trilogy, while reading the seven elements of 'self' in Chapter Thirteen of Vol. II is useful, too, especially the section about the 'Individualism' element.

Sadly, we cannot avoid people's interferences and all the bad information in society that affects our lives somehow, including our jobs, marriages, and investments. Thus, the need for vigilance about the severe impacts of this rising general social disorder has placed a huge burden on our psyches. Then, we must also ensure our minds and actions are not infected and we have not become an advocate of this social epidemic, e.g., as a pushy salesperson selling useless stuff to people. Our efforts for ultra consciousness, and cynicism to curb the influence and pressures of these social barriers and chaos, have become too exhausting and depressing. Now, this vigilance is an added responsibility for us for running a simple life, not losing our integrity and identity, and preventing our 'self' from being shattered within this vile social structure.

2. Destiny

Our instincts and commonsense drive us to play an active role in forming our future. Yet, we realize that no matter how diligently we make proper plans and decisions to endure the tyrannies of the rising social chaos, the outcomes of our decisions and actions often remain beyond our control. Sometimes, things keep going wrong no matter how hard we plan and decide. And sometimes things happen in our favour despite our silly decisions. Therefore, the question is, "Is destiny something we can, i) depend on at all, or ii) affect even slightly with our actions and decisions, e.g., when we perform all kinds of analyses and make diligent, timely decisions for living well and happy?"

We all have felt the existence of some strange (maybe even playful) power that either blesses or punishes us for no apparent reason, although sometimes we feel the immense wisdom behind the bizarre course of events leading to amazing outcomes. While we attribute these weird coincidences merely to the randomness of the universe or people's superstitions, some of us cannot stop feeling that something more fundamental might lie behind them.

So, are we at the mercy of destiny, or we should rely on, and blame, only ourselves for the outcomes of our major decisions? Should we merely try to do our best, but then leave everything to destiny? 'Just take the risk and do not worry,' could be one type of personal life philosophy. If the risks of our major decisions are unpredictable and unanalysable, then what is the point of trying so hard to measure or even fuss about some imaginary outcomes too much? Should we admit our severe limitations for building our lives (and fates) or believe in having full control of things; or something between these two extremes? Does either fate or faith, or a divine mix of them, play any role in any of these scenarios?

The dilemma we are facing is that either our perception of fate is naïve, or our efforts to plan and make our major life decisions diligently is futile—unless fate and personal efforts are connected based on some sacred principles beyond human comprehension!

These types of spiritual curiosities erupt, as we try to build our fundamental thoughts and life philosophies. They feel relevant for exploring our doubts and dilemmas, including the role of destiny, and developing a viable personal belief system. How much faith we should have in fate is a vital personal decision, yet it must also constitute a major chapter in itself when we write our unique life philosophy. Overall, however, we should always remember that regardless of the type of our life philosophy, the outcomes of our major life decisions could potentially destroy our lives forever—or conversely, guarantee a tranquil existence. And that we would feel (and must admit) the ultimate responsibility and guilt for not being proactive enough in our decision making efforts.

Mostly, we can always say that, "Since the consequences of major decisions and actions always remain uncontrollable, we all need *a meticulous foundation of thoughts* even more to gauge our decisions wisely in the first place." This does not merely suggest that we should be more thoughtful or diligent in analyzing things. Rather, it implies that, i) the format of our life philosophy and foundation of thoughts should be well-planned and quite useful for supporting our major decisions, and ii) we must learn to cope with the potential risks associated with our beliefs and decisions, including our choice of a life path and philosophy as well as the depth of our faith. This means that the foundation our thoughts must also enable us boost our spirits for facing our likely failures and stressful calamities rather patiently and graciously with some degree of divine resignation. This well-construed foundation of our thoughts must particularly align 'life' and 'self' requirements delicately.

Actually, it seems many (often conflicting) factors should be aligned within our foundation of thoughts—including spirituality mixed with the likely role of destiny, for building a sensible life philosophy and making sounder decisions towards some likely ('self' oriented) means of happiness. We should just try to fathom what really matters at the end and not only today. We can set our priorities around those divine values and thoughts that become relevant in the third phase of our lives when arrogance and spite do not hinder our judgments as much as they do during youth.

Then again, some people might argue, rather sensibly, "Why should I even believe I'd reach the third phase of my life? I might die tomorrow. Let's be happy now." Anyway, the crucial point is that the way we often assess the consequences of life's significant decisions cannot be, and would not follow, the same criteria we use for mundane decisions. And those criteria most likely do not seem relevant and important to us later, either, when (and if) we reach the latter phases of life.* Therefore, for this reason alone, we cannot just 'live in the now,' or based on the perceived world values and criteria per se. Instead, we should apply the criteria that would make sense in the third phase, which are also usually more in line with humans' authentic needs within the context of the real world's values. We can use 'self'-control to mitigate our Ego and Model's obsessions for social compliance and making life's major decisions merely based on materialism and rivalry. It would also be wise and more prudent to believe in reaching the third phase of our lives. If we live healthy, most of us should face the reality and pains of existence in all three life phases. Actually, the foundation of our thoughts must stress on this perspective to force us plan our lives for all three phases on a proactive life path.

---

* Three life phases and 'Forward Thinking' are further elaborated in the next chapter beyond the preliminary discussions on pages 235-7.

3. Personal Negligence

Personal negligence causes most life failures for many reasons, including our shoddy perceptions of social disorder and destiny. Our personalities, actions, and life plans are to blame, while we are also lazy or naïve about social chaos and peoples' intentions, or ignore 'self'-awareness as a basis for mental growth. Personal negligence also manifests in our low morality or interest to adjust our attitudes and mentalities to get along with others easier. Thus, the rest of this chapter discusses the topic of personal negligence.

Of course, the idealistic suggestions in this chapter about the benefits of gauging both our 'negligence' and 'ignorance' do not impress, or help, people who are genetically malicious or turned into ardent villains and narcissists. These sick people never grasp their idiocy or the meaning of morality, never mind caring about the harm they are causing humanity besides fooling themselves. Yet, the rest of us have a capacity to adjust in some ways in order to think and act somewhat more productively and peacefully for personal sake at least. We just need an incentive to begin thinking in the right direction for personal and social salvation.

The Morality of Our Actions

The fact that our actions and reactions harm others and us is not a big surprise considering humans' crooked nature. So much direr is our reluctance to admit and make up for our malicious actions, especially if they have harmed others. It would have not been too much of a crime, either, had our actions been mostly due to our mistakes or innate ignorance. Yet, the growing fad for intentional arrogance and persistence for idiocy reveal the depth of genetic deformity and malice so endemic now. People's rampant show of *rather deliberate* inferiority beyond average humans' evil is now just shameful and pitiful. It is also a huge 'personal negligence.'

We may even have valuable thoughts and intentions on some occasions, yet our shaky characters prevent us from turning them into worthwhile decisions and actions. A simple example is our political leaders' shallow promises to do all sorts of services for the desperate public (which are precious thoughts and intentions), but they eventually fail to act honestly, mostly for safeguarding their profitable political careers. Even when they start with good intentions to help people, their actions become mostly self-serving with so little selfless motives. They only stir more desperation and doubts in society when they lie, manipulate voters with their luring propagandas and empty promises, and abuse democracy. Even worse, we elect them to save a few dollars on our taxes perhaps, instead of worrying about so much corruption and the collapse of the entire social system in a few decades.

When most leaders all over the world behave so greedily and irresponsibly, as puppets and agents of conglomerates, how can anybody expect the rest of us, we commoners, ever think and act a bit more honestly and compassionately for our own sakes and possibly saving the doomed destiny of humanity, too? We have difficulty transforming even our random significant thoughts into actions, as it requires certain personal qualities, such as integrity, principles, sacrifice, confidence, and perseverance, which many of us have lost during our social encounters. After all, plenty of character and morality is needed to refuse the social incentives for corruption, and instead focus on some worthy thoughts, plans, and actions that require selfless mentality and leadership.

Staying vigilant about our negligence and mistakes is tough, but we can learn to do so gradually by reflecting on our actions and relationships' shortfalls consciously and conscientiously. If only we stop being so self-centred and needy, we get a chance to grow our self-awareness and morality, especially when we notice how badly we are hurting others. We might at least stop being so spiteful, which has been hurting us personally the most, anyway.

Most importantly, gauging the morality and motives behind our actions and reactions can help us learn a lot about ourselves as lost souls in confusing, chaotic societies, and the way we see and discharge our social responsibilities. We could do so at least for keeping our own sanity. It always pays off, personally at least, to become a bit ethical mostly by curbing our zeal for pomposity.

On the one hand, expecting people adjust their set mentalities and learn humility through 'self'-awareness sounds naïve! On the other hand, leaning about humans' innate deficiencies, which are boosted in society, make us more conscious of our idiosyncrasies as a member of this tormented species. Then, we might possibly make some adjustment to live easier. The following psychological analyses are mainly for boosting one's motivation to change.

The Capacity to Adjust and Act

We may have strong beliefs and profound thoughts to build our principles and decision-making criteria. We may even be a great philosopher and an advocate of certain worthy causes in society, and yet often fail in our encounters, because we cannot refine our simplest attitude. For example, our Self may induce the soothing thought of forgiving someone, for our own sake, despite his/her proven guilt. However, we hesitate to go to our friend or spouse and tell him/her how we feel and our willingness to move on. Our spoiled Ego keeps resisting and preventing us from actually doing something a little different for a change. Or, we might have realized, through our rare 'self'-driven thoughts, that we have made a mistake. Yet, when we must admit and express it openly, our false pride, or the idea of admitting guilt, stops us from doing the right things for our own sake at least. The notion of 'How others may see our passivity' agitates our Egos or Models. These types of mental conflicts and resistance hinder the transformation of our noble thoughts (e.g., forgiveness) into soulful actions.

Fear and insecurity are other causes of our failure to adjust our mentalities and begin a self-searching routine. We get intimidated fast or invent juvenile justifications for our lethargy to cleanse our mindsets. Often, we even doubt the value of our earlier decision to improve our attitudes and soon revert to our old, evil habits. The sources of our fears and insecurities that overwhelm us are numerous and too complex to discuss here. They are usually also justified for coping in society and staying practical. For example, we may not like our boss or job, but the sensible fear of losing our source of income and not finding another job forces us to compromise our integrity and beliefs and bear our boss's selfish expectations or intimidation. Another example is our desperate compromise about the quality of the person we may accept for friendship or marriage when we are lonely. Now just imagine the humility of feeling obliged to work in a debilitating job only to humour a nagging wife and a bunch of unappreciative kids—perhaps for a few more years before they leave us with all kinds of accusations and ingratitude, anyway.

Surely, too many forces hinder our abilities to revamp our mentalities and turn our noble thoughts into actions. However, our mere awareness of these inevitable mental traps might at least help us a bit to subdue their effects and maybe alleviate our stress somewhat, too. Thus, some rather deep psychological issues may be worth mentioning briefly in this section. We might even learn to defeat our chronic resistance to adjust our attitudes. Especially, we might finally do something about our laziness or impatience when we learn about those self-imposed barriers for personal growth and peace. With 'self'-awareness and courage to see our weaknesses, we can prepare ourselves to act before our identities and minds are shattered. We might find solutions for stressful, dull routines we follow helplessly and only whine about.

Although the levels of personal intelligence and potentialities are vital, hereditary factors for building a proactive personality, a variety of simple flaws also make us impatient, biased, or unable to focus and persevere for achieving worthwhile objectives. In the end, our big range of genetic flaws pushed by the rising social havoc infects our personalities and dampens our spirits severely. Yet, we deny even our simple quirks, such as jealousy and spite, to adjust our attitudes and thoughts. We just flow with the current and hope to survive financially and emotionally with no clue about who we are and how some tiny adjustments in our attitudes can improve our lives and relationships drastically.

We move on from one project to another in hopes of soothing our spirits, but we never finish them or soon they feel boring, futile, or not enough inspirational. Accordingly, our potentialities and thoughts never turn into worthwhile and meaningful actions. Our self-image and objectivity also decline due to our inability to induce 'self' driven thoughts and incentives. This epidemic sense of vanity has ruined our chances for keeping even a little peace and sanity, let alone capturing that elusive success and happiness that we are all desperately seeking. Even our *idealistic* ideologies and philosophies are often just for either hiding our failures and dejection or serving our rigid mentalities and selfish desires.

As if reality is not tough enough to face every day, often our paranoia also paralyse our thinking and decision-making abilities. Our erratic perceptions of reality turn into bizarre illusions that overwhelm our whole existence. Our paranoia and illusions feel like inescapable 'facts' of life in our disturbed heads and cripple us completely at the end. For instance, not finding a decent job is a modern life reality, but also presents one major source for our rising paranoia and insecurity about the whole structure of life, including the socioeconomic aspects of it.

The bottom line is that our muddled mindsets are not only preventing us to manage our personalities and lives effectively, but also ruining our chances to think outside the box and free ourselves from the hold of the ostentatious social norms and our own evil urges. Our spoiled personalities stir vile thoughts and decisions. In return, our petty thoughts damage our personalities further. Only Ego and Model thrive all along to drive our actions, which then makes the value of our thoughts and decisions highly questionable, too, if not vain altogether. Only occasionally, when Self happens to get a break, our thoughts become significant and we initiate some worthy actions.

Our low characters and high frustrations cause extreme harm to others regularly as well. Still, we merely blame other people's actions and attitudes without giving even a slight thought to the possibility of our own defects contributing to so much personal conflicts and suffering, while also raising the overall social chaos. We always exonerate ourselves quickly and move on. Therefore, everybody suffers the dire consequences of humans' obsession to live selfishly and mindlessly according to their shoddy choices, judgments, and decisions. Even when our conscience (Self) tries to induce our noble thoughts and feelings, e.g., by condemning our urge for revenge, we personally sabotage our chances with our egotistical habits. We rarely recognize the value of following a more tranquil life direction, as our frantic, selfish urges always interfere and cause more chaos, confusion, and distress for us and the whole society. Our rigid, demented personalities do not let us develop a solid foundation of thoughts and make life's important decisions more patiently and compassionately.

All the above sources of personal negligence are evident in the growing level of senseless crimes that are spreading fast all over the world in all aspects of humanity. They demonstrate the inevitability of humans' demise only due to the accelerating dominance of Ego and Model in new societies ruining people's psyches and spirits (Self).

Still, despite humans' vile nature and all the social hindrances around the glob maiming us, perhaps some hopes still exist for many people to develop right mindsets, firm convictions, and real commitments to transform their profound and *practical* thoughts into worthy actions. We could personally learn to nurture a more 'self' driven life path. Our new thoughts and goals for a simpler lifestyle could not only subdue our Ego and Model driven urges, but also help us cope with demented social demands easier. We can also take calculated risks in line with our life philosophy and by grasping divine opportunities that come around only in special stages of our lives, and most likely only once in our lifetime. Yet, we should also be prepared to accept the unforeseeable outcomes of our risky decisions for pursuing a less conventional lifestyle, e.g., by choosing self-employment in hopes of 'self'-realization or merely for avoiding the hassles of working for others.

Changes and Adjustments

We conceited humans are quite stubborn and opinionated due to our nature and social teachings. Once our brains are conditioned and our three personality aspects are developed, we refuse to see things differently. We block viewpoints and communications that contradict our mentalities or threaten our psyches. We stop others harshly from expressing their opinions, because they trigger our insecurities and sound ridiculous to us.

Accordingly, we all look naive often when we expect people to change. To the youths, particularly, ideas outside their limited mindset sound absurd, especially the notion of forward thinking and how human priorities and thoughts usually differ in the latter phases of their lives. Overall, we cannot expect ourselves or others to change our personalities or outlooks, or understand the value of humility, as a 'self'-driven person with a lifestyle more akin to his/her inner needs.

Of course, some people change slowly, as they age and reset their life purposes according to their wiser views of existence. In rare instances, people change unexpectedly or rather fast, too, for the better or worse for all kinds of personal and psychological reasons. They change consciously or unconsciously for adapting to new demands, ideas, or situations. In such cases, a person's motivation and determination for change fuel him with adequate force, since he is convinced that change is logical, necessary, and fruitful for his physical and mental health. Still, his *scant* capacity for change depends on his intelligence, depth of idiosyncrasies, life experiences, priorities, and social pressures on him.

At the same time, most of us feel the necessity of making some personal adjustments in order to bear social living better at least. In fact, making some simple *adjustments* might prove more productive than struggling in vain, or getting uptight about our inability, to change ourselves.

Adjustment is quite different from changing, although they are complementary principles. Especially, knowing that we cannot readily 'change,' our second best choice is to know what and how we can adjust to make up for our inability or unwillingness to change. Accepting the principles noted above, (i.e., that we can learn to adjust without changing), is a divine form of change by itself. We could introduce this concept in the foundation of our thoughts as a valuable life routine and philosophy.

Sometimes, we feel obliged to make these small adjustments. And sometimes, we are struck by a miracle and feel a genuine *desire* and *motivation* to take actions for reducing our stress and improving our relationships. Thus, despite our rooted dogmatism and inherent difficulty to grow the motivation to change even slightly, we often can adjust ourselves in three ways:

1) We adjust our *thoughts* when we challenge our life path and perhaps revise our mentality gradually, too. Despite our high opinion of ourselves and addiction to certain norms, we may now suddenly realize that a more sensible lifestyle along with a rather flexible, objective mentality is worth entertaining. We now want to nurture some inspiring thoughts in our head at least. This is the *adjustment of thoughts*.

2) Often we feel the necessity of adjusting our *attitudes* to get along with family and people, despite our differences in thoughts and beliefs or our misgivings about society. For example, if we were trying to convert to a 'self'-driven individual, always a great risk exists for being misunderstood or rejected by family, friends, and society as a whole. Thus, we adjust our attitude to cope with the fallout of being, and being seen as, somewhat different from the mainstream, and even the possibility of being rejected. We adjust our attitude mostly for our own sake. This would be the *adjustment of attitudes*.

3) Sometimes, we feel unhappy with our current *situation* or past *actions*, regardless of the ingenuity of our fresher thoughts and beliefs. Thus, we adjust our subsequent actions or decisions to correct the matter, or get ready for their outcomes emotionally and mentally at least, e.g., after we finally accept that our job or marriage is not going to work out in the long run. Often, we might

have to adjust the situation, as the outcomes of our prior decisions or actions have been unsatisfactory, if not torturous. This is the *adjustment of actions or situations.*

We may make these three types of adjustments separately, or in some combination, since we cannot change our personalities or fundamental beliefs. These adjustments can make our encounters and lives easier without losing our integrity and values. They are also complementary, so if we have problems in one area, we can make adjustment in the other one(s) in order to create a balance.

A wise person adjusts in at least one of these areas in order to make living easier for himself. Without this ability, and admitting the need for continuous adjustments and flexibility, we would be in danger of extinction by endless waves of disagreements and oppositions. We would clash with ideas and people constantly, and hurt ourselves for people's lack of understanding.

Learning to adjust is a major life lesson and decision, but we normally resent flexibility, especially in the earlier phases of our lives. We prefer to be stubborn and supposedly protect our pride and standards. However, dogmatism and pride are merely signs of naivety beyond the person's obvious arrogance. We are often wrong about those issues we feel quite certain about. There are usually ways of making life easier for others and ourselves by choosing some practical adjustments in terms of our approaches towards people and situations. Instead, we suffer a lot because of our false pride, stubbornness, and inflexibility.

For example, let us say we are in a relationship that feels odd because of partners' differences in personalities and values, etc. If we believe separation is not a viable option, for this instance, the 'situation' is nonadjustable. If a partner has a solid foundation of thoughts, s/he does not wish to compromise his/her values, either; or convince him/herself to ignore his/her beliefs. Surely, partners cannot adjust their principles to accommodate each other. Thus, the only possibility to keep this relationship would be to adjust his/her attitude, which is a skill s/he can learn if s/he is keen about salvaging his/her relationship. Now, if even one spouse cannot convince him/herself to adjust his/her attitudes, their separation option would have to force itself to *adjust the situation* at least.

We are familiar with these adjustment options intuitively and do them subconsciously and passively. However, it is important to make these adjustments quite consciously and actively after we decide which one of the three types of adjustments is most viable on different occasions and for the kind of person we are.

We would adjust our thoughts only when we are convinced new thoughts are prominent and superior to the older ones. A person with high principles cannot, and should not, do it because somebody, even his/her spouse, is demanding it. Normally, we adjust the situations and our actions first, if we can, in order to prevent further mistakes. Yet, if good reasons exist to try to keep an otherwise substandard situation, we could try to adjust our attitudes. We can study the best combination of adjustments that can work for correcting a matter or instance. If it still does not work, we can try another combination of adjustments and test it. During the process, we learn a lot about ourselves and how to compromise for teamwork, which is like adjusting our thoughts for good reasons. We usually adjust in order to stop stalemate and our continuous doubts about our options. Still, we should know what adjustments are needed and pursued actively; why and how.

In the earlier phases of life, we do not envision how restricted our actions and possibilities for adjustments would become when we move into the second and third phases of life. We assume innocently we can make adjustments anytime as freely and easily as we could when we were young and free of responsibilities. We do not realize that, as we move up into the future phases of life, we get trapped in the consequences of our earlier decisions and actions, and it would become gradually more difficult, and often impossible, to make adjustments to our situations and actions. We do not wish to adjust the foundation of our thoughts, either, as it would be like losing our identity and integrity altogether, which is especially too risky and unhealthy at old age.

For instance, we strive to take on a special role in the family as a caring parent or spouse. Soon we become an adjusted person formed merely to fit our family's needs, to keep a certain job (that we might even resent), to maintain certain friends, or to pursue a superficial lifestyle. These routines become part of our identity as a fixed mark of our being that remains mostly nonadjustable. In particular, we cannot change or adjust our children just because their attitudes offend us. We cannot lose the companionship and love that we exchange with each family member. We cannot change our *situation* or the nature of things or activities around us, since we love our families and do not wish to abandon or hurt them. Thus, our only option is to adjust our *thoughts* and/or our *attitudes* somewhat in order to make our lives tolerable.

We can say that many of our sufferings in life come from our naivety to assume we can stay in charge of our actions and situations throughout our lives and that we can adjust them easily when necessary. The reality is that we would not have the luxury of reversing or adjusting our situations as much as we desire once we reach the latter phases of life. We get trapped. We might and could try to adjust the situations in these latter phases of life *only if absolutely* necessary, but most likely at high risks and costs. If we cannot make adjustments in 'situations' to escape life traps, luckily we can often adjust our 'attitudes,' and perhaps even our 'thoughts' in some extreme circumstances, to curb the pressures of binding situations and our inabilities to execute some kind of adjustments. Our deep insecurities and humans' inherent defects, including our logic's shortfalls discussed in Volume II, are other big sources that obstruct our desires and attempts for some form of adjustment.

The need for making personal adjustments has been reiterated in this trilogy to stress how our social actions are usually passive, subconscious, naïve, immoral, and a sign of low self-awareness.

Awareness and Actions

'Self'-awareness makes us both conscious and proactive to make better life choices, instead of remaining dogmatic with our views, procrastinating out of indecision, or relying on destiny too much. Low 'self'-awareness sabotages our decision-making ability, thus it could be deemed another serious 'personal negligence.' In fact, a big purpose of self-awareness is to anticipate and get ready for destiny's interferences in our lives for better or worse, especially the latter. 'Self'-awareness is also for gauging the morality of our actions and their possible effects on others, while reminding us of the importance of some life decisions and actions. We begin to see life dilemmas and choices clearer with better control over our actions and their outcomes along with a better understanding of their meanings and value; we gauge the causes of our failures and successes more sensibly. Through self-awareness, including our beliefs and reserved trust in destiny, we feel in charge with more confidence and less anxiety about so many issues in the world that we had taken too seriously as matters of life and death in the past. We relax somewhat and take life easier along with our less expectations from society and simpler needs.

Most of all, awareness does not refer to mythical wisdom or a (supernatural) state. It is not the same thing as awakening, either, that has a higher divine source, although they evoke each other within a person gradually. 'Self'-awareness, especially, refers only to the degree, depth, and longevity of our reflections on humans' fundamental thoughts and life experiences. It is simply a higher level of consciousness and comprehension of factors surrounding life's realities leading to full 'awareness' of our essence. Then, we might even be awakened and reach enlightenment, too.

Perhaps using a simple example can clarify the overall role of self-awareness (higher consciousness) for increasing the level of our comprehension and appreciation of the universe, especially its sacred beauties:

We listen to music with different degrees of attention at any time, even when listening to particular pieces that usually give us a special feeling. Sometimes, we enjoy it only in the background, while running our errands or reading a book. We hear it, enjoy it somewhat, and relax, etc. In these instances, we are aware of the music, but our degree of consciousness and comprehension is low. Sometimes, we make a point to listen to music per se, by going to a concert hall or in seclusion at home. In such cases, we pay more attention, grasp, and appreciate the music much better. Preventing mental interruptions increases our attention span and we let the music carry us. Sometimes, we might lose our attention and slip into a daydream, get distracted, or doze off, perhaps by the romantic feelings that the music is creating. This is an average awareness level, even though we pay attention and money (if we go to a concert) to listen to music.

At a full awareness level, however, we receive every single note, feel (absorb) it, and anticipate the next one. During full awareness, in fact, we discern and synthesize many notes that are emitted simultaneously at every tiny instant. We not only follow the notes, but also grasp their relationships in harmony with the overall orchestration. While partly absorbed in the music, we stay highly conscious of each note and moment and in the manner we relate to the whole tune. This is almost like a conductor's job leading the orchestra with full attention to every single note and instrument that should emerge in a fraction of a second.

In the awareness mode, we do not forget ourselves, although we often try to clear our minds from trivia and life pressures. In fact, we become extremely conscious and alert of our being, as we get dissolved in the process, e.g., following the notes that are pouring out at an extremely high speed. We become the carrier of notes that our brain can receive at high speed, while blocking any other thoughts or distractions that might ruin our concentration. The span of attention should be long enough for full appreciation and comprehension of the depth of the message completely, or else we must start all over with still higher efforts and attention.

With alert listening, we hear the first note and stay focused for the length of the music with genuine appreciation of our experience. Long periods of full attention, which is needed for major pieces of classical music, can boost our awareness and enjoyment once we learn to follow the music. This is, of course, only one aspect of the classical music that makes it attractive to some people. A conductor's or a soloist's long pause at the end of a performance shows his/her attempt to return to his/her normal awareness level after spending a long time within the realm of full awareness.

Learning and boosting our self-awareness is a lengthy, delicate project during certain periods of contemplation or meditation. It requires devotion and practice much more than what an orchestra conductor or soloist usually masters in order to attain excellence through his/her high levels of concentration.

Naturally, the value and depth of any experience or thought grows substantially when it is fully comprehended and absorbed. That is why awareness can introduce us to such divine dimensions of life (and 'self') that are not visible or sensible under normal moods, conditions, and regular levels of consciousness.

For self-awareness, we ask ourselves some basic questions regularly about our being and routines, and then draw upon our foundation of thoughts to find the answers objectively during a peaceful period of meditation. These questions and meditations help us assess the significance of our major decisions and plans along with our criteria. Is our decision or action hasty or tainted by our pride, spite, family or social conditioning? Is it in line with our life philosophy and 'self'-control principles? We like to know which aspects of personality (Ego, Model, and Self) are in charge of our judgments regarding this decision or action. If it is Ego or Model driven, we like to find out why we cannot resist or avoid them. We like to know how to distinguish noble actions from vain, unimportant, and irrelevant ones, especially if they may hurt others or us. We could apply these simple awareness principles to many important encounters in society and with our 'self.'

Many shallow activities in new societies (such as obsession for fashion, shopping, travelling) have been taken as the signs of modernity or necessities of living, but they are merely distracting us from attending to more fundamentals of life, including our grasp of 'self' for becoming a better human being. Focusing so much on trivia beyond the minimum level needed for relaxation only lowers our characters and chances for tranquility. Instead, we could use our precious energy, nerves, and time on significant thoughts and productive decisions of life more often. By learning to use the right criteria for 'self' growth, we could acknowledge, and stress on, those major life decisions and plans that we have so far handled so casually. We merely want to stop dwelling on our obsessive habits, superficial needs, and showy lifestyles.

Through 'forward thinking,' we learn how trivial some of the things we do in life would prove to be. Conversely, we can learn how to build a fulfilling life by doing certain activities akin to our spirits with high potential for stirring inner satisfaction, which we have neglected all along. High awareness about important things, and relinquishing insignificant ones, is simple and practical, once we put our 'thoughts' into it, abandon our superficial habits, and find the right criteria for making our major life decisions. One simple test is that almost all Ego driven activities and thoughts are unessential. The same thing is true about a great majority of Model motivated thoughts and actions. Through self-awareness, it becomes easy to detect Ego and Model oriented thoughts, thus reduce their **significance** in our lives when we must make serious decisions properly or when we doubt our decision criteria.

Significant things in life are so by their own natural existence and manifestation. They are not the creations of our fantasies and naïve values. And they are not urges pushed by Model and Ego. However, we cannot make this simple distinction as long as we are entangled with mundane and trivial matters we have chosen as our biggest challenges and problems. The test of 'significance' lies in the genuine feelings of joy and a lasting inner satisfaction that comes from some experiences, such as watching a sunset with full awareness. These authentic feelings are never found in other experiences—an enlightening fact that necessarily reflects the insignificance of most activities we do habitually. Moreover, significant experiences release a large level of energy that is heartfelt and continues rather consistently throughout our lives. They lift our spirits, whereas trivial experiences only consume our energies without giving back anything in return, other than perhaps some short-lived pleasures and egotistical satisfaction— the two most cherished obsessions of naïve humans, nowadays!

As we push superficial activities and feelings out of our lives, our senses become sharper gradually for finding those significant things in life that boost our authenticity, make us touch our souls, and make us feel the whole world with our souls. Through these experiences, we build a high level of awareness to differentiate all the significant things in life even more diligently. The discussions of facts and myths in Part II revealed how all those things we accept as 'facts' indeed cause our sufferings, and all the things we view as 'myths' can become the sources of healing and inner joy as we feel the significant facets of our being. Those discussions can provide a starting point to heighten our awareness about the significant stuff of existence.

Conversely, by discovering the mysteries of the real world, as mostly hidden in Nature and myths about the universe, we might also raise our self-awareness and spiritualism.

Then again, we cannot develop a natural and practical life based on myths alone. That is why we need high self-awareness, a solid foundation of thoughts, and a sensible life philosophy to integrate all these realities of existence, including its demoralizing or joyous facts, as we try to survive within a dwindling society we have so proudly built around such vile symbols of civilization crushing our spirits.

Naturally, a main reason for some decisions being considered 'major' is their prominent potentials for mapping the path of our lives and preventing lifelong disappointments and sufferings. Accordingly, adopting the 'self'-control principles and adapting ourselves to the requirements of that unconventional, and rather lonely, lifestyle are major life decisions all by themselves. We should be prepared for the inevitable hardships of adjusting our mentality to live closer to the boundaries of the real world, rather than within the illusions of the perceived world. This big mental adjustment is another *major* life decision by itself.

Although we cannot expect anybody attain 'self' awareness readily, we all can approach it gradually with sincere efforts and beliefs. We must be truly convinced, though, that pursuing a 'self'-driven lifestyle is a viable option for us in the long run.

Again, the suggestions in this chapter about changing ourselves or adjusting some aspects of our thoughts, attitudes, or situations would ordinarily feel like commonsense that we are all familiar with already. Yet, they also sound absurd to most of us, because we already trust our wisdom and personality totally with no need for self-awareness! Even if we happen to entertain the slightest doubt about our perfection, we normally have no patience, time, or interest to study ourselves. Therefore, we all feel comfortable to keep thinking and planning our lives merely in line with social norms rather hypnotically. We trust social values and lifestyles too much with inadequate care about the looming disasters and disappointments humans will be forced to face soon without mental preparation. Sadly, our educational systems have been unequipped to teach us life's essential necessities and prepare us for accelerating social burdens, while we keep relying on people and society more every generation for financial and emotional supports. We do not get the guidance and incentive to learn about our 'self' as an independent individual or our roles in societies for coexistence. As a result, humans and humanity have reached a dangerous stage in history in total confusion.

CHAPTER TWELVE
'Forward Thinking' Philosophy

The three fundamental questions people ask themselves during their lives' three phases were noted on page 237 as follows:

Phases of Life	Underlying Philosophical Questions
Youth	What will be (my life like)?
Middle Age	What is this (that is happening)?
Old Age	What was it (all about)?

These questions have now passed the test of history and would remain valid forever, because the overall human nature would not change, anyway. We like to make life miserable for one another and we are not made to get along for a long time. Therefore, hardships, exploitations, and agonies of life would continue forever and the three fundamental questions in the three phases of life would stay intact. Actually, these three questions become even more pertinent in the future while societies continue to deteriorate so rapidly. We could verify the validity of these questions in any era by talking to people in different phases of their lives and capable of speaking intelligently and honestly. We can expect the same feelings and answers even though we might believe to be wiser and more modern in the new era.

Naturally, nobody should rely on the wisdom of one person or group to build his/her life philosophy, anyway. While a specific individual's wisdom is valuable if we can trust his/her faculty, our interest is mainly in the uniform messages of a large group of thoughtful people in the third phase of their lives with proven intelligence and objectivity, perhaps as scholars and philosophers. Meanwhile, we can also check with normal people in the latter phases of their lives and see how prevalent these three main life messages are amongst the public with varied intelligence levels and lifestyles. Then, if we are somewhat convinced about the value of using the messages that people convey in their three life phases, we might consider the idea of 'forward thinking' while we might still have a chance to benefit from that wisdom.

Forward thinking is only a philosophical notion to set our life priorities and outlooks based on the three fundamental questions everybody faces in the three life phases. The idea is to view the world and existence's fundamentals according to our prospective wisdom after years of living and experiencing all aspects of life. Logically, the information content and value of our experiences are cumulative, thus our wisdom *supposedly* increases with age. Especially, our mentalities, priorities, and life outlooks improve. (This seems like a plausible assumption for most people, as long as one's mental health is intact and before aging ruins a person's sense of judgment and reasoning.) In all, we may assume that our wisdom in the third phase of life is more valuable and reliable than the one we have in the earlier phases when our emotional and logical senses are both fragile and clashing too often. Yet, we believe to be the smartest person in the world during adolescence. We are usually most arrogant and stubborn about our viewpoints when we are least experienced, most impatient, too passionate, and immensely vulnerable. In fact, we can say that almost all our helplessness and sufferings in life are the steep price we end up paying for our stubbornness and naivety during the earlier phases of our lives, especially the first one.

The wisdom and insight at each phase of life surely depends on a person's intelligence and thought processes. Yet, by the third phase of our lives, we have faced all the doubts and decisions of life, made many mistakes and adjustments to our thoughts and attitudes, experienced the pleasures of life, and perhaps learned something about our spirituality and actualization needs. We are more realistic about our dreams and have leaned more towards our Self, since Ego and Model cannot serve us as much as before. We finally realize the value of Self for bringing us harmony and tranquility. We grow deeper insight about life's essentialities and meaning. We learn to come to terms with ourselves and reach for our souls, instead of pursuing superficial goals. Unless inflicted with dark life outlook and values due to severe hardships and failures, an intelligent person learns objectivity and gains wisdom as s/he ages.

Of course, this huge expectation for personal growth through life phases is not realistic for narrow-minded, ignorant people who do not have the time or mind to ponder their life dilemmas and purposes as diligently as an enlightened person does more keenly. Without adequate growth and self-development in line with the points noted in this book, the chances for attaining a high degree of personal judgment needed for forward thinking would be quite limited for most people. Yet, everybody gets somewhat smarter after enough trials and errors throughout his/her life and learning a few good things about the reality of existence.

Nevertheless, the objective of forward thinking is to listen to the depth of the messages that most people in their third phase of life convey about existence by thinking or asking the question of, 'What was it all about?' There is no specific advice in this phrase, but only a fundamental and philosophical expression about life in line with a better grasp of both our personal whims' and social values' vanities. All we need is attention and basic trust in the messages erupting from the phrase, 'What was it all about?' However, if it is the sentiments in the third phase of life that we want to 'forward-think,' we must also adjust our misperceptions of old people and their wisdom. We should actually mature enough to imagine ourselves as an old person soon and asking the same question with a great deal of pain and regrets.

As a young person, however, we dissociate ourselves from older people and their pains. We cannot even grasp, consciously enough, the notion of getting old and fragile ourselves. Ironically, even people in their middle or old ages put a distance between elders and themselves, desperately hoping to come across young and alert. Youths are too proud of their fresh, youthful values and outlooks to listen to an older person's wisdom. Our subconscious fear of death also makes us anxious around older people. All the traditional respect for the grownups' wisdom has been eradicated in modern eras due to the fast rise of arrogance and superficiality that society pushes on the youths deliberately. Surely, the general scepticism about the values and viewpoints of older people is partially valid, since with old age come senility, depression, and health issues. Usually, these factors make their judgments less trustworthy and more depressing than ever. Yet, while they still have their senses intact, old people's question of, 'What was it all about?' is a reliable conclusion about the frailty and vanity of life. Sadly, most people, mainly elders, cannot articulate their feelings and wisdom. Yet, they are all thinking the points stressed in this chapter, at least subconsciously. We can see it in their gloomy, tired faces behind their mocking words and grins, anyway.

Surely, forward thinking would remain mainly a hypothetical notion at this point for only a small group to absorb and practise effectively. However, getting even a sense of the messages in this philosophy can help everybody to some extent. Not many people can capture the real intention of 'living in the now,' either, for example, yet we all incorporate this raw ideology in our personal philosophy, too, although often erroneously.

Maybe someday—in the 50th century perhaps—humans grow a magical intuition or techniques to foretell their future thoughts and states of mind. However, for now, we may use 'forward thinking' philosophy only to enhance our awareness and to inject some doubts in our minds about the essentialities of life, as we see them, nowadays, in our *allegedly modern* cultures.

We cannot realistically expect the youths to think like their parents, let alone their grandparents, or really feel and grasp the wisdom that comes only from lifelong experiences. All we can do, as also intended here, is to open their thought horizons to give a benefit of a doubt to the collective wisdom of people who all ask the same question, 'What was it all about?'

When we are young in the first phase of our lives, we are full of ambitions, plans, and yearning for pleasures. This is a natural attitude and expectation to the extent it matches our instincts and basic needs. Beyond this crude intuition, our outlooks reflect the conditioning norms, materialistic standards, and pleasure-seeking priorities of the modern society that we learn to imitate. We have turned into robots who follow the crowd and social trends with little 'self'-control over the processes and directions of our lives, although we believe to be in charge and independent. As a young person, in particular, we are both naive and proud. We want to try our own logic, ways, and values, yet deep in our unconscious, we feel committed to follow some standard life plans. We allow these standards and plans direct the course of our lives. We have some ideas regarding independence and breaking away, yet the criteria of success and the fake essentialities of life keep us trapped within an imposing, ominous social structure. They are the same crude values that all generations appear to adopt at each phase of life—the kind of mentality that keeps them dependent on their superficial habits and pretentious people around them— except that shallowness has grown fast with every generation. In the first life phase, we are optimistic about future, sometimes even despite our cynicism about society and people. We believe we are smart and capable of building a good life—money, love, fame, and everything else we admire as the criteria of success.

The main characteristic of this phase is the attitude of forward looking (not 'forward thinking') and wondering *what our lives would be like*. Life's essentialities are set with the same criteria we have used to delineate the formula of success. In fact, in our minds, success and happiness are synonymous. Most likely, we do not even dwell on happiness and the path leading to it, since we imagine success brings us happiness automatically—a major assumption that proves to be wrong in the second and third phases of our lives. Meanwhile, we fill our lives with short-term pleasures just to keep ourselves amused, and because everybody else is doing the same stuff. The path of life in the youths' eyes is quite clear. It consists of having more pleasures (for replicating happiness) while striving for, and looking forward to, more love, pleasure, and success.

Our cultures have been so deformed that they define 'success' only within materialistic criteria. Our immediate perception of the word 'success' is money, fame, luxuries, power, sexuality, and extravagance. What we do to get to this point does not matter, and what we feel even when we are there still does not matter. All we are used to perceive and gauge is one's level of pleasure, wealth, and fame as valid symbols of a person's level of success and happiness. In fact, we have become so naive and conditioned that when we hear that someone is not happy despite his/her fame and wealth, we get extremely surprised.

Strangely enough, we reject the idea that a person is actually not successful because he is not happy (despite his/her money and power). That is, we believe that if somebody is successful, according to our cultural interpretation, s/he should be happy, but not the opposite (as noted in the previous sentence). Naively, we insist that this person is really successful, but unable to appreciate it or be happy. Facing such a perceptually untenable, paradoxical situation, we then struggle to modify our position and assume that happiness is something that we can buy with our success, rather than being an inherent state of satisfaction erupting from 'real' success. We try idiotically to redefine the relationship between success and happiness. Thus, even in our minds and perceptions, we are inconsistent in relating happiness and success. Although 'success' and 'happiness' are synonym in common perceptions, we readily refute their relationship when someone's happiness does not materialize despite his/her success. Therefore, the only justification we offer to reconcile this inconsistency is that s/he does not know how to buy happiness with his/her success. We merely blame him/her and pity his/her stupidity!

Success, as defined through various social symbols, and in the way we have imposed it on ourselves in our cultures, is actually synonymous with suffering, instead of happiness. We suffer a lot emotionally and physically by working hard so many hours and worrying about our profits and competitions, and at the end, all we can show for it is stress, loneliness, and crushed Egos. Even when we achieve our objectives of making our wealth at any cost and by winning major competitions, we find our success at best only a business target; once we reach that target we have to shoot for a higher one. In the midst of all these struggles for success (higher targets), we become increasingly ignorant about the real meanings and sources of happiness, while hypnotically believe we are happy or it would happen soon.

In all, we have spread a big misperception in our culture about success. Accordingly, we condition ourselves, particularly in the earlier phases of our lives, to follow odd objectives and lifestyles for becoming successful and happy. Forward thinking is merely for reassessing these old habits and crooked social values about success and happiness. We should adjust our thoughts on this important issue at least for the sake of being objective and sincere with ourselves. Accordingly, four cautionary points are important to stress here about the subtle, vital intention of forward thinking:

1. Forward thinking's subtle message about life's shallowness, especially within the present socioeconomic structure, should be viewed merely as a philosophical thought and wisdom to make the best of our existence. It certainly is not for justifying our laziness, self-pity, or cruelties.
2. Although 'forward thinking' messages in this chapter might initially sound negative and depressing, their ultimate goal is

to increase our chances for happiness (or at least contentment) by seeing life realistically and working harder in setting and attaining worthwhile personal objectives. This important point is further explained below.

3. Throughout the three life phases, we all seek various forms of pleasure to mitigate our sufferings temporarily. This might even turn into an addiction if we believe that analysing life, planning, or worrying is futile or stressful. We strive to 'live in the now' as much as possible. Yet, building this type of carefree mentality or a sense of resignation is not the intention of 'forward thinking' philosophy at all.

4. A young person who feels life's futility must realize that s/he is in a special (temporary) state of mind that everybody faces sporadically at any age or phase of life. These sentiments are unrelated (or sometimes only auxiliary) to the main theme of 'forward thinking' and philosophical thoughts that most of us hold in each phase of life.

Now, let us review the main messages of 'Forward Thinking' during the three life phases.

Phase Three Reference

The ultimate question of, 'What was this life all about?' strikes us harshly in the third phase of our lives. Thus, the idea behind the philosophy of 'forward thinking' is to familiarize ourselves with this inevitable, dreadful discovery as soon as possible in our lives. Then, we might consider adjusting our mindsets and plans based on this cruel reality. Many profound messages could be deduced from this fine, ultimate question, such as:

- We would all sense the question of, 'What was it all about?' when we reach the third phase of our lives.
- We would feel disappointed and doubt our wisdom all along —during our past life stages—especially in terms of our futile worries and struggles for some juvenile semblance of success.

- Life is indeed too short, even shorter than what we had often heard and imagined.
- Our criteria of success and its outcome do not prove useful and meaningful, but rather quite irrelevant and foolish for reaching even a relative sense of fulfilment or happiness.
- The outcomes of our plans often turn out differently.
- Our views about life and people change, often drastically.
- We recognize the absurdity of positive thinking.
- We realize our naïveté to trust certain values, thoughts, people, and the sources of success and happiness.
- We feel major regrets, helplessness, and sadness for the loss of an otherwise *(possibly)* beautiful life.
- We feel the ultimate blow—that no hope of escape from our present life entrapment exists, nor much is left to do.
- We finally accept that we are alone in this life regardless of all the friends and family surrounding us.
- We throw in the towel and accept our defeat with desperation and an eventual resignation for the remainder of our lives.
- We blame our foolishness and passivity for not realizing all the above facts much sooner.

Obviously, these gloomy messages and afterthoughts are indeed too harsh to adopt as life's reality, especially for young people who are blooming with all kinds of optimism and enthusiasm. How can we tell them about the sad reality that would prove to be the *truth*, but sounds too depressing and cynical? And even if we built the guts and tried, how can we expect them to understand the depth of these messages wholeheartedly without giving up on life? The wisdom and intention of this insight is most likely not even clear to us. We often misinterpret these messages and believe that they are merely intended to portray the futility of life and our struggles to succeed. However, this is **definitely** not the intention.

The purpose of exposing ourselves to these gloomy messages is merely to raise our awareness. In fact, the objective is to see the futility of wasting our lives on those petty things and plans that we have learned to consider essential for success. The ultimate purpose is to become wiser, build a more fulfilling life path, find the real means of achieving happiness, and see the beauty of the natural world. The interpretation of the messages should be based on an initial understanding of the purpose of 'forward thinking.' The idea is to prepare ourselves, *to some extent*, for the inevitable shocks in life, thus sail through this rough journey as smoothly as possible with minimum scars, regrets, and expectations. Most of all, surely the idea is not to encourage 'living in the now' more actively in hopes of eluding life's harsh realities. On the contrary, the main message of 'forward thinking' is to plan our lives very diligently 'for a very long time in the future' by identifying and studying life's essentialities regularly.

If not fully appreciated, 'forward thinking' messages might seem counterproductive for setting the right criteria for living and justifying our efforts. They might create even more doubts about the purpose of living just by keeping ourselves amused with work, all kinds of pleasures, etc. We might get confused when no substantive joys and goals seem to exist for following the air of forward thinking messages. What should our new values be, then, if we suddenly consider social norms and values questionable, if not harmful altogether? These are legitimate concerns. Yet, we can defeat these hurdles if we contemplate the forward thinking messages along with the goals we have set within the foundation of our thoughts and philosophy for boosting our spirits. Those principles can replace unessential values with meaningful beliefs and finer goals. The process of adjusting our thoughts, outlooks, and actions is for smoothing the transition from the common way of thinking and living to some new innovative ones. The idea is not to abandon our social values and customs completely, but just elude phony habits and hollow lifestyles in the chaotic perceived world by adjusting our thoughts, beliefs, and actions. At the same time, making people, especially the youths, interested in this rather stoic or unconventional mentality—to abandon their excessive self-gratifying aspirations at least—is an extremely tough job, if possible at all?!

Many other aspects of the 'forward thinking' can be studied to get a fuller appreciation of its messages and goals. For example, it reflects that all our crude ambitions and wearing efforts to boost our Egos would *particularly* prove foolish and funny. At the end, our fat Egos would burst and we would realize the emptiness of it all, not to mention our dire sense of stupidity. Therefore, once we adjust our attitudes, we learn to remain indifferent to people's routine suggestions or offences that our Egos react to harshly, like occasions when somebody says we are 'wrong' about something. Usually, we spend a lot of energy and time to fight back and prove that we are not 'wrong.' We learn that, in the final analysis, from the forward thinking viewpoint, it does not really matter whether somebody thinks we are right or wrong as long as we keep an objective perspective of our thoughts and deeds. Only our objectivity and integrity matter in this world, not other people's selfish or naive opinions of who we are. Our only goal is to find the means of boosting our energies and beliefs to remain focused, which is mostly for keeping our sanity and objectivity.

With forward thinking, we would find it much easier to curb our fears and insecurities about the love we do not receive, the jobs we cannot find, promotions we do not get, the wealth we have not accumulated, etc. We can better control our anger about losing our spouse who proves to be extremely insensitive and ignorant, or when we realize how s/he disregards or misjudges our love, etc. We can witness and withstand our kids' apathy, wickedness, and cruelty. We can see that our shallow senses of success, even when achieved, do not give us mental satisfaction, a sense of 'being', true happiness, and peace of mind. We realize that customary social achievements are not essentialities of life to be overly concerned about or lose our energies on. In fact, many of presumed life fundamentals in our presumed civilized societies only heighten our entrapments and insecurities. Through forward thinking, we can reassess our life's essentialities and authentic beliefs by building our foundation of thoughts and finer priorities for tangible (partly spiritual) objectives.

Phase Two Reference

The question, 'What is this (life about)?' that hits us in the second phase of life also provides some great messages. Mainly, the question implies that we are right in the middle of a mess and feel trapped. However, in this phase of life we are still hopeful and believe to be clever enough to elude the traps. We still think there are ways to get out of this situation somehow and things would eventually start to make sense. We still think we might have done something wrong that could be corrected, e.g., by divorcing our spouse and finding a new one. We are assuming that the same lifestyle, values, and principles that we have followed so far are good enough to rescue us from our present entrapments, too. We think of success and happiness in the same way and according to the same criteria. The following messages of the question, 'What is this?' become clearer and gloomier as we age in this life phase:

- We are facing a major flaw in our plans and perceptions of life, which we had envisioned and adopted in the first phase of our lives eagerly.
- We are truly surprised to encounter such harsh outcomes at the prime of our lives.
- We feel the mess we are in and our big dilemmas seriously.
- We become anxious and frustrated, and do not understand why our plans, logic, and wisdom do not work.
- We doubt the validity of our criteria of success as well as our naïve notion of presumed automatic happiness.
- We notice the rising social chaos and people's hypocrisy more clearly and feel sad about the whole situation and humanity.
- We are still confused about the meaning of our experiences and remain doubtful about the roots of our problems. Yet, we seem to have no other options for living. Instead, we just feel

more obliged feebly to follow the same path and values and hope for the best.
- At the same time, we blame our past mistakes and wonder if we could find a way to correct them.
- We also blame others and bad luck for our failures, although sometimes feel our naivety and dip into self-pity as well.
- Sometimes, we question our lifestyles as well as the meaning and purpose of everything happening around us with deeper cynicism.
- The lingering sense of questioning things and reflecting on our routines keeps intensifying. We do not know who to trust or turn to for guidance.
- Our dilemmas feel more overwhelming and serious every day, while we keep looking more diligently for alternatives to get out of this mess. We feel sadder and more helpless every day.
- Our doubts about our future and options keep growing, while the outlook feels depressing. Still, we force ourselves to push forward and hope for a more manageable future or a miracle to save us. (Only in the third phase of our lives our doubts and hopes finally deplete and we sense the frailty and shallowness of our dreams altogether.)
- We encounter the biggest question of our lives, 'Is this what life supposed to be?'
- Yet, we still strive to remain rather optimistic and keep looking for solutions, despite our growing cynicism about the bizarre manifestation of life.
- We just get deeper in the same old habits, e.g., working harder and seeking more pleasures, for handling the tough dilemmas erupting in this life phase.

The question 'What is this?' in life's second phase shows that a big part of the optimism and enthusiasm of phase one diminishes and a sense of reality kicks in. We face the walls of resistance, disappointments, and discouragements in society and life overall.

Surely, some beautiful experiences keep us going. Some precious moments might bring us some fleeting happiness and pleasures, thus make up for our depressions, delusions, and confusions a bit. Yet, our dreams of a happy life and success begin to feel like just a horrendous mirage. Looking so promising and fulfilling from a distance in Phase One, they prove hollow, tedious, and illusive when we actually reach and touch them in Phase Two.

The big, shocking discovery in Phase Two is about our view of success and happiness. We realize that we have no realistic set of criteria outside the conditioning and restricted social norms. We realize happiness does not erupt automatically from success according to our naïve initial imagination and expectation during Phase I. In fact, we might realize that we inflict sufferings upon ourselves in pursuit of that elusive 'success,' and that our endless struggles for success only add to our pains and stress. We feel that our present mentality and approach have created a big variety of entrapments. We suffer for the lack of a meaningful sense of purpose and success, despite our incessant struggles for it, and, even when we have captured all the symbols of success. Thus, we conclude that something should be wrong with the present definition of success. So now, we feel obliged to rediscover the meaning, and means, of 'success' before it is too late and we get completely old and useless.

We realize in Phase Two that we have been misled to assume we can direct and shape our lives any way we desire. We realize that following the values we have learned and practised has kept us at the mercy of external forces and other individuals as our sources of satisfaction—but also the main roots of our sufferings. The consequences of our erroneous major life decisions, e.g., a bad career or marriage, are haunting us. We now realize how we have missed our life opportunities due to those wrong decisions. We might find out that our authentic needs and happiness are not achievable within the raw standards and lifestyles that everybody follows rather blindly. We might at least imagine the possibility of a more meaningful life, question our daily routines all along, and maybe find some motivation to seek other options that could give us freedom, wisdom, 'self'-control, and peace. Whether we act on our findings and seek a different lifestyle, or at least make some serious, mental adjustments, is a crucial decision. However, most often, people do not or cannot make a tangible adjustment.

When we are in our second life phase and ask the question of, 'What is this?', we should remember that, by following the same life routine, the next question awaiting us would be, 'What was it?'; and that would, in fact, come around very soon. A motivated person might be able to turn his situation around by adjusting his foundation of thoughts, attitude, and actions, once he truly grasps the messages of the forward thinking. He can redeem himself just by pausing his routine life long enough to grasp and internalize these awakening messages.

By forward thinking during the second phase of our lives, we want to sensitize our mentality and enhance our resilience and wisdom. We also want to reassess our foundation of thoughts and personal life philosophy in hopes of detecting the causes of our failures so far. We hope to find a better philosophy of life in order to redeem our Selfs and elude the questions of, 'What is this?' and 'What was it?' for the rest of our lives.

But we should also beware of the pitfalls of making drastic life changes before building our foundation of thoughts and setting valid criteria for success mainly for satisfying our authentic needs and boosting our spirits. In particular, becoming more easygoing or 'living in the now' is not going to help the matter. Many of us take drastic actions to relieve ourselves from the agony of the question, 'What is this?', e.g., when we are depressed about our jobs or marriages. We call this mid-life crisis. Yet, quitting our jobs or divorcing our spouses and still following the old criteria for finding a new job or spouse would most likely lead to more frustration and failures. Seeking more pleasure or losing sight of our responsibilities would not solve the problem, either, but in fact makes us even more susceptible to the ultimate blow in the third phase.

Phase One Reference

We ask the question 'What my life will be like?' in the 1st phase of our lives. Without the *forward thinking* insight, we only keep *forward looking* to the future with all kinds of dreams and hopes that society pushes us to believe are legitimate and deserving for any person who follows some prevalent, idiotic rules of success. Accordingly, personal failures and depression augment the rising social mayhem towards the ultimate socioeconomic collapse that has been discussed enough in this and other books. We will only stagnate and suffer a lifetime, while the haunting questions in the second and third phases of our lives await us.

On the other hand, the question 'What my life will be like?' in phase one would take a different meaning and form within the 'forward thinking' domain. This question would be redundant in any phase of one's life if we have established our foundation of thoughts and life based on the awakening messages of forward thinking. In that circumstance, life essentialities would not change from one phase to the next, except that they feel profounder and truer. Therefore, looking forward to future outcomes and risks are meaningless in the manner we would normally see them in the perceived world. In fact, this awakening thru 'forward thinking' in our first life phase also brings us to the threshold of the real world, where only our wisdom grows, while life realities remain consistent—as frigid, dry facts. The truth does not change; it merely becomes clearer and feels harsher to us with time. Thus, we learn to become more flexible in our minds and attitudes to withstand the gloomy truth about life's unchangeable rigidity. We do not see success and its criteria in the customary way, and thus, it cannot be measured now or in the future. In the real world, the only interpretation of success would be 'self'-control for finding peace and happiness or at least curbing our sufferings. The real test of success lies only in finding a decent response for the question 'What was it?' when we are ready to die.

Sadly, only rarely any of us might have a valid answer!

In all, forward thinking in the first life phase is only for raising our levels of awareness and tolerance about every circumstance and each thought that would prevail in the future phases of life. If we somewhat understand, in Phase One, the main messages of forward thinking, then we might be mentally prepared to handle these disappointing facts when they actually hit us. Furthermore, if we could really adjust our thoughts, attitudes, actions, and the criteria of success in the lower phases of life, we would raise our chances for tasting some semblance of peace, fulfilment, passion, enjoyment, and true happiness in the following life phases.

Forward thinking could trigger a mild state of awakening. We could stay in this domain for a tangible amount of time to attain the real sense of it, rather than passing through it quickly like a tentative contemplation. We can even reach for a high platform of awareness by absorbing these questions truly and internalizing the meanings of those subtle messages. We could reach out for a state of permanent and full awareness, which would lead to deep awakening and the path of wisdom.

A parallel question that emerges during forward thinking is, 'What becomes of my soul (after my earthly existence)?' And we know already that at best only a few individuals (saints) might have known the answer to this bizarre question, if at all. Forget everything religions have told us throughout the human history. The question about the future of our souls would always remain unanswered, as the greatest doubt and mystery for us all, most likely even if we reached the summit on the path of wisdom. A lasting soul, if at all possible, would surely not be the same type of life experience and feeling that we envision and talk about our spirits now. Most likely, it would be so isolated and unlike to our earthly life that cannot have any relation to our present senses, existence, naïve contemplations, or a vision of a continuation of our being. Soul is probably a form of energy teeming around, if that, and then released from, a contained mass we call existence.

In particular, forget about afterlife and similar thoughts that all prophets have pushed into too many naïve people's minds! What a pity!—not only what they have done, but more so our inability as humans to elude those naïve perceptions ruining our indolent, susceptible heads. Then, you also wonder about the quality of all these leaders around the world allegedly trusted to guide humans into brighter futures! *What a pity, really!!*

The whole process of life remains full of mysteries, doubts, and decisions. Despite our initial exposure to forward thinking ideas or similar thoughts or experiences, we remain doubtful about our viable life options. We can neither convince ourselves, nor find the courage, to break away from the norms that so conveniently accommodate our conditioned minds. We do not seem to grasp truly the messages that are in front of us. We simply forget or send them to our unconscious. How many times have we felt our vulnerability and nothingness and quickly forgotten them and returned to our expressions and feelings of superiority due to Ego domination? How many times have we promised our spirits to change our ways of life when we visited a cemetery, went to the funeral of our young friend, witnessed the miserable lives of crippled and helpless people all over the world, and saw pictures of masses of children dying in millions from hunger, wars, and neglect? How quickly we lose our compassion and awareness and return to our deep-rooted greed and self-serving thoughts and attitudes!

How soon we forget is no wonder. How our rowdy doubts control the whole domain of our thoughts and render us helpless is no wonder. What is of tremendous wonder is our inability (and unwillingness) to retain a state of self-awareness more regularly and appreciate the gloominess of the world we have created out of ignorance! If only we learn to internalize our sporadic, simple awareness experiences, we might eventually find a basic path of wisdom, to make the rest of our lives somewhat easier to go through. What is of immense wonder is our resistance to ponder, understand, and let a simple philosophy of 'forward thinking' rejuvenate human spirits and the foundation of human thoughts!

Epilogue

As explained in the Author's Note, my main intention for writing this trilogy was to communicate better with my beloved children about the facts of life in hopes of helping them think and live healthier. Thus, my failure for many reasons to raise their interests to read the manuscript was both disheartening and educational. Then again, their resistance to ponder some radical ideas outside the norms matched this trilogy's theories about the youths' rising, deplorable apathy for both life's realities and adults' advice. Most likely, my views had sounded silly to my anxious kids relative to illusive social trends ingrained in modern lifestyles these days. My wife's disagreement with my outlook had also restricted my influence over my children all those years. Her beliefs were, of course, in line with the mainstream's values, i.e., an illusion of a fantastic world built around materialism, egotism, individualism, competition, superficiality, etc. How could I tell my kids that they were being spoiled; or keep arguing with my wife about it? How could I prove that they were filling their brains with values that would cause them only confusion and stress all their lives? I tried not to alienate my children with my messages that contradicted their mother's and the whole society's views. So I kept quiet a lot and stashed the manuscript in a corner. *Instead, all that despair and family education made me write many more books!*

A decade later, I retrieved the manuscript and reread it with surprise. Over this period, I had become even more sceptical about social affairs, the waning state of humans' 'self'-realization, and the misery we are inflicting upon humanity so hastily. I was glad that my rather moderate opinions were not printed, since the situation appears to be getting out of hand so fast now. People's chances for communication (especially between parents and their kids) and the possibility of finding peace of mind in our modern societies felt even more remote without revamping our mindsets vastly. My initial manuscript's goal had been to tell my kids about life being essentially a tricky process of adaptation for survival, which needs lots of compliance and resilience, though we should at least try to raise our self-awareness for 'self'-realization, too.

Now, however, active resistance towards current norms and lifestyles feels even more urgent before social health and integrity are abolished for good. Now, it feels foolish to merely try to cope or comply with the status quo. Lots of resilience is still required to endure life's rising hardships and live effectively in society, while resisting modern lifestyles' superficialities and humans' thirst for self-gratification. We should still learn how to live as independently as we can, both financially and emotionally, based on a solid foundation of thoughts, a personal life philosophy, and self-awareness. We should make many tough decisions, develop a less hectic life path, and elude the lure of materialism, all in hopes of some personal salvation. Surely, social adaptation and cooperation are still necessary, although it feels more imperative every year to play a bigger role in revamping personal and social mentalities before the word 'humanity' sounds just like a useless and ironic semblance of humans' arrogance and ignorance. *All this idealism is just a reflection of the author's naiveté, of course!*

It might be helpful to develop a 'social sickness' index to gauge the overall health (sanity) of society based on its citizens' level of stress, marital failures, job dissatisfactions, phoniness, wasteful consumerism, etc. Developing this index scientifically is easy if the public show interest about such information and then some responsible authorities or scholars take on the responsibility of collecting the relevant data and doing this vital measurement probably once a year. We only need to be honest in terms of gauging the causes and effects of our crooked lifestyles and the impact of capitalism. This index could also reflect humans and governments' degree of success or failure in developing social conscience, propagating a reliable foundation of thoughts, and defining some fundamentals about a fairer and healthier society for humanity's sake at least. Maybe soon we realize the necessity of putting less stress on measuring only economic factors, such as GDP, wealth, and employment, etc.—which by the way only confirm the growing failures of capitalistic systems and human mentalities, anyway. Now, we must emphasize on measuring the extent of social sickness and misery that is getting out of hand.

If the author were asked to suggest a subjective rating of this (social sickness) index at this point, he would suggest 7 on a scale of 1 to 10, where ten would be a picture of total social madness. If we can learn to become better people and less selfish, it would probably be possible to bring down the index of social sickness to around 4 in about three centuries, which would be an amazing accomplishment. However, this is only another wild imagination by this naïve author. We will never stop screwing up one another, our societies, and the world until we are all totally insane, phony, and dysfunctional. We are fast moving toward 8-9-10 in not so distant future.

A philosophical question raised in this trilogy is, 'Why live when life has become so meaningless and full of suffering?' This topic was partly tackled in Chapter Two, but it must be reiterated that living might give us a chance to laugh or feel 'self'-realized, or maybe even play a role in bringing the sickness index down to 6 or lower. Dying eliminates these opportunities, *especially the ambitious goal of lowering the social sickness index!* Besides, what we think and feel today (about living—as Shakespeare was eager to sort out, too) would most likely be different from the way we would think or feel in the future, especially if we learn to pursue a path of self-awareness and see a bit of the *real world* without any travelling! In fact, our present mentality and practice to travel so often to all corners of the world, as another gimmick to forget our pains and ourselves for a while, has only distracted us from our main mission in life to learn about the real world and ourselves only through meditation and inner exploration.

Of course, when suffering feels unbearable to some people, they could decide to end their miseries, hopefully after weighing all their options calmly over months or years, instead of acting hastily in a moment of emotional or mental setback. *Maybe they could go away on a trip again, for now!!* Still, anytime we doubt the purpose of living, we must remember that living is merely for getting those small victories now and then, at the expense of the never-ending struggles and hardships of existence. Some of us might even succeed to discover that 'being' is still a privilege in spite of the agony of living in such humiliating societies.

On the other hand, life hardships, especially for those of us blessed to live in modern societies, are mostly of our making when we insist on living in our phony worlds. We are personally responsible for the way we have confused ourselves by insisting to live in this weird perceived world. We are personally guilty for supporting such phony, meaningless social mechanism revolving around humans' naïve impressions, ideals, ambitions, laziness, ignorance, and self-pity. Merely our crooked genes and lifestyles are causing our sufferings, as they push us to follow certain life routines like helpless addicts. We simply cannot avoid the same selfish, greed-ridden thoughts for more pleasures and power. Our egotistical pursuit of materialism obstructs our mental capacities and chances of building a solid foundation for decision-making and managing our doubts regarding the harsh reality of existence, while our lifestyles are also getting too exhausting and stressful.

As a basic wisdom, we may finally agree that humans' natural qualities do not match their common (idealistic) perceptions of themselves, and that this wide mental incongruity accounts for most of our personal and interpersonal problems. In addition, the characteristics of societies we have developed gradually around our naive mentalities make it impossible for us to converge with either our natural or idealistic view of humans. Nevertheless, it appears as though we should face the same old cliché, 'Who are we?', as disgruntled humans, even more seriously now, just for detecting the origins of our personal and social problems. Our findings would then make us wonder with even more surprise, 'Why have we become this way...? Really...?'

Under the present circumstances, it is very hard for parents to advise their children about life. They are doomed if they support their shallow, fanciful dreams and the youths' overall growing expectations from life and relationships. And parents are doomed if they try to push their kids a bit towards a more practical and simpler lifestyle in hopes of minimizing their predictable pains. We get blamed for both not letting them live freely and warning them about their misperceived ideals. How can we tell our kids that all their dreams, nowadays, including love, trust, freedom, dependence, fame, and all the rest of all those good imaginations are only sure ways of losing more chunks of their independence, identity, and integrity? But then, how can humanity be sustained if not even parenting is understood or practiced?

Surely, living in the 'perceived world' according to our ideals or fantasies feels more natural and easier, almost like going to the movies to relax our busy minds awhile. Yet, our absorption in the 'perceived world' has now besieged our spirits, identities, senses, and judgments. Our love of our phony identities and lifestyles has caused our chronic depression and stress, just because we are now so helplessly attached to the prevalent features of social living.

Like everybody else, I personally live in a fantasy world too often as well, although I have learned how to enjoy it without getting too serious or uptight about its capacity and meaning. I dream mainly about peace of mind for my children and all the people in the world. I dream about people's mentalities changing someday to envision novel, meaningful norms for our societies. I dream about my books making sense to at least a small group of people, who would in turn advocate practical ways of living in a healthy, peaceful world. These dreams and writings keep me busy and alive and they are my ways of thanking my creator. *I also dream that He is happy about what I am doing for Him!!*

Yes, I believe in God or the creator, which somehow exists in a form and format not comprehensible to us now or ever. This private belief comes merely from a personal appreciation of an imaginary 'real world,' contrary to corny religious ideologies. I believe everybody can have a sincere relationship with his/her creator without resorting to religions, which are at best absurd imaginations about a specific entity called God and the fake truth they wish to force about supernatural. We have used this naive concept of God too much, and invented all types of perceptions and ideologies around it, to fulfil certain social needs and perhaps induce some morality. However, we have failed to create even a uniform God to bring us together or enhance morality. Instead, we worship too many kinds of Gods and we fight one another forever over whose God is a better one and which one has sent us the right messages. That is exactly how Arabs behaved around a variety of wooden gods before Mohammad and Islam emerged; and now we are acting in a more confusing, wilder manner with no prospect in sight. Anyway, my extensive views about God and spirituality are delineated in Volume II of this trilogy.

Back to my personal objective for writing this trilogy, it does not seem like ever happening! My wishful thinking about a deeper and more effective communication with my children through this trilogy at least has not *yet* borne fruits with no light in the horizon. The prospect for direct communication is also evaporating very fast. Only more heartache about this matter singes my spirit. My naïveté has been proven to me again and again in assuming that the youths may find it in their interests to be more thoughtful for handling their life dilemmas and decisions. Instead, they merely seem quite adamant to make their own mistakes and the modern world less civilized. Genetics and parents' conflicting viewpoints combined with societies' lack of direction keep hindering the development of a uniform learning environment for the youths, nowadays, especially when parents wish to spoil their kids as a show of their modernism. The competition in society to give children all the privileges they supposedly deserve and more is too stiff to allow any one parent teach the reality of life and its hardships to his/her children. Thus, kids grow up to believe life is a place to find happiness, which they also imagine comes from pleasures, sexuality, wealth, and arrogance.

By the way, even my efforts all those years to minimize my advice and demonstrate my reserved liberalism backfired, as my kids took it as a sign of my apathy, aloofness, silent treatment, or resistance to spoil them like normal parents! Gosh, parenting is so confusing and futile, nowadays. We should submit to our kids' desires fully to elude being perceived as a bad parent; that is how every generation is becoming spoiler. *Instead of teaching some basic wisdom about life to my children, I have been learning so many depressing, deep lessons from my family all along!*

Anyhow, not much we parents can do, but wait and hope our kids would *magically* find the wisdom of living and maybe even the secret of happiness. As a tortured father, sometimes I spell the biggest curse on my children when I say, "I hope you have many kids of your own." Then again, I feel guilty about my innocent curse also affecting my grandchildren who must live in a horribly chaotic world in the years to come. I believe my children get the gist of my sarcasm. To be sure, however, I have advised them subtly a few times to not have any kids even if they are lucky enough to find a compatible companion.

The heartbreak of loving your kids so much, while watching them suffer in society, nowadays, is too much, not to mention the pain of their rising apathy towards their parents. It seems futile, anyway, creating more helpless souls that must endure so much disappointments and hardships in horrid societies. I ask my kids to be smart and less selfish in this regard at least, although I really like to have a dozen grandchildren when I get selfish myself!

Let us hope the points raised in this trilogy occur to the youths somehow, they get a chance to ponder the sad reality about the looming demise of humanity, and do lots of self-analyses, too. Volume II discusses many topics for building a personal sense of spirituality and boosting our spirits, instead of trusting religions or juvenile positive thinking mottos blindly. Volume III reviews the structure of human life and the immense task of handling a bunch of major decisions and doubts for living—i.e., 'life' decisions.

Nevertheless, the following conclusions might be a suitable summary or words of wisdom *(my precious two cents!), to the youths especially,* by someone in his/her third life phase:

1. **Just one wrong decision in life, such as a bad marriage, can ruin one's life.** Thus, this trilogy stresses on the importance of both making timely life decisions and honouring positive doubts that intend to keep us alert about our major decisions.
2. Any healthy person over the age of twelve should be ready and feel responsible for his/her actions and decisions. This requires building the right mentality during adolescence for analysing and pursuing many difficult tasks of existence.
3. Seeking advice and help from people, parents, or even God, is wise, but it is good only for strengthening our information base and self-confidence. The final decision and subsequent blames and victories are all ours.
4. Everybody, especially the youths, encounters vast amounts of doubts and dilemmas about social living and existence, and must make many risky decisions. S/he needs the wisdom to weigh his/her options and make timely, objective decisions ultimately, instead of looking for excuses to procrastinate.
5. Despite our efforts to make the best choices and decisions, we would often feel the whole universe and life are running erratically, mostly against our needs and objectives.
6. Our achievements seem subject to other people's judgments and approvals, but if we wish their acceptance, we must often become a lot like them, speak in their phony languages, and thus sacrifice our identity and creativity in the process.

7. Do not argue when people contradict you or express different opinions about issues. Instead, encourage them to open up, just to give yourself a chance to learn more stuff about life and people in general, while raising your wisdom to prevent being influenced by charlatans and bad information.
8. The effects of genetics and humans' limited logic and mental capacity cannot be helped. Learn how best to deal with them.
9. Luck and destiny play a large role in everybody's life. Yet good things may happen to us, too. Thus, we should be ready —without becoming a dreamer—for luck finally knocking on our doors as well. We do not want to be held back by our own personal weaknesses, too, including poor health, habits, and relationships.
10. Nobody truly knows who s/he is, let alone knowing or caring about who we are. We cannot understand others, either.
11. People would often misjudge and mistreat us. This includes our spouses, kids, friends, bosses, colleagues, neighbours, etc. Relying merely on our own judgments and convictions, would not be easy or wise, either. Thus, objectivity to balance our perceptions and viewpoints against others' is often useful —no matter how ridiculous and unfair they sound to us..
12. Life would never be fair and fairness is just a human fantasy.
13. Sadly, the modern society and people are mostly damaged or evil, thus incapable of showing compassion, responding to our needs, or even grasping our basic logic and needs.
14. We can never help people change or even see the need for it, nor would we change ourselves, unless we go through a long process of self-awareness and build a deep desire to become a selfless and self-reliant person merely for our own sakes.
15. Yet, we can often adjust our attitudes, thoughts, or situations to cope with the world a little easier in some kind of harmony.
16. Humans' ability to communicate and relate has declined in modern societies due to rising arrogance, narrow mentalities, and shallow lifestyles. Thus, finding our soul mates is getting too difficult, despite our lifelong search for a reliable mate.

17. Building an independent mindset is crucial, especially if we are keen to maintain our personal beliefs and identities. Yet, it helps to find a companion to share life's hardships together.
18. Sadly, separation and solitude are becoming deeper facts of the 21st century, as relationships' instability keeps growing.* Still, we must nurture our marriages as much as we boost our inner-strengths to live alone independently if necessary.
19. Beyond the times of creativity, life is made only of physical and mental hardships with some occasional chances for joy and pleasures along the way, if we are lucky.
20. In particular, working for others, mainly in organizations, is stressful and often against a normal person's enthusiasm for independence and integrity. Thus, learn the *means of coping* in such environments to minimize the chance of losing your identity and self-respect.*
21. Since most people should do some work for subsistence, try to see it only as an acceptable background or necessity for chasing your sensible dreams in life on the side at least. Take work as neither a burden, nor a main objective of your life.*
22. Always be careful about your health. Cherish your body and mind, as they are your best friends and assets. We all forget them until they are gone and we suffer their loss badly.
23. Always enjoy and thank god for your passions and creativity, as they are your second best assets, after health, and the only tools that may soothe our souls and keep us going in life.
24. Without personal creativity, we would always feel lonely and desolate no matter how many friends and family surround us.
25. Staying practical by adapting to societies' norms is as vital as enriching our spirits a lifetime in a rather stoic lifestyle. Our potentialities and wisdom are useful for running a simple life and feeling 'self'-actualized. Thus, be ready to give up some of your freedom, passion, and time for creativity in order to adapt and attend to urgent duties towards family and society.

---

* Means of coping in our marriages and organizations are discussed in Volume III.

26. Plan your life to be independent at a practical level, but also remain flexible and compassionate towards others. Despite the social corruption and humans' inherent impurity, keeping some degree of social attachment helps our minds and spirits.
27. Always live within your means, so that you are never a slave for money or eager for extravagance.
28. Control your habit of buying things for fad or boosting your mood. Instead, find the right ways of enriching your spirit.
29. Minimize purchasing things that you cannot pay for by the end of the month. Avoid waste and consumerism, especially for fashion that has become another big source of corruption and pollution. Of course, the credit to purchase your home is necessary, but try to keep it below 70 percent of the property value, while your mortgage payments stay below 30 percent of your monthly net income. Repay it as quickly as possible, too, and stay debt free, and thus less needy.
30. The most important and rewarding challenge in life is to learn humility and become a good person, despite humans' crooked nature and all the pressures to be arrogant like others and stir more conflicts and agony in a world of illusions and idiotic ideals.

Now, my humblest advice is that advising people is often a waste of time and silly for many reasons, especially how they resent us for it, regardless of their initial reactions and the outcome. In fact, humans' aversion to advice and insisting on making their own terrible mistakes feels bizarre and pitiful. Even more bizarre, we all rush to advise others like big experts about everything, which ironically makes the general aversion to advice partly justifiable!

Still weirder, while I have finally learned not to volunteer my two cents to people, I keep writing more books with messages that sound like futile advice, even in fictions, albeit I try to remain humorous and realistic at least. Still, writing has helped me a lot to learn about myself and how to live both independently and compassionately, while learning humility the most. Meanwhile, a barrage of doubts and dilemmas turn in my head often about my habits and efforts to help my kids and possibly humanity as well:

Am I gonna smarten up enough, especially about my idiotic obsession for writing alone? In fact, it feels odd making many enemies, mostly out of people I've loved and felt obliged to help; or when they had asked for my opinion (for teasing me possibly) and I'd indulged them as honestly as I'd been able... Especially, I've felt both hurt and stupid a lot when they had often attacked me immediately, instead of thanking me for my sincere opinions! In fact, they had resisted even hearing a word I was saying or showing the slightest interest to grasp my meanings.

Anyway, I have promised myself not to offer any more direct advice, except for my general comments in my books. Then again, even this meek resolution of mine has backfired! A disheartening situation for me, nowadays, happens when somebody asks for my advice directly about an urgent decision he/she is facing. I simply do not oblige him/her even when I feel that his/her decision has a good chance of leading to a disaster for him/her. Now I know—or at least have become too paranoid to believe—he/she is asking for advice just for getting a chance to attack me again!

"I really don't know," I usually tell him/her, when in fact I know perfectly well, or at least I think so!

Well, people have made me this way and it is sad, as I said. Gosh! How could I let them do this to me?

Naturally, my passion for writing still overrides my intention to keep my opinions all to myself. Apparently, I cannot do much about this particular situation, although I am glad that at least I usually do not have to also confront the readers directly and get their condemnation of my guts, and maybe sounding preachy in my books sometimes, too! I have received enough of these *kind* feedbacks from my cranky family and friends all along already! Thank you very much!

I just hope at least some of you can see why I have become this way!

www.ingramcontent.com/pod-product-compliance
Lightning Source LLC
Chambersburg PA
CBHW020349170426
43200CB00005B/102